Invincible green suburbs, brave new towns

MANCHESTER
UNIVERSITY PRESS

Invincible green suburbs, brave new towns

Social change and urban dispersal in postwar England

Mark Clapson

Manchester University Press
Manchester and New York
Distributed exclusively in the USA by St. Martin's Press

Published by Manchester University Press
Oxford Road, Manchester M13 9NR, UK
and Room 400, 175 Fifth Avenue, New York, NY 10010, USA

Distributed exclusively in the USA by
St. Martin's Press, Inc., 175 Fifth Avenue, New York, NY 10010, USA

Distributed exclusively in Canada by
UBC Press, University of British Columbia, 6344 Memorial Road,
Vancouver, BC, Canada V6T 1Z2

British Library Cataloguing-in-Publication Data
A catalogue record for this book is available from the British Library

Library of Congress Cataloging-in-Publication Data
Clapson, Mark.
Invincible green suburbs, brave new towns : social change and urban dispersal in postwar England / Mark Clapson.
p. cm.
Includes bibliographical references and index
ISBN 0-7190-4135-X (cloth).
1. New towns–Great Britain. 2. Suburbs–Great Britain. I. Title.
HT169.57.G7C53 1998
307.76'8'0941–DC21 97-24841

ISBN 0 7190 4135 X *hardback*

First published 1998

01 00 99 98 10 9 8 7 6 5 4 3 2 1

Printed in Great Britain by
Bookcraft (Bath) Ltd, Midsomer Norton

To mum, dad, Sharon and Heather

Contents

Tables

Acknowledgements

Richard Croucher read an earlier draft of the manuscript and made many helpful suggestions and criticisms. Nick Tiratsoo has been a great help with sources. My wife, Caroline, read a number of chapters and made some very constructive comments. I am very grateful to each of them.

Thanks also to Sarah Fielder at the Department of the Environment for her assistance with the *English House Conditions Survey*, and to the staff at the British Library, the British Library of Political and Economic Science, the City Discovery Centre in Milton Keynes, the University of Luton library, the library at Northern Shell Tower, Docklands, and the Jennie Lee library at the Open University.

Abbreviations

CCPR	Central Council for Physical Recreation
CES	Centre for Environmental Studies
CHAC	Central Housing Advisory Committee
DNS	Direct Nominations Scheme
ICS	Institute of Community Studies
ISS	Industrial Selection Scheme
LCC	London County Council
MHLG	Ministry of Housing and Local Government
MKDC	Milton Keynes Development Corporation
NCSS	National Council of Social Service
NETS	New and Expanded Towns Scheme
NFCO	National Federation of Community Organisations
OPCS	Office of Population Censuses and Surveys
PEP	Political and Economic Planning
WEA	Workers' Educational Association

1

Myths and misunderstandings

> We were a slum rich in life, and now we've become a very boring, decent council estate.[1]

This chapter has four aims. First, it will define exactly what this book is concerned with, namely, the migration of the urban working classes in England to the new housing developments which came into being beyond the town and city centres. Second, the chapter will demonstrate that the urban dispersal of the English working classes met with much hostility and misunderstanding from more than a few social critics and cultural commentators who should have known better. The fears and criticisms which were generated by the new estates were stimulated by an extraordinarily pervasive anti-suburban myth in English culture. The third part of this introduction will demonstrate that, with a few notable exceptions, social history has neglected the historical significance of the outward migration of the working classes. Fourth, the chapter will outline the structure of the book, and discuss the key sources used throughout.

Some definitions: suburbs and new towns; new estates and neighbourhoods

The sociologist Peter Willmott, basing his definitions upon official housing categories, divided postwar housing developments into four: suburban 'peripheral projects', new towns, expanded towns and central redevelopment areas. Each will be discussed in turn.

New estates on the suburban fringes came under the category of 'peripheral projects', undertaken by local authorities or private developers largely on greenfield or infill sites in existing settlements.

The interwar years witnessed the first mass phase of local authority, or public sector, housing for rent. A major aim of the new council estates was to provide accommodation for slum clearance families. The 1920s and 1930s also witnessed a massive expansion of suburban estates comprising houses for owner-occupation built for sale to mortgagees by speculative volume builders. The Second World War interrupted the expansion of these peripheral projects, but they continued once the conflict was over.[2]

'The suburbs' is a term which evokes images of sprawling and homogenous residential areas away from the town and city centres. Yet there are a number of important defining characteristics of the suburbs. These have been itemised by the sociologist David C. Thorns. First, whilst located beyond the heart of the town, the suburb has been within its urban agglomeration. Second, the urban geography of the suburb was intermediate between the town centre and the countryside. Third, the suburbs were usually within commuting distance of the centre, and commuting has long been a major facet of suburban life, because the majority of suburban estates were residential developments built away from places of employment. Fourth, and in relation to this, they were usually dependent upon the town or city centre as a source of goods and services, that is, for shopping, leisure and other practical needs.[3] Thorns drew upon the work of the urban historian H. J. Dyos, who had studied the suburbs of Victorian and Edwardian London, to characterise the social functions of suburbs as 'providing the environment for the satisfaction of many needs of the family, and containing some facilities for leisure pursuits'.[4]

These basic social and spatial components of the suburbs are central to the working definition adopted throughout this book. As Thorns argues, however, whilst suburban areas could share these characteristics, they were not all the same. Spatially, for example, they varied in size, and in distance from the town centres. Nor were they socially homogenous. They varied enormously in terms of their occupational class composition. Moreover, most postwar developments have been planned, but many prewar suburbs were not. Hence, Thorns's Anglo-American 'suburban typology' divides suburbs into, among other categories, planned middle-class and planned working-class residential, and unplanned middle-class and unplanned working-class residential, suburbs.[5] The planned working-class suburb is the focus of attention within this suburban typology.

This is an important point because it illustrates that the middle-class near-monopoly of suburban living has been largely broken since the 1920s, and especially since 1945. This has been a profound consequence of the working-class penetration of the suburbs, whether through local authority council rehousing schemes, or via owner-occupation for the most affluent sections of the skilled working class. For both owner-occupiers and council tenants, however, the suburban new estate has been the major agency for this transition in the socio-residential patterns of English towns and cities. The new and expanded towns have also made a considerable contribution to the fortunes of the dispersed working classes. Care in definition, however, is required when the suburbs and the new and expanded towns are discussed in relation to dispersal.

The new towns – sometimes incorrectly referred to as satellite towns[6] – constituted the second category of urban residential development. They were brought into being by the 1946 and 1965 New Towns Acts. In England, the 1946 Act produced eleven new towns, eight of which were designed to relieve London of its congested slums and inadequate housing stock by drawing people away from the capital. Further programmes of new towns were begun in the early and late 1960s. Unlike many suburban developments, the new towns were planned to be economically self-sufficient, thus providing enough employment to prevent the long-distance commuting and the 'journey to work' problem associated with suburbs.[7] The residential areas of the first wave of new towns were termed 'neighbourhood units' by planners, rather than new estates. Unlike the latter, neighbourhoods were to contain a balanced mix of both working- and middle-class heads of household. Here too, the new towns were a reaction against the interwar suburbs, in this case their alleged social segregation.[8]

The third sector of urban dispersal was the so-called expanding towns, brought into existence by the Town Development Act of 1952. By the provisions of that Act, a number of existing towns, the largest of which included Northampton, Swindon and Salford, were to be considerably extended by planned large-scale economic and residential developments. As with new towns, their rationale was dispersal for the relief of the congested inner city. Both expanded towns and new towns were seen into existence by development corporations. These were unelected corporations, appointed by government.[9]

The fourth urban context for major housing projects was not intended to disperse but to consolidate urban populations. These were the 'redevelopment areas', which are unfortunately better known today as the inner cities. They tended to be the areas of the central towns and cities devastated by Nazi bombs or long-term urban decay. A detailed history of the redevelopment areas is beyond the scope of this book. Their relationship to urban dispersal, however, has been much discussed. Many critics of dispersal projects have argued that the redevelopment areas have been starved of people and jobs by relocation, and that this has rendered many areas impoverished twilight zones. The 'inner city' is now a term synonymous with deprivation and social problems.[10] Others argue that dispersal had little or no effect upon the socio-economic destiny of the inner city.[11] The relationship between dispersal, sometimes called decentralisation, and redevelopment areas will be further discussed where relevant to the subject matter of this book.

The peripheral projects and the new and expanded towns have added greatly to English urbanisation, and accommodated many millions of people, as Chapter 2 will demonstrate. These residential areas, so often ignored by social history, are the contexts for a social history of working-class urban dispersal since 1945.

The design and layout of housing estates and new towns is important, too. For as anyone may observe when looking at suburban housing estates and new towns, they have been largely, but not wholly, characterised by low-level houses and dwellings, and relatively low densities of population, when compared to many high-rise comprehensively redeveloped inner urban areas. In this, the new estates and the new town neighbourhoods both shared, admittedly in an often bastardised form, a common heritage in the influence of garden suburb and garden city planning and design principles. Late Victorian and Edwardian garden city and suburb experiments were comprised of cottage-style terraced houses, and semi-detached and detached houses. Many town planners and local authorities did much to feed these designs into the interwar and postwar residential projects. This is discussed more fully in Chapter 2.

It will also be shown in Chapter 2 that many people were relocated to these areas by government housing policies. However, the vast majority moved out voluntarily to the new accommodation and superior environmental conditions offered by these urban contexts. The new estate and the neighbourhood units of new and expanded towns were the destinations of the vast majority of those who moved.

During the 1950s, however, the term 'new estate' became a general catch-all term for almost all new residential areas in both new and older towns. Moreover, the new estate became synonymous with 'the new working class' as opposed to the older 'traditional working class' of the slums and the redevelopment areas. Yet, despite the tangible material improvements enjoyed by newcomers to the new estates and the neighbourhoods of the new and expanded towns, many writers were both critical and wary of these widespread changes. Their criticisms must be set within the context of a pervasive anti-suburban ethos in England. Literature is largely to blame for this myth.

The myth of suburbia and 'subtopia'

For the writer Fay Weldon, the city of the invention – the city of the literary imagination – evokes close similarities with the real city. The literary imagination produces cities with central districts, 'dreary new suburbs', respectable streets and red light districts. Weldon's adjective for the new suburbs may have been used ironically, for she also argues that some literary suburbs may be safe and salubrious, or seedy and frightening.[12] Yet the predominant tone of literary representations of English suburbia and new towns makes it difficult to treat uncritically Feldon's view that it is in literature that 'you find *real* history, and not in text books'.[13] For, with a few exceptions, for example R. F. Delderfield's *Avenue* novels, or Stevie Smith's affectionate depictions of her London suburb,[14] the English suburbs have long been the subject of superficial and negative generalisations inspired more by the animus of the writer than by any balanced notion of life there. Those generalisations, furthermore, are evidenced in other sources. Newspaper columnists, especially those working for the broadsheets, range from sarcasm to *schadenfreude* when inferring triviality, double standards, narrow-mindedness or misery from suburban life.[15] Also, a wide range of postwar journals, films and television programmes have poked fun at the suburbs and new towns. They are the unoriginal heirs to the anti-suburban tradition.

Since the late Victorian period critical and elitist attacks on 'Englishness' and also on 'mass society' by novelists and poets targeted the suburbs as miserable expressions of both. The suburbs were castigated or lampooned as quintessentially 'English' because they were supposedly torpid and conformist.[16] The attack on the suburbs was undertaken by writers on both the Left and the Right of the political spectrum as uniform and ungainly sprawls of streets and streets of silly little houses with silly little gardens. The suburbs were allegedly full of 'clerks', a pejorative catch-all term. This mockery stemmed from George and Weedon Grossmith's caricature Mr Pooter, the narrator in *The Diary of a Nobody*, first published in 1892, and continued to George Orwell's Stanley Bowling in the 1930s novel *Coming Up for Air*. It has been seen more recently in the 1970s television sitcom *The Fall and Rise of Reginald Perrin*. Clerks lived routine and uneventful lives dictated by the times of commuter trains and the monotony of office life.[17] According to their literary critics, they were passive creatures, devoid of finer feelings and high culture. They tended their little gardens, were mesmerised by advertisements for material things, and obsessed by the petty symbols of respectability and status. Towards the end of the 1930s, Orwell half hoped and half feared that the dozy tranquillity of the clerkish English suburbs might be shattered by bombs.[18] John Betjeman's 1937 poem on the suburban development of Slough appeared to welcome that prospect.[19]

Soon after the war of 1939–45 ended, these disdainful stereotypes were quickly resurrected. The writer R. J. Cruickshank, for example, contrasted the lively and fatalistic 'children of the ruins' in blitzed inner London with the 'subdued' inhabitants of the 'squalid and irrational' north London suburbs. The latter, when faced with grave national news, replied: 'we must cultivate our gardens'.[20] (This was a highbrow allusion to Voltaire's *Candide*.) The cosy claustrophobic world of John Betjeman's and Julian Barnes's *Metroland*, the sullen interiors of houses in Barbara Pym's leafy streets of North Oxford, the soullessness of Angus Wilson's fictional new town of Carshall, the 'subtopian cliché' of Keith Waterhouse's fictive Yorkshire suburb of Stradhoughton, and the punkish reaction against Bromley in Hanif Kureishi's *The Buddha of Suburbia*, are among the more famous of many novels which despaired of the suburbs and the new towns.[21]

The example of Stradhoughton, the suburban estate which stimulated the dreamland of Billy Liar, indicates that cultural criticism gained a new term in its anti-suburban lexicon during the 1950s. 'Subtopia' was originally intended, as a term coined by the architect Ian Nairn, to critically describe the design and environmental aspects of suburban and new town housing developments. Moreover, the destruction of the English countryside by new estates of low-density and low-rise housing angered many, including some within the architectural and planning professions. 'Subtopia' signified neither the utopian New Jerusalem promised by politicians and planners in 1945, nor the urban nightmare of 'dystopia'. England was, instead, being reduced to 'a universal subtopia, a mean and middle state, neither town nor country ... a universal condition which spreads both ways from suburbia'.[22] To provide an exciting new alternative to subtopia, some modernist urbanists sought to encourage local authorities to break with traditional building materials and low-density overspill schemes. Instead, they called for high-density, compact housing experiments constructed with plastics, concrete, metal alloys and technologically enhanced heavy-duty materials, notably reinforced Canadian aluminium.[23] Nairn shared such views. He was, moreover, also critical of the new towns, which he felt had failed to achieve a true urbanity. He found a critical ally in an ex-manager of Stevenage Development Corporation, Clough Williams-Ellis, who felt the new towns fell far short of being pioneering rehousing projects and 'exemplars of urbanity'.[24]

These professional debates were originally conducted within architectural and planning journals, but the term 'subtopia' was increasingly influential from the mid-1950s. John Betjeman, for example, made a number of commentaries on the subtopian aspects of Metroland in the *Spectator*.[25] The Ministry of Housing and Local Government (MHLG), under whose auspices the postwar housing programmes were planned and constructed, became offended, by the mid-1960s, at the frequency with which such negative terms as subtopia, 'cultural deserts' and the like were applied by the media to new towns and planned new housing developments.[26]

Subtopia came to possess a social connotation alongside its original environmental meaning. Similarly critical but general impressions of suburban and new town life became easy targets for many writers, both in highbrow journals and in more populist media. As Stuart Laing has argued, in the later 1950s and the first half of the 1960s the new estates and the new towns became synonymous with 'the new England' of increasing affluence, consumption, conformity, conservatism, passivity and dearth of the type of culture which many intellectuals felt the working classes *ought* to possess.[27] In relation to these perceived changes, the new estates and new towns also became synonymous with the 'new working class'.[28] As the working classes moved away from their 'traditional' proletarian heartlands in the town and city centres to a new home in a new housing development, they were seen to absorb and embrace increasingly materialistic, home-centred and individualistic values as opposed to collectivist ones. This analysis reflected a strong sense of disappointment felt by the Left during the 1950s and 1960s. A number of articles in sociological and political journals held the planners and their new housing developments responsible for a qualitative decline in the social life of the 'traditional' working-class areas by the creation of dull new suburbs and new town 'ghettos'.[29] For some, notably the political scientist Mark Abrams and the sociologist Ferdynand Zweig, the new working class was becoming middle class, adopting a suburban lifestyle long associated with the bourgeoisie, hence the term *embourgeoisement.*[30] Raymond Williams, the literary critic and historian of culture, simplistically compared a horizontally oriented working-class collectivism with an atomistic and divisive middle-class privatism and individualism, and argued that as the working classes became more affluent the former was being eroded by the latter.[31] Key socialist thinkers, for example Stuart Hall, were wary of the notion of *embourgeoisement*, yet felt the new working class was becoming increasingly home-centred or 'privatised', materialistic, and also politically conservative as a consequence of these changes. They pointed to the voting behaviour of suburbs and new towns to prove it.[32] Here, the affluent working class appeared to be forsaking the socialist vote.

The suburbanite also stood accused of yet another problem, or rather a profound existential condition: anomie. This is a condition of rootlessness and unsatisfied desires which may lead to dysfunctional behaviour. John Burke's 1960s novel *The Suburbs of Pleasure* reworked the themes of mass society and the indoctrinated suburbanite.[33] Its subject matter was similar to William H. Whyte's influential *The Organisation Man*, first published in 1956. This book described the American corporate status seeker, both at work and at home, to wit, 'his dormitories – the great package suburbs that have sprung up outside our cities since the war'.[34] The organisation man was transient: on the move as in on the way up. And his ostensibly 'classless' suburban lifestyle was, for Whyte, betrayed by his car, the bearer of his speedy mobility and a symbol of his rootlessness. Alongside the automobile, other status symbols bore witness to the skill and expense with which people made themselves feel superior to others.[35] Another influential American polemic was David Reisman's *The Lonely Crowd*, first published in 1950. It argued that within the wealthy American suburbs, life for the white-collared elite was driven, competitive, only superficially sociable. Wealthy suburbanites were constantly striving to live to aspirations and wishes dictated by advertisements or by their neighbours. They were 'other-directed', as opposed to being inner-directed. Hence they were unfulfilled.[36] Zweig felt that the affluent British worker was becoming increasingly 'other-directed' in Reisman's sense.[37]

Reisman and Whyte were not simply attacking the suburban way of life: they were adopting a polemical position which viewed the suburbs as the most profound condition of the 'new America'. In its growing love of the 'car culture' and of mobility in general, America was in danger of becoming a rootless and anomic society.[38] That raised warnings for Britain. As the blurb on the back of the Penguin edition of Whyte's *The Organisation Man* put it: 'All of this is of direct interest to us, for what is happening in America is happening here'.[39] Writing in *Socialist Commentary*, Tosca Fyvel felt that similar changes, 'affected by American styles, by the insistent advertisers', were growing in Britain.[40] Fyvel was not alone. Christopher Booker, the journalist and cultural critic, has shown how Reisman's and Whyte's analyses of the suburban condition found favour with a generation of disillusioned postwar intellectuals in Britain. The allegedly egregious suburbanites were central to the gloomier prognoses of the 'what's wrong with Britain?' school of cultural criticism and highbrow journalism.[41]

Suburbanites increasingly made appearances on the television, a rapidly growing item of consumption. The BBC's 1960s police serial *Z Cars*, for example, was set in 'Newtown', and possessed more than a few similarities to the Merseyside housing development of Kirkby.[42] New towns attracted the attention of television producers and screenplay writers, too. From 1965 to 1969, the BBC soap opera *Newcomers* dealt with the crises and compensations of a family who moved to 'Angleton'.[43] However, it was slapstick and situation comedy which provided the most commonplace representations of the suburbs, sending up all sorts of sad, ludicrous, bored, well-meaning, ill-meaning, anti-social or overly sociable subjects. Many of postwar Britain's most successful actors and scriptwriters have been involved (see Table 1).

Table 1 A selection of suburban sitcoms on postwar British television

Title	*Channel*	*Years*	*Actors*	*Scriptwriters*
Hancock	BBC1	1956–60	Tony Hancock	Alan Galton Ray Simpson
Hugh and I	BBC1	1962–67	Terry Scott	John Chapman
Beggar my Neighbour	BBC1	1967–68	Pat Coombes Reg Varney June Whitfield	Ken Hoare Mike Sharland
Bless This House	Thames	1971–76	Diana Coupland Sid James	Carla Lane
Happy Ever After	BBC1	1974–78	Terry Scott June Whitfield	John Chapman Eric Merriman
The Good Life	BBC1	1975–78	Richard Briers Paul Eddington Penelope Keith Felicity Kendal	John Esmonde Bob Larbey
George and Mildred	Thames	1976–78	Yootha Joyce Brian Murphy	John Mortimer Brian Cooke
Citizen Smith	BBC1	1977–80	Robert Lindsay	John Sullivan
Reginald Perrin	BBC1	1976–79	Leonard Rossiter Pauline Yates	David Nobbs
Keeping up Appearances	BBC1	1990–	Patricia Routledge	Roy Clarke
One Foot in the Grave	BBC1	1990–	Annette Crosbie Richard Wilson	David Renwick

Source: This table is based on information in T. Vahimagi, for the British Film Institute, *British Television: An Illustrated Guide* (Oxford, 1994).

The juxtaposition of opposites was one device for getting a laugh at the expense of suburbanites. In *Citizen Smith*, for example, the alleged conformity and conservatism of suburban Tooting was the back-cloth for the pathetic revolutionary pretensions of the 'Che Guevara' of the Tooting Popular Front. In *Reginald Perrin* the repetition of commuting and office life, and the boredom and pointlessness of which suburbia is so often accused, were the recurring themes. The snobberies and pretensions of suburbia were given a novel format in *The Good Life*. A young couple, the Goods, aim for self-sufficiency in Surbiton by turning their garden into a farmyard, thus angering their extremely status-conscious neighbours who possess a perfectly manicured back garden. And the promiscuous suburban woman with her socially inept husband was the theme of *George and Mildred*. In *Whatever Happened to the Likely Lads?*, a late 1960s and 1970s sitcom, albeit one which was not centrally concerned with suburban life, resolutely proletarian Terry was contrasted with social climbers Bob and Thelma on the Elm Lodge housing estate, and their sex-mad or snobbish neighbours. In television plays too, for example *Abigail's Party* by Mike Leigh, first shown in November 1977, the bored, frustrated, *nouveau riche* Beverley was the subject of a merciless attack on her suburban values and lifestyle.[44] Alison Steadman, who played Beverley, also starred as the suburban housewife with a problem husband in the television adaptation of one of Nigel Williams's *Wimbledon* novels during the mid-1990s.[45]

The sex-mad woman in boring suburbia has continued to be a staple of popular novels, and also of soft porn. Examples of the former are Leslie Thomas's *Tropic of Ruislip*, first published in 1974. Women writers also explore the idea that there is something promiscuous or even unhealthy about a suburban woman's sexuality, as is shown for example by Judith Astley's *Pleasant Vices* or by Fay Weldon's *Life Force*.[46] Newspaper book reviewers often tend to emphasise the salacious, or to use such literature to re-affirm their own jaded views of the suburbs: '[her] self consciously "naughty" obsession with sex was the perfect expression of a suburban mentality ...'.[47] Men's (hetero) sex magazines have actively endorsed such stereotypes. In 1992 *Men Only* offered its readers the 'sex secrets of bored suburban man mad housewives'.[48] One such secret has, since the 1960s, been wife-swapping, described by *Penthouse* as 'the primary indoor sport of suburbia'.[49] During the mid-1970s, one intrepid *Penthouse* writer went to 'a very suburban pub in Sussex' to meet none other than John and Norma, 'two experienced swingers'.[50] In the mid-1990s, the *Sunday Mirror* could offer its readers adult videos entitled 'British couples in suburban sex', although what was specifically suburban about the 'nookie quota' of these couples was not specified in the advertisement.[51] Instead, the noun 'suburban' when coupled with sex automatically implied something naughty.

British rock singers have been more than willing to perpetuate these stereotypes. There have been three impressive bursts of creativity in British rock music: the beat bands of the mid-1960s, the punk and new wave era from 1976 to 1979, and the Britpop bands of the mid-1990s. Each has thrown up its suburban caricatures. During the 1960s, for example, the Bonzo Dog Band lampooned excessive privatism and the do-it-yourself mentality in 'My pink half of the drainpipe'.[52] Manfred Mann's 1966 hit 'Semi-detached suburban Mr James' lamented the loss of his erstwhile partner to a life of toast buttering for her status-seeking husband.[53] Such titles hint strongly at why the suburban couple of the 1960s have been condemned as 'Mr and Mrs Average',[54] yet many suburbans were not 'average' (whatever that means). John Lennon and Paul McCartney hailed from the Liverpool suburbs, and in 'Penny Lane' provided a rare vision of the sunny optimism which many suburbanites must have felt in the so-called 'summer of love' of 1967.[55] And the Kinks' Dave and Ray Davies, who as young boys in the later 1940s and 1950s moved with their family from the 'awful' overcrowded dwellings near Kings Cross to Muswell Hill, via Finchley, drew upon the north London suburbs for their affectionate songs of London life.[56] The Kinks also explored, in their early 1970s album *The Muswell Hillbillies*, the experiences of 'the working class families who were forced out of the inner city and rehoused in the cheaply built suburban new towns that were to become the slums of the future'.[57]

During the later 1970s, punk and new wave bands indulged in a dramatic and exciting anti-suburbanism which was influenced by the American new wave, notably such 'bombed out suburbanites' as the New York Dolls.[58] A hostile or mocking attitude towards the suburbs featured in many songs, with perhaps the Members' single 'Sound of the suburbs' being the most famous.[59] Some punks hailed from the suburbs, such as Paul Cook, the drummer with the Sex Pistols, who grew up on a West London council estate.[60] Siouxsie Sioux was raised in Chislehurst, a south London suburb. In 1978 Siouxsie and the Banshees' 'Suburban relapse' depicted a woman whose 'strings snapped' when she was washing the dishes or minding her own business.[61] Sioux hated the suburbs for their apparent dullness and 'old people ... always going on about Hitler'. In order to agitate them she stuck swastikas on her clothes.[62] The anti-suburban element of punk and new wave continued into the 1980s. 'Suburban relapse' may usefully be compared with the violent symptoms of alleged suburban monotony and frustration in such 1980s tracks as the Pet Shop Boy's 'Suburbia', the Police's 'Synchronicity 2', or the Style Council's 'Come to Milton Keynes'.[63]

The 1990s Britpop boom has demonstrated scarcely any lyrical originality in its tragic or maudlin tales of suburban life. For Suede, women tend to be enslaved with children in far-flung suburban homes or forgotten satellite towns.[64] Blur sing of sad couples moving to a brand new town to be with people just like themselves, or, in the aptly titled 'Stereotypes', of a 'frisky' woman who lives in the dreaming suburbs. Another Blur song, 'Ernold Same', crystallises some classic anti-suburban themes. Narrated by Labour MP Ken Livingstone, it depicts a sad commuter at the same station, getting on the same train, and doing the same work every day.[65] According to *Q* magazine, Blur's singer-songwriter Damon Albarn 'can be applauded for capturing the essence of the painful longing and commuter-numbed nothingness of suburban cul de sac existence ...'.[66]

Yet although these varying sources have resorted to mockery, or relied upon a well-rehearsed pessimism about social life in the postwar new housing developments, they did at least understand that something worth writing or singing about was happening there. They were, in that sense, quicker on the uptake than social historians have been. With a few notable exceptions, this profound postwar transition has been largely ignored by social history.

Social history and urban dispersal

For the purposes of this discussion, the canon of social history may be divided up into general survey studies of postwar British or English society and specific studies. Within the former category, suburban housing estates are mentioned briefly, at best.[67] And when they do catch the attention of historians, a tendency to accentuate the negative is strongly evident, and this fails to challenge the anti-suburban orthodoxy. François Bédarida, for example, writes of the 'peculiar frustrations' of suburban life: privacy, loneliness, frustration, and the standardisation of exteriors and interiors.[68]

As the local historian Nigel Todd argued in 1975, 'although the rise of suburbia has been spectacular it is still a neglected historical theme',[69] a point which is also germane to the new and expanded towns. What little social and urban history does exist, moreover, is almost wholly concerned with middle-class suburbs and weighted more heavily towards the prewar period.[70] Whilst a number of important studies emphasising the need to study the suburbs have been published since 1975, the historiography has been mostly conducted by urban and not social historians.[71] There is, then, as Tom Jeffrey has argued, strong justification for a historical investigation of 'the often unrecognised but undoubtedly important migration of the working class to the suburbs'.[72]

Some oral historians have, however, understood this. Stephen Caunce has noted 'the crucial moment' of the interwar suburban council estates in offering working-class folk the 'space and facilities they had never had before'.[73] A number of oral historians have explored the experiences of moving out from the town and city centres into a new home in a new housing development, notably Catherine Hall for interwar suburban development in Birmingham, Stephen Humphries for postwar London migrants, and Elizabeth Roberts for North West Lancashire during the period from 1940 to 1970.[74] In addition, a number of local oral history projects on migration to the new estates and to new and expanded towns have been undertaken by community oral historians.[75]

Hall and Humphries demonstrate, for interwar Birmingham and postwar London respectively, that on balance migrants to new housing developments from poorer areas were happy with the move. Both historians, however, note the difficulties in settling down which were experienced by some migrants, especially women, often based all day in their new home, and no longer in close contact with their local friends and relatives. Roberts takes this perspective further. She argues that 'an erosion of community norms' has taken place, and that means the demise both of close-knit extended families and of local support networks of neighbours.[76] Writing in review of Roberts's work, the eminent community historian Carl Chinn characteristically got to the heart of the matter:

> In an understandable search for privacy, we have become too private. We have abandoned the communal space. In our striving for respectability we have sought to mould working-class women into the domestic ideal. We have shied away from their strength and sought to make them pliant. [We] have taken power from them in the home, and we have deprived them of their influence on the street.[77]

Yet as Chinn was also well aware, many working-class families sought a new home in a suburban residential environment. Indeed, his parents had moved from Sparkbrook to the suburbs during the mid-1950s. Chinn's father, a street bookmaker, was following a path well-trodden by his working-class profession since the 1930s, a path increasingly pursued by the postwar working classes in general. Chinn's work on council houses in Birmingham illustrates the rewards which many felt at moving into a new estate home.[78]

It is Chinn's former perspective, however, which represents an orthodoxy in social history. For a similar emphasis on disempowerment haunts the work of the social historian Eric Hopkins, whose view is that the growth of affluence, better housing and improved living standards generally have eroded the collectivist working-class ethos and the positive imagery which went with it.[79] The work of the writer and sometime popular historian Jeremy Seabrook is perhaps the apotheosis of this perspective. For him, something has gone tragically wrong in postwar England, and that something is the loss of a traditional, collectivist working-class community. The forsaking of the lessons learned in the common experiences of poverty and hardship, and the loss of pride in their community, are abiding themes in Seabrook's work. Instead, he argues that the fundamental ties that bound people together have been eroded as society has grown increasingly affluent, consumerist and, apparently, individuated and privatised. Dispersal was inextricably linked up with these changes, and the postwar new estates played host to dispersal. For Seabrook, then, the new estate is a desiccated world, ghosted by the lost world of working-class solidarism. It turned many men into selfish and violent animals. It confined women to lonely domestic drudgery.[80] As we will see in Chapter 5, however, there was a considerable level of research and debate about women's problems when moving which provided some highly qualified and complex evidence about 'suburban neurosis' or the 'new town blues'. With the exception of work by Barbara Brookes and Jane Lewis, and by Alan A. Jackson, however, there has been little previous historical attention paid to the issue of suburban neurosis.[81] This, in turn, relates to a further lacuna within social history: the failure of social historians to contribute to the debate about the quality of women's lives in planned towns and cities.

With some notable exceptions, then, social history has largely reiterated and added emphasis to the negative view of the suburbs and the new and expanded towns. It is time for a fresh examination of the relationship of social change to urban dispersal in the postwar period. This will provide an altogether more optimistic appraisal of social change. In order to undertake this complex task, some key themes are central to each chapter of this book. These themes, and the manner in which they are examined historically, are the subject of the final section of this introduction.

The structure of this book

The premise of Chapter 2 is continuity. We cannot fully understand the structures of postwar social change without an understanding of the wider, longer-term historical context. Hence the historical origins of postwar urban dispersal are assessed. These lay, originally, in the middle-class migration to the suburbs as a response to the degraded conditions of the industrial cities and towns of Victorian England. The garden city and garden suburb experiments are discussed as responses to the problems of Victorian and Edwardian towns and cities. Their influence on both municipal council estates and the postwar programmes of new and expanded towns is discussed. These experiments were essential to the formation and consolidation of a town and country planning profession in England for whom dispersal into planned new communities has been a major *raison d'être*. Chapter 2 also highlights working-class suburban migration prior to 1939. It demonstrates how these developments, in combination, laid the basis for postwar urban dispersal. Finally, it assesses the extent of these great internal migrations since 1945. The major primary sources for this chapter are planning and sociological materials. These are utilised within a wider historical account based upon secondary histories of planning and urban growth.

Chapter 3 looks at the reasons why people moved out to the new estates and the new and expanded towns. Chapter 4 discusses their experiences when settling down. Mostly, these chapters utilise official studies of migration made by planners, materials from housing managers, sociological studies of the working-class experience of moving house, and oral testimonies.

Chapter 5 assesses the problems incurred by the move to the suburban new estate or the new and expanded town, problems which were almost wholly associated with women migrants. A number of sociological, socio-psychological and medical studies examined the phenomena known as suburban neurosis and new town blues. These are discussed in synthesis with governmental appraisals of the problem, and also with literary and fictive sources which were concerned with the feelings of many working-class migrants, almost all of whom were women, and many of whom were unhappy with aspects of their new life.

Chapter 6 assesses the nature of social life on the working-class new estate, and argues for a flexible and nuanced framework which seeks to understand this without relying overmuch, as social historians are wont to do, upon the notions of localism and neighbourhood as the linchpins of community. By synthesising a wide range of planning materials, sociologies, local press reports and oral testimonies, it hopes to show that the ability of people to connect with and interact with each other has remained strong. Planning materials might be accused of willing the often positive results they reported, but that was rarely the case. Some of the most enthusiastic exponents of dispersal were also the most wary of its potential hazards.

Chapter 7, in conclusion, aims to show that the experiences of working-class migrants to new housing developments should not be viewed as marginal to the consciousness and action of the postwar working classes, but as central to them. The chapter argues that there are lessons to be learned from these experiences, because spatially towns are continuing to grow. Moreover, further new towns are mooted for the next century. Important historical lessons may be learned from the experiences of the pioneers who moved onto the new estates and into the new and expanded towns of postwar England.

Notes

1 R. Gosling, *Personal Copy* (London, 1980), p. 218.

2 P. Willmott, 'Social research and the new communities', *Journal of the American Institute of Planners*, 33:6 (1967), p. 388. Ministry of Housing and Local Government (MHLG), *The Needs of New Communities: A Report on Social Provision in New and Expanding Communities* (London, 1967), pp. 4–14; see also F. M. L. Thompson, 'Introduction: the rise of suburbia', in F. M. L. Thompson (ed.), *The Rise of Suburbia* (Leicester, 1982), p. 2.

3 D. C. Thorns, *Suburbia* (London, 1972), pp. 31–3.

4 Ibid., p. 33.

5 Ibid., p. 83.

6 New towns have a greater level of economic and administrative independence from the centres of established cities than satellite towns. See L. F. Schnore, 'Satellites and suburbs', in W. M. Dobriner (ed.), *The Suburban Community* (New York, 1958), pp. 109–11.

7 K. K. Liepmann, *The Journey to Work: Its Significance for Industrial and Community Life* (London, 1944), p. 89.
8 Willmott, 'Social research', pp. 389–90.
9 F. Schaffer, *The New Town Story* (London, 1972), pp. 53–66, 246–7.
10 P. Lawless, *Britain's Inner Cities: Problems and Policies* (London, 1981), pp. 216–34.
11 C. Hamnett, 'Social change – London', *Urban Studies*, 13 (1976), pp. 269–70.
12 F. Weldon, 'Letter one: the city of invention', in *Letters to Alice on First Reading Jane Austin* (London, 1993), pp. 11–14.
13 Ibid., p. 13.
14 R. F. Delderfield's *The Dreaming Suburb* and *The Avenue Goes to War* were published together in one volume as *The Avenue Story* (London, 1964); S. Smith, 'A London suburb', in S. Smith, *Me Again: The Uncollected Writings of Stevie Smith* (London, 1988), pp. 100–4.
15 See, for example, S. Barwick, 'In the circles of Pooter's inferno', *Independent*, 28 March 1992; A. Brown, 'Dead bored and other common problems', *Independent*, 8 August 1992; W. Hutton, 'Angst in Acacia Avenue', *Guardian*, 2 August 1994; J. Legatte, 'Out of the closet and into the commuter belt', *Guardian*, 12 April 1993.
16 J. Giles and T. Middleton, *Writing Englishness, 1900–1950: An Introductory Sourcebook on National Identity* (London, 1995), pp. 195–6, 208–9, 231–9.
17 J. Carey, *The Intellectuals and the Masses: Pride and Prejudice among the Literary Intelligentsia, 1880–1939* (London, 1992), pp. 46–70; K. Flint, 'Fictional suburbia', *Literature and History*, 8:2 (1982), pp. 68–9.
18 G. Orwell, *Homage to Catalonia* (London, 1971), p. 248.
19 J. Betjeman, 'Slough', in R. Skelton (ed.), *Poetry of the Thirties* (Harmondsworth, 1985), p. 74.
20 R. J. Cruickshank, *The Moods of London* (London, 1951), p. 5.
21 J. Barnes, *Metroland* (London, 1990); B. Pym, *Crampton Hodnet* (London, 1986); A. Wilson, *Late Call* (Harmondsworth, 1992); K. Waterhouse, *Billy Liar* (Harmondsworth, 1985); H. Kureishi, *The Buddha of Suburbia* (London, 1989).
22 I. Nairn, *Outrage* (London, 1955), p. 365.
23 Alcan Industries Limited with Gordon Cullen, *A Town Called Alcan* (London, 1964), pp. 1–2; I. De Wofle with I. Nairn, *Civilia: The End of Suburban Man* (London, 1971), passim; J. Harlow, 'One new town', *Universities and Left Review*, 5 (1958), pp. 18–20.
24 C. Williams-Ellis, 'To hell with subtopia', *New Statesman and Nation*,

23 March 1957, p. 372; see also De Wofle with I. Nairn, *Civilia*, passim.

25 See the 'City and Suburban' columns of the *Spectator*, 15 February 1957, p. 204; 22 February 1957, p. 237; 1 March 1957, p. 276. Also, see below, Chapter 3, p. 64.

26 MHLG, *The Needs of New Communities*, p. 21.

27 S. Laing, *Representations of Working Class Life, 1957–64* (London, 1986), pp. 3–30.

28 D. Lockwood, 'The new working class', *European Journal of Sociology*, 1:2 (1960), pp. 251–5; D. Lockwood, 'Sources of variation in working-class images of society', *Sociological Review* (New Series) 14:3 (1966), pp. 257–9.

29 See, for example, T. Fyvel, 'The stones of Harlow', *Encounter*, 33 (1956), pp. 11–17; G. Gibson, 'New town ghettoes', *Socialist Commentary*, April 1959, pp. 12–14; M. Muggeridge, 'England, whose England?', *Encounter*, 118 (1963), pp. 15–17; M. Young, 'Must we abandon our cities?', *Socialist Commentary*, September 1954, pp. 251–3.

30 M. Abrams, 'The home centred society', *Listener*, 26 November 1959, pp. 914–15; F. Zweig, *The Worker in an Affluent Society* (London, 1961), pp. 205–12.

31 R. Williams, *Culture and Society, 1780–1950* (Harmondsworth, 1984), pp. 314–18.

32 S. Hall, 'The supply of demand', in E. P. Thompson (ed.), *Out of Apathy* (London, 1960), pp. 56–97; on this debate in general, see S. Fielding, '"White heat" and white collars: the evolution of "Wilsonism"', in R. Coopey, S. Fielding and N. Tiratsoo (eds), *The Wilson Governments, 1964–1970* (London, 1993), pp. 29–33.

33 M. Seymour Smith, review of J. Burke, *The Suburbs of Pleasure*, in *Spectator*, 3 March 1967, p. 252.

34 W. H. Whyte, *The Organisation Man* (Harmondsworth, 1965), p. 246.

35 Ibid., pp. 246–303.

36 D. Reisman, *The Lonely Crowd* (Yale, 1970), pp. 19–22.

37 Zweig, *The Worker in an Affluent Society*, p. 210.

38 Reisman, *Lonely Crowd*, pp. 17–23.

39 Whyte, *Organisation Man*, back cover.

40 T. Fyvel, 'Thoughts about suburbia', *Socialist Commentary*, January 1961, p. 22.

41 C. Booker, *The Neophiliacs: A Study of the Revolution in English Life in the Fifties and Sixties* (London, 1970), pp. 144, 161.

42 J. B. Mays, 'New hope in newtown', *New Society*, 22 August 1963, pp. 11–13.
43 T. Vahimagi for the British Film Institute, *British Television: An Illustrated Guide* (Oxford, 1994), p. 139.
44 Ibid., p. 191.
45 N. Williams, *The Wimbledon Poisoner* (1990); N. Williams, *They Came From SW19* (London, 1992); *East of Wimbledon* (London, 1993). *The Wimbledon Poisoner* was shown on BBC television in 1994.
46 J. Astley, *Pleasant Vices* (London, 1995); F. Weldon, *Life Force* (London, 1992).
47 Quote from the *Independent*, 15 February 1991, in review of Wendy Perriam's television programme on Surbiton. See also the review of Weldon's *Life Force* entitled 'Suburban silliness' in the *Independent*, 25 July 1992.
48 *Men Only*, 57:1 (1992), front cover.
49 *Penthouse*, 8:12 (1973), p. 68.
50 *Penthouse*, 10:10 (1975), p. 79.
51 *Sunday Mirror*, 9 October 1994.
52 The Bonzo Dog Band, 'My pink half of the drainpipe', on *Cornology: Vol. 1: The Intro* CD (EMI, 1992, 0777 7 99596 2 4).
53 Manfred Mann, 'Semi-detached suburban Mr James', *Ages of Mann* CD (Polygram, 1993, 514 326–2); D. Ree, B. Lazell and R. Osborne, *The Complete N.M.E. Singles Charts* (London, 1995), pp. 174–5.
54 J. and M. Stern, *Sixties People* (London, 1990), pp. 219–31.
55 I. MacDonald, *Revolution in the Head* (London, 1995), p. 177.
56 D. Davies, *Kink: An Autobiography* (London, 1996), pp. 1–6.
57 Ibid., p. 147.
58 J. Savage, *England's Dreaming: The Sex Pistols and Punk Rock* (London, 1992), p. 59.
59 The Members, 'The sound of the suburbs' single (Virgin Music, 1979, VS242).
60 Savage, *England's Dreaming*, pp. 72–3.
61 Siouxsie and the Banshees, 'Suburban relapse', on *The Scream* CD (Polydor, 1989, 839 008–2).
62 Savage, *England's Dreaming*, pp. 146, 241.
63 The Pet Shop Boys, 'Suburbia', on The Pet Shop Boys, *Discography* (Parlophone, 1991, TCPMTV 3); The Police 'Synchronicity 2', on *The Police: Greatest Hits* CD (A & M Records, 1992, 540 030–2); The Style Council, 'Come to Milton Keynes', on *Our Favourite Shop* CD (Polydor, 1985, 825 700–2).

64 Suede, 'The power', on *Dog Man Star* CD (Nude, 1995, 3CD).

65 Blur, 'Stereotypes' and 'Ernold Same', on Blur, *The Great Escape* CD (Parlophone, 1995, 7243 8 35235 28)

66 *Q*, September 1996, p. 114.

67 See, for example, P. Johnson (ed.), *Twentieth Century Britain: Economic, Social and Cultural Change* (London, 1994), pp. 16–17; A. Marwick, *British Society Since 1945* (Harmondsworth, 1987), pp. 19, 28, 31 and 34.

68 F. Bédarida, *A Social History of England, 1951–1990* (London, 1991), pp. 233–4.

69 N. Todd, 'The uses of contemporary suburban history, 1918–1950', *Local Historian*, 11:5 (1975), p. 285.

70 See, for example, D. Reeder, *Suburbanity and the Victorian City* (Leicester, 1980), passim; S. Martin Gaskell, 'Housing and the lower middle class, 1870–1914', in G. Crossick (ed.), *The Lower Middle Class in Britain, 1870–1914* (London, 1977), pp. 159–80; S. M. Gaskell, '"The suburb salubrious": town planning in practice', in A. Sutcliffe (ed.), *British Town Planning: The Formative Years* (Leicester, 1981), pp. 16–61; Thompson, *The Rise of Suburbia*, passim.

71 H. J. Dyos, *Urbanity and Suburbanity* (Leicester, 1979), passim. A. A. Jackson, *Semi Detached London* (London, 1991); A. A. Jackson, *The Middle Classes, 1900–1950* (Nairn, 1991), both passim.

72 T. Jeffrey, 'The suburban nation: politics and class in Lewisham', in D. Feldman and G. S. Jones (eds), *Metropolis. London: Histories and Representations Since 1800* (London, 1989), p. 191.

73 S. Caunce, *Oral History and the Local Historian* (London, 1994), p. 120.

74 C. Hall, 'Married women at home in Birmingham in the 1920s and 1930s', *Oral History*, 5:2 (1977), pp. 62–83; S. Humphries and J. Taylor, *The Making of Modern London: 1945–1985* (London, 1986), pp. 80–107; E. Roberts, *Women and Families: An Oral History, 1940–1970* (Oxford, 1995), passim.

75 See, for example, Age Exchange, *Just Like the Country: Memories of London Families Who Settled the New Cottage Estates, 1919–1939* (London, 1991). The Living Archive Project, in Wolverton, Milton Keynes, possesses a considerable tape archive on the experiences of moving to, and settling into, the new city.

76 E. Roberts, 'Neighbours: North West England, 1940–70', *Oral History*, 21:2 (1993), pp. 43–4.

77 C. Chinn, 'Women in their own words', *Social History Society Bulletin*, 20:20 (1995), p. 32.

78 C. Chinn, *Better Betting With a Decent Feller: Bookmakers, Betting and the British Working Class, 1750–1991* (Hemel Hempstead, 1991), pp. xi, 185–6. See also above, Chapters 3 and 4; p. 70.

79 E. Hopkins, *The Rise and Decline of the English Working Classes: 1918–1990* (London, 1991), p. 277.

80 T. Blackwell and J. Seabrook, *A World Still to Win: The Reconstruction of the Postwar Working Class* (London, 1985), p. 110; J. Seabrook, 'Milton Keynes: a mirror of England', *Observer Magazine*, 5 October 1978.

81 B. Brookes and J. Lewis, 'A reassessment of the work of the Peckham Health Centre, 1926–1951', *Milbank Memorial Fund Quarterly, Health and Society*, 61:2 (1983), pp. 330–2; Jackson, *Semi Detached London*, pp. 137–8.

2

The origins and extent of postwar urban dispersal

This chapter is in four parts. First, it looks at the reasons for the growth of the suburbs in the Victorian and Edwardian years. It assesses the origins of the garden city and garden suburb schemes as reactions to both suburban sprawl and to the degraded hearts of England's larger industrial towns and cities. The influence of garden city and garden suburb experiments upon the design of suburbs and new towns is emphasised.

The second part of this chapter describes the continuing spread of suburbanisation between the wars. This was manifest both in the classic era of semi-detached, privately purchased suburban homes, and in the instigation of large new municipal housing estates comprised largely of homes for rent and built in the outer areas of established towns and cities. This section will, furthermore, point to the growing influence of the town planning profession between the wars, and its promotion of contained development via new towns to counteract suburban sprawl.

Third, and following on from the previous discussion, the impact of war and reconstruction on postwar dispersal is assessed. For war brought about the consolidation of the town planning profession and promoted its influence. Many planners and politicians advocated the introduction of new and expanded towns as central to the postwar reconstruction of Britain. Prewar developments are stressed in this chapter because they influenced the shape of postwar housing developments and laid the basis for postwar dispersal.

Fourth, then, the chapter assesses the extent of the continuing postwar spread of peripheral projects, which, as F. M. L. Thompson argued, 'replicated the established suburban mode of attaching new building estates and complete fresh suburbs to the existing built-up area'.[1] It then illustrates the extent of migration to new and expanded towns. Finally, the chapter ascertains which working-class groups moved out.

Victorian and Edwardian suburbanisation

Suburban areas of towns and cities were nothing new to the nineteenth century. Lewis Mumford, an influential writer on the history of cities, argued that suburbs had grown from the centres of towns and cities in classical civilisations, and Byzantine, medieval and many early modern cities were characterised by suburban growth.[2] In nineteenth-century England, however, particularly from the 1820s, they took on their first truly modern form: the suburban extension of the industrial town and city.[3] The spatial spread of suburbanisation was stimulated by middle-class money and aspirations, by the purchase of land away from the urban cores so that new developments of suburban residences could be built exclusively for those who could afford them. Improved transportation, initially the increased private ownership of the horse-drawn carriage, enabled the comfortably-off Victorian householder to commute between home and the centre of town, as the town centres became increasingly reserved for business and commerce. The spread of the railways from the 1820s expanded suburbanisation by reducing commuting time. The extent of railways in Britain increased from a few score miles during the 1820s to over 18,000 miles of track by 1914.[4] Most significant for this discussion was the growth of the urban railway system, which occurred mostly from the 1850s. Intra-urban networks and local branch lines enabled people to live on the margins and work in the centre. From 1863, the London Metropolitan railway system, later to become the Underground, accelerated and extended this trend in the capital.[5] The introduction of the tramways during the 1870s and after furthered suburbanisation, too.[6]

The nineteenth-century suburbs have been interpreted in a negative way as a bourgeois reaction to a bourgeois creation, a response to the degraded, overpopulated, unsanitary and ill-regulated slums of the capitalist industrial city.[7] As workers migrated to the industrial centres to seek work in mills, mines and workshops, they found rented accommodation in often cheap, jerry-built and tightly clustered terraces of housing. Many thousands of families also lived in lets: rooms of larger houses which had been vacated by the evacuating middle classes and sold on to landlords.[8] The wealthy and aspiring middle classes – industrial, commercial, professional – became increasingly ensconced in the suburban rings around the town and city centres. Some moved even further afield to far-flung rural retreats or seaside residences.[9] These patterns in the geographical spread of housing have continued to the present day.

Suburbanisation had both a social and a spatial impact. The beleaguered proletarian dwellings of the town and city centres, huddling close to the factories and commercial areas of the Victorian town, often degenerated into slums, 'that relatively inert mass stranded behind suburban frontiers'.[10] For Marxist critics of the suburbs, the middle classes were deserting the poor. The wealth of the town was also being diverted outwards, creating a legacy of inner urban decay which clung tenaciously to the English town well into the twentieth century. Conservative historians have also been critical. Writing long before the onset of the Thatcherite era of urban deregulation, Roy Lewis and Angus Maude (the latter an MP during the 1950s and 1960s) noted the problems of the pre-regulated city:

> As the northern towns grew, without services or government, the middle classes prospered at the cost of suppressing their humanity, of refusing to see what went on about them. When the towns became too insanitary, they built suburbs for themselves and cultivated the suburban values which go with them.[11]

A further consequence of suburbanism, which has also attracted considerable criticism, was the increased distance it placed between home and work. It thus appeared to extend the separation of home and work which was characteristic of advanced capitalist society. The social and personal implications of this were imaginatively anticipated by Charles Dickens. For example, in *Great Expectations*, first published in 1860, the character of Wemmick lived with his aged parent in a new suburban villa in Deptford, South London. He was a decent, docile, do-it-yourself home-lover, but at his City offices in Little Britain he had transmuted into an evil plotter. That Jekyll and Hyde transformation occurred *en route* between home and office. For the historian of literature Angus Calder, Wemmick may be viewed as 'a prophetic parody of the divided existence of present-day commuters who, after a day at the office working for the firm, "relax" by working wholeheartedly at improving their own homes'.[12]

The cult of home improvement was an important aspect of Victorian suburban domesticity. So was the garden. The home-based or privatised family, which was central to Victorian values, found perhaps its highest and most materially well-endowed expression in the suburbs. The proximity of a house with a garden to the fresh air and fields of the countryside, in combination with access to the cultural and practical facilities of the town (a mere tram or train ride away), formed the basic elements of suburban culture. Whilst noting the social, economic and environmental impact of suburbanisation, urban historians have recognised that the suburban home offered 'a fuller life for many city dwellers' in its comforts and compensations, and as a decent location within which the family could flourish.[13] This theme is further pursued in Chapters 3 and 4.

During the 1860s the bourgeois creation of the suburbs ceased to be a bourgeois monopoly. The faster expansion of the urban railway networks contributed to a democratisation of the outlying residential rings. In London, for example, the introduction of the metropolitan railway system from 1863 ushered in an era of cheaper mass transport. This was continually augmented by the extension of lines by other railway companies. Thus began the process by which a small but significant proportion of the more affluent working classes could move to the suburbs. In Edmonton in North London, for example, the extension of the Great Eastern Railway beyond Liverpool Street Station in 1872 brought with it an influx of working-class East Enders who could afford both to live in the cheaper rental houses, and the rail fares.[14] This process, a trickle in the 1860s and 1870s, was accelerated by government policy, notably the introduction of the working men's Cheap Trains Act of 1883.[15] New 'workers' suburbs' sprang up along the burgeoning railway networks. As John Burnett notes, the poorer suburbs were generally located closer to the city, where fares and housing rents remained cheaper.[16] Furthermore, cheap suburban housing was often the product of excessive building activities. This sometimes led to gluts of housing which had to be let at reduced prices in order to recoup some of the outlay costs.[17] The very poorest of the working classes, however, continued to cling on to a precarious existence in the slums and rookeries of inner London.[18]

A minority of workers could afford to move to the suburbs. For example, in late Victorian Brixton, south of the Thames, the Labour leader Herbert Morrison was in his own way representative of the aspirant working classes who could afford the higher rents of the 'dormitory estates'. Morrison's father was a policeman, a denizen of the respectable, uniformed working class who mixed with the affluent artisans and mechanics in small and distinctive pockets of, by working-class standards, superior housing.[19] Morrison grew up in a two-down, three-up terraced house 'on the edge of London'. Evincing an attitude that has long since been criticised as 'suburban', he wrote of 'the cult of respectability' in terms of occupation and place of residence, and proudly described his 'modest home' as 'the envy and admiration of the neighbours, though with little reason on grounds of practical considerations'. Beyond his home, however, 'one came to the suburbs of the richer people'.[20]

Lewisham was one such richer middle-class suburb of South London. The arrival of the railways from 1849 had transformed this rural parish into a network of large and middling-sized terraced town houses.[21] A contemporary of Morrison's, the writer and journalist Thomas Burke, who hailed from a well-off family, wrote fondly of the beauties, comforts and stability of his South London suburban 'village' home.[22] These two boys lived in adjacent suburbs, but their home and family circumstances differed. Such socio-economic diversity was endemic to London's railway suburbs: by street, within streets, and by area and borough. This social and economic differentiation, writ large, became increasingly significant with the growth of cheap trains and trams from the mid-1880s. The gathering pace of suburban differentiation was mapped by Charles Booth and his team of researchers in their great survey of *Life and Labour of the People of London*. This was begun in the mid-1880s and completed in 1902.

As David Reeder has shown from his work on Booth's survey, the suburban areas of London were by no means static and homogenous, but dynamic and in some areas unstable. Booth emphasised the 'powerful centrifugal forces' which shaped London's expansion. His survey illustrated how earlier suburbs were transcended by subsequent housing developments. Earlier Victorian suburbs sitting just outside the centre became pressurised for living space, as overcrowding accompanied the relentless process of outward migration. Hence, once outer suburbs became inner suburbs. Moreover, suburban arrivals at an outer London village could generally improve the economic fortunes of that village, but marginalise the poor of the parish.[23]

Life and Labour was an important developmental moment in the empirical tradition of British social investigation. One of Booth's avowed intentions was to glean systematic socio-economic and demographic data which could be drawn upon for the purposes of ameliorative social policies.[24] Other sociologists, notably B. S. Rowntree and Marion Bowley, refined social survey techniques to produce both systematic and vivid pictures of town life. That point serves as a reminder of the importance of sociology as a primary source for historians of the social changes and continuities in urbanisation. The following chapters make extensive use of sociology.

Booth, however, was but one important figure who sought solutions to the problems of the late Victorian city. The rapid and extensive urbanisation of England had created towns and cities which were characterised by extremes of wealth and poverty, of comfortable affluent areas contrasting with insanitary and overcrowded slums. Hence the slum was at the centre of the Edwardian crisis of national self-confidence. The 'new' Liberal reforms of 1906–14, whose key innovations were the introduction of national insurance, of unemployment payments, and of non-contributory old age pensions, represented attempts by central government to alleviate social and economic deprivation in the poorest areas.[25]

Coterminous with the growth of both empirical social investigation and increasing government intervention was the development of a town planning profession. These two traditions were to some extent synthesised in the work of Patrick Geddes, a leading planner and advocate of garden cities, who was adamant that new plans for new cities should be prefaced by a survey into the economic, demographic, social and even historical characteristics of the area. Only then would the requisite information be available to plan for the reconstruction of a region or a locality. Geddes's ideas influenced a number of key advocates of planning, notably Lewis Mumford and Clarence Stein.[26]

The influence of town planning during the early twentieth century can be seen in the increased centralised intervention engendered by the 1909 Housing and Town Planning Act. Planners were also involved in a number of pioneering local authorities who had attempted to clear slums and provide houses in the later Victorian years, and the 1909 Act attempted to expedite and extend these developments. It gave powers of compulsory land purchase to local authorities in order that they might acquire land for building, and to facilitate removals from slums. It also empowered the Local Government Board to enforce inactive local authorities to build houses.[27]

Before the First World War, however, slum clearance schemes remained *ad hoc* and small-scale. And whilst there were some significant public housing schemes, there was nothing on a mass scale.[28]

The influence of town planning ideology and action was more in evidence in some significant private initiatives and experiments in housing provision and urban improvement during the Edwardian years. Their origins and enactment lay in a combination of utopianism and practical mutual self-help schemes. These were the garden city and garden suburb schemes, associated with the ideas of Ebenezer Howard. He proposed the dispersal of parts of the population from overcrowded and polluted urban areas to new garden cities. These were to be placed in the countryside, but they were intended to be small, self-contained, socially mixed and balanced town communities in their own right. They were to provide their inhabitants with the amenities of the town and the healthy benefits of the countryside, but without the squalor and overcrowding of the former or the supposedly atavistic elements of the latter.

Howard, furthermore, wanted to preserve the countryside by preventing unplanned and untidy suburban sprawl. Planned garden cities, he argued, as self-contained communities, and with the best of town and country, would obviate the need to live away from work, and hence reduce the outward thrust of urban development. Such thinking was echoed in the organisational heirs to Howard: the Garden Cities and Town Planning Association and the Hundred New Towns Group, for example, which were comprised of leading Edwardian and interwar planners.[29]

The two famous private experiments to result from Howard's thinking, about which much has been written, were the Garden City Pioneer Company Limited, which gave birth to Letchworth in the early Edwardian years, and Welwyn Garden City, which was built between the wars.[30] They reflected the influence upon Howard of a number of successful Victorian factory villages provided by model employers.[31] Howard also shared with many of his reforming contemporaries an idealised image of pre-industrial 'Merrie England'. He contrasted this seemingly static and stable organic rural settlement with the instability of the expanding, shifting metropolis and, it was argued, the artificial, social and spatial segregation of the classes. There was, moreover, a practical consideration: overcrowded and overstretched cities strained resources and services, and burdened tax-payers and rate-payers. Hence planned communities were viewed as solutions to the ills of the urban-industrial complex. Lower housing densities, parks and gardens, proximity to the countryside, and the provision of adequate practical and cultural facilities within the town, would provide for a healthier and more fulfilling life.[32]

Social mix, however, did not really translate into residential mix. Whilst Howard's garden city was to contain a representative cross-section of the national community, at the micro level there was no next-door-neighbouring between the affluent middle classes, the lower middle classes and the affluent artisans. And there was certainly no room for those whom Booth had termed the 'vicious, semi-criminal poor'. This 'residuum' was never decanted to Letchworth. Instead, for some deemed to be the undeserving or dangerous poor, the destination was, literally, a labour colony on the coast of England.[33] The other classes were represented in Letchworth, but in houses and streets akin to their income and occupation.[34]

Howard's vision of low-density layout was complemented by a traditional domestic architecture which owed much to some of the Victorian model villages, with their cottage architecture and concern for attractive layout and amenities. The architects Barry Parker and Raymond Unwin became influential within this tradition. They designed and planned buildings and estates for Letchworth, and for a number of other pioneer garden suburb schemes.[35] By 1914, Parker and Unwin were leading architects and estate planners.

Alongside the garden city experiments, the garden suburb movement provided some important exemplars of planned suburban estates. It also pioneered some important examples of 'voluntary corporate action' as the basis of estate life[36] in the Edwardian period. A pioneer of the garden suburb ideal was Henrietta Barnett, co-founder with her husband Canon Samuel Barnett of the Settlement in Toynbee Hall, East London, in the 1880s. Henrietta Barnett wanted to provide housing in planned out-of-town estates which were to be brought into existence by the collective self-help of the tenants themselves. This was 'co-partnership'. In common with the social principles advocated by Howard, the garden suburb was to be socially mixed and balanced. It was intended that by placing the workers in with the allegedly example-setting middle classes, a general raising of the manners and morals of the people would occur. Hampstead Garden Suburb, designed according to Parker and Unwin's plans, was the fruit of Barnett's work.[37]

Against Barnett's hopes, however, Hampstead Garden Suburb developed into a largely middle-class enclave.[38] It would be mistaken, despite this, to view the garden suburb idea, the co-partnership principle, and the practical examples to which they gave birth, as essentially middle-class. For these ideals were advocated by and pursued by undeservedly less well known activists from the affluent and skilled working class who wanted to provide those sections of the working classes with the benefits of planned estates of cottage-style houses which were situated away from the slummy, smoky city centres. The carpenter and trades unionist Henry Vivian, for example, was the leading founder of Ealing Tenants' Limited, which built the Brentham Estate in West London. Vivian was, furthermore, a founder of a builders' co-operative, and he applied his strongly held belief in collective endeavour to a mutual scheme for raising the capital required for the estate and sharing its profits.[39] Co-partnership tenants frequently raised capital in the form of loans from building societies – themselves originally institutional expressions of working-class collective investment and mutual self-help[40] – and commissioned architects and builders. Association with a local co-operative society was often useful to these ends, too.[41] The principle of co-partnership was given everyday expression in the shared enjoyment of a tranquil and planned garden suburb, with an active social life. Self-help was the key. Tenants' associations were to be responsible for maintenance in Brentham, for example, and a horticultural society was formed to promote self-sufficiency in the growing of fruit and vegetables.[42] This may also be viewed as one of many open-air leisure activities which were becoming fashionable with the wider suburban public of the pre-1914 era, and which included cycling, tennis, bowling and other sporting clubs.[43]

Many new garden suburbs were brought into existence by co-partnership associations. Of the fifty-eight garden suburbs in existence by 1914, thirty-eight had been developed along co-partnership lines.[44] And the associative principle provided the organised social life of these estates. Associations were expressions both of mutual self-help and of sociability. Michael Harrison has shown that Burnage Garden Village in Edwardian Manchester demonstrated that co-partnership was perceived by tenants as an opportunity to manage 'the whole social and recreative life' of the estate, and an association and clubhouse soon came into being to provide for that.[45] S. M. Gaskell argues that garden suburbs 'developed a sense of identity [and] a pattern of community life which was to become a model for twentieth-century planners'.[46]

The rents of the architect-designed houses at Brentham were between six and twenty-one shillings per week, excluding rates. In Burnage, they varied from upwards of five shillings to eleven shillings and sixpence a week, again exclusive of rates. This put them beyond the budgets of most of London's and Manchester's working classes.[47] Hence rent levels ensured a measure of exclusivity, which itself may be interpreted as an expression of social identification within groups who defined themselves against others. (This point is returned to in Chapters 4 and 5.) The minority presence of the working classes in the peripheries, however, was to end with the so-called 'bastardisation' of the garden suburb model.[48] The years after 1918 witnessed the mass penetration of the working classes into the suburbs, largely via municipal estates for rent, but also, for the most securely employed workers, through the ownership of a house on a privately built estate.

The growth of suburbanisation between the wars

The inappropriately named Great War of 1914–18 brought to a halt most slum clearance and municipal housing projects begun in the period immediately before August 1914. The war thus exacerbated housing problems. In February 1917 Lloyd George appointed the Second Reconstruction Committee to plan for an extensive programme of working-class housing once the war was over, and reports from other bodies, notably the Local Government Board's committee on working-class dwellings, revised upwards the scale of housing required after the cease-fire.[49] This report, known after the Chairman of the committee, Sir John Tudor Walters, also adopted elements of the garden suburb models for estate layout and domestic architecture, and utilised these in its recommendations for the design of future working-class housing. The Tudor Walters report also advised on healthier minimum standards for light, space and room size, and allowed generously for household amenities, notably indoor lavatories, bathroom and kitchen equipment, and larders in kitchens.[50]

After the Armistice, the continuation of the housing problem was given an added urgency by the need to house soldiers, and also by the demonstrations and rent strikes of 1919. In consequence, the Minister for Health, Christopher Addison, was responsible for the 1919 Housing and Town Planning Act. This provided for a subsidy from central government to local authorities to promote the construction of essential new housing. The subsidy principle was the clearest commitment by the state thus far to the provision of houses, and was an important dimension of increased government collectivism between the wars. The Addison scheme provided for over 213,000 houses; 170,000 were constructed by councils, and 39,000 by private builders. Growing costs and the financial problems of the early 1920s curtailed Addison's programme, however.[51]

The government's proactive role in subsiding housing provision continued with Neville Chamberlain's 1923 Housing Act. This Act switched subsidies away from the council to private builders, and allowed for a lowering of the grant eligibility, which in turn meant many smaller and more cheaply built houses let at lower rents. The following year, the Labour government passed the Wheatley Act, which restored subsidies directly to the councils, thus strengthening their role as housing providers once more. The subsidy principle was continued until 1933, when it was phased out by the Conservative-dominated National government, which fastened more fully upon the problems of the slums.[52] Slum clearance had accompanied many local authority rehousing schemes, but only 11,000 slum dwellings were cleared in the 1920s. Labour's 1930 Acts and the National government's 1933 Act made slum clearance and five-year rehousing schemes a priority: between 1932 and 1939 local authorities rehoused about four-fifths of those living in slum dwellings.[53] The legislative foundations of postwar housing developments had been laid.

Of the four million dwellings built between 1919 and 1939, 1.5 million were built by local authorities.[54] Most towns and cities gained the large interwar municipal estates which are such a familiar part of England's present urban landscape. Some of these developments were huge, for example St Helier near Wimbledon in South London, Edgware in North London, Wythenshawe in Manchester, Speke in Liverpool, and the Kingstanding estate in Birmingham. Dagenham, a London County Council (LCC) estate built near Becontree in Essex, was the largest, numbering over 17,800 houses and 103,300 people by 1932.[55] Dagenham, however, in common with many of these large-scale developments, was not primarily a slum clearance estate, although many residents came from cramped inner London housing. It was comprised largely of skilled and semi-skilled manual workers, over one-fifth of whom worked at Ford. The remainder were employed largely in transport and other manufacturing concerns.[56]

The new council estates such as those at Dagenham provided superior working-class housing to the inner urban areas. Both sociology and oral testimony provide many examples of the joy with which working-class people greeted a new home. Sentiments such as 'it was just like a palace' were not uncommon.[57] However, whilst most women welcomed their new home, some were greatly inconvenienced by poor transportation and insufficient leisure and shopping facilities.[58] Hence a widely held belief developed that the estates had become 'dormitories' due to their geographical location, which was often a lengthy bus or train ride away from the major source of employment, from shopping and entertainments, and from relatives. The visible lack of street life when compared with the colourful slums led many to view dormitory estates as social failures.[59]

Historians are fortunate that sociologists ventured onto some of the new estates during the 1930s to ascertain the nature of local life and social relations in these new communities. The findings of Ruth Durant for Edgware ('Watling'), or of Terence Young for Dagenham, for example, affirmed that new estates suffered from a lack of amenities, especially in their early days. Yet they dispelled any simplistic view of a dormant lifestyle, noting the role of organised associations. Some had formal problem-solving aims, but others were informal and based around a variety of interests and leisure activities.[60] There was, therefore, a certain continuity with the associative life of the Edwardian garden suburbs, but it was now increasingly to be found on predominantly working-class council estates. This discussion is returned to in Chapter 6.

The growth of council estates between the wars was related to major changes in tenure. They were in no small part responsible for the decline in renting from private landlords. Local authority rentals grew to account for 10 per cent of the housing stock by 1938.[61] Yet a greater independence in tenure, enabled by home ownership on owner-occupied estates, largely destroyed the predominance of renting from private landlords. These were mostly but not solely middle-class estates.[62] Hence the 1920s and 1930s have been viewed by social and urban historians as the classic era of semi-detached suburbia, or 'Dunroamin'. 'Dunroamin' was one of countless affectionate names chosen for a house by its owners. It symbolised a sense of home and of place that a new semi-detached or terraced home, with its often rusticated motifs and front and back gardens, offered to its inhabitants. Other names such as 'Acacia Villa' or 'The Hawthorns' hinted at rural influences, and the taste for the *rus in urbe* was exploited by private builders, as can be seen in the rural affectation of the names developers chose for their estates. The very word 'estate', moreover, was redolent with comfortable country domesticity.[63]

The new owner-occupied suburbs were significant in another very important way: Dunroamin was a motor car suburb. Public transport by bus and train continued to play an important role in commuting, but the car enabled people to enjoy more flexible travel routes. As Stevenson notes, by 1914 there were 140,000 motor vehicles in Britain. By 1939 there were three million, and two million were private vehicles.[64] Many new estates sprang up alongside arterial roads and service roads often stretching out for miles into the countryside. This was 'ribbon development' which motivated many people to act. The Campaign for the Preservation of Rural England, for example, included Patrick Abercrombie, a planner who was also passionate about the need for countryside conservation. Planners' pressure groups such as the Hundred New Towns Group, the Garden Cities and Town Planning Association and the Greater London Planning Committee lobbied for legislation to halt the spread of the metropolis. Abercrombie and Unwin, for example, argued strongly for a 'green girdle' around London, a plea taken up by Herbert Morrison, leader of the Labour-controlled London County Council, with his 'green belt' scheme of 1938. Other attempted restrictions of ribbon development included the unsuccessful Restriction of Ribbon Development Act of 1935, a product of the 1932 Town and Country Planning Act.[65]

Interwar critics such as the cartoonist Osbert Lancaster sneered at the 'by-pass variegated' of the suburban semi with its car on the drive,[66] but there can be little doubt of its popular appeal. The houses were within commuting distance of the town centre, and not far from the countryside. As one man, the son of a clerk in a London linoleum company during the 1930s, remembered: 'The single most important thing about its situation was that it stood on the Kingston bypass [but] we had to walk only a few hundred yards from our house to find countryside'. His mother and father named their house 'Wayside'.[67]

The internal combustion engine was adopted by industry, too. Between the wars, the new industries enjoyed greater mobility in location enabled by the extension of electricity and the growth of motorised transport. Companies chose to locate on out-of-town greenfield sites where rates and rents were cheap and motor access was easier than to the city centres. If Ford in Dagenham demonstrated that, so too did the location of the Hoover Factory in Perivale, Middlesex. This was symbolic both of the suburbanites' consumption of labour-saving devices and of the increasing spread of 'Metroland' over rural Middlesex.[68] As J. B. Priestley lamented in *English Journey*, the metropolitan suburbs were at the forefront of new trends in domestic consumption which were often American in origin. He was no fan of wirelesses, giant cinemas, dance halls and cafés, 'where the smooth wide road passes between miles and miles of semi-detached bungalows, all with their little garages ...'.[69]

Dunroamin, in all its local interwar variations, played host to the beginnings of a major expansion in the tenurial trend to popular owner-occupation. Between the end of the First World War and 1938, for example, the number of owner-occupied houses rose from about 10 per cent to 32 per cent.[70] Yet this broad statistic requires qualification. Only a small and relatively affluent elite of the skilled working classes and those in the better-paid service sector jobs could afford home ownership, 'and even then at the cost of self sacrifice and thrift'.[71] The repayments on a mortgage from a building society or on a local authority loan removed a significant part of many people's wages. Many annual incomes, moreover, most noticeably in the depressed industrial areas, were insufficient to raise a loan in the first place. Hence, as Swenarton and Taylor argue, there was no working-class 'incorporation' into home ownership by 1939.[72] The newly constructed suburbs of the middle classes contained the highest levels of owner-occupation between the wars. The 'boom' had begun, however, and it was to continue into the postwar years.[73]

Most English towns and cities were extended by Dunroamin-style developments. They were most extensive, however, in London, the South East and the Midlands. The geography of the owner-occupied suburbs is significant, for these were the regions where the rise of the new manufacturing industries was most extensive: the motor car, household durables and light engineering industries. The growth of the service sector, of finance, retail, distribution and administrative employment, was most extensive in the London and South East region. Two-thirds of all new jobs created in Britain between the wars were located in the metropolitan area, and the distributive trades showed the most rapid growth, from 1,661,000 workers in 1920–22 to 2,436,000 by 1938. More generally, white-collar work rose from 12 per cent of the occupied population in 1924 to over 15 per cent by 1935. In contrast, the nineteenth-century sectors of industrial manufacturing, mining, iron and steel, and shipbuilding, located in the North of England, were in decline.[74] This contrast between the depressed areas of the North of England and the prosperous suburbanising South and Midlands was a regional problem, which politicians attempted to relieve by public works schemes, notably by the euphemistically named Special Areas Acts of 1934 and 1937, which were designed to encourage investment in the depressed regions.[75] There was no reversal in the economic fortunes of the depressed areas, however. Instead, people voted with their feet and moved to the growing regions to look for work. This was the beginnings of the phenomenon of the 'drift to the South East', a drift which added to the population of the region over and above the 'natural' increase of births over deaths.[76] Suburbanisation and the new towns programme would become most extensive in this region. The economic fortunes of both would be bound up with the new light industries, but increasingly the service sector. As Peter Hall has argued, the interwar growth of the service sector would continue during the postwar years, and especially since 1970.[77]

In 1940 the *Report of the Royal Commission on the Distribution of the Industrial Population* (the Barlow Report) showed that between 1921 and the outbreak of war the population of London and the Home Counties had increased by over 18 per cent. Other areas of new industrial growth, such as the Midlands, grew by less than 11 per cent. In the North Eastern counties of Durham and Northumberland the population had declined by 1 per cent, whilst the South Wales coal field areas lost 9 per cent of their population.[78] The Report suggested that the continuing growth of the capital might undermine the economic recovery of other regions of Britain.[79] It called for the location of industry and new investment to be guided to the economically retarded 'special' areas of the old industrial heartlands. Its solution to the chronic congestion of inner London was to disperse population and employment into the regional hinterland.[80]

Barlow had actually begun work in 1937, yet his was the first wartime report. Others were to follow. They reflected the growing influence of planners in the political administration of Britain which war helped to bring about. Prior to 1939, the planning profession had only a limited influence, but war extended and consolidated the influence of planners within the emergency system of 'experts' created by the coalition government.

War, planning and reconstruction

The war began in September 1939. Once the 'phoney war' of late 1939 to mid-1940 was over, and as the bombs devastated housing and factories in the industrial areas, there was an early grasp of the need to take urgent action once the conflict had ended. Peter Hall's *Urban and Regional Planning* emphasises the significance of a number of wartime and immediate postwar planning reports which established the nature of, and parameters for, future planning action.[81]

The Dudley Report of 1944, entitled the *Design of Dwellings*, 'was intended to do for postwar housing what the Tudor Walters Report had done for interwar housing', and to adjust former standards to meet new needs and raised expectations.[82] The Committee, chaired by the Earl of Dudley, had gathered evidence from a number of witnesses, including women's organisations, on what people wanted from their house, and on how homes were used for cooking, eating, leisure and other aspects of what might be termed the reproduction of the household. Dudley recommended generous-sized living rooms, dining-kitchens and a range of improvements to accommodate the growing expectation for convenience and luxury: bigger and better-equipped kitchens, ventilated larders, cupboards, even a small refrigerator as standard, although the latter item was omitted from most municipal housing schemes as costs spiralled.[83] The recommendations of the Dudley Report were given expression in the government's *Housing Manual*, which set the minimum standards of public housing until the Parker Morris Report of 1961.[84]

In 1944 the *Greater London Plan*, researched and written by Forshaw and Abercrombie, was published. It has two major points of relevance for this discussion. First, it gave explicit and practical recognition to the principle of dispersal as a solution to the problems of London's overcrowding. Hence it adopted the leitmotif in Barlow's report. Abercrombie's vision entailed a system of concentric centrifugal 'rings' of development for the capital and its hinterland which would sit over and around the complex and ungainly metropolitan area, and contain it. As Gordon Cherry has argued, the *Greater London Plan* was a bold and simplistic solution: in order to salvage and redevelop inner London's largely Victorian core, reduced population densities and the outward movement of industries were required. This movement was, metaphorically speaking, to jump over the 'suburban ring' and 'green belt ring' and culminate in a series of planned and contained new towns, and in out-county estates, built in the fourth 'outer county ring'. It was intended that over one million people, with the requisite employment, would be dispersed. A further anticipated benefit was the reduction in the number of journeys to work within the capital.[85] Abercrombie's Plan was endorsed by a wartime study of the journey to work problem, which supported the call for self-contained new towns.[86]

How would the new towns be designed, however, as places in which to live? Here the second major aspect of Abercrombie's recommendations was in the advocacy of the 'neighbourhood unit' principle in the design of housing developments. Technically, the neighbourhood as a concept in planning emanated from the United States, but it was one which was implicit in the ideas for social mix and social balance promulgated by the leading advocates of the garden suburb and garden city movements on both sides of the Atlantic.[87] In interwar England, Barry Parker's Wythenshawe, for example, had been designed to local neighbourhood principles, and by 1933 25,000 people were housed in three neighbourhood units there. As a planner, Abercrombie was well versed in these experiments and felt that the neighbourhood inculcated local pride, facilitated local control and organisation, 'and is the means for resolving what would otherwise be interminable aggregations of housing'.[88] In other words, the neighbourhood was an antidote to atomistic dormitory sprawl.

This idea gelled strongly with the sense of a new national community and of social mixing which many politicians and planners felt had been fired up by the war effort. For example, Sir Charles Reilly's neighbourhood estate plan for Birkenhead excited many on the Left who felt it provided a model not simply for the reconstruction of the built environment but also for community reconstruction, for the facilitation of local pride, and for resolving the problems of dormitory estates.[89] Local authorities and new and expanded town development corporations would adopt neighbourhood units, to varying degrees of success, in the design of the largest postwar peripheral projects and new towns.[90]

The subsidy for these developments would come from central governments. It must be remembered here that over and above the extensive damage to homes caused by aerial bombardment, the ability of local authorities to build houses was severely curtailed during the conflict. There resulted, in consequence, an official imperative to ensure that the central–local government partnership in house building and slum clearance, established between the wars, would become as efficient as possible. The subsidy from Westminster to local councils was affirmed by both Labour and Conservative parties during the war.[91]

The aforementioned concepts of dispersal and of the neighbourhood unit, however, would find their most systematic expression in the programme for the new towns. This was evidenced in the work of John Reith, appointed head of the New Towns Committee by the incoming Labour government in 1945. The Reith Committee fully endorsed the need to decant population from the congested inner areas, and to encourage economic growth in the host areas in order to create self-contained self-sufficient new towns.[92]

Dispersal and its social implications were no monopoly concern of planners and politicians. The National Council of Social Service (NCSS), a statutory organisation concerned to ameliorate social problems through social policies and through practical on-the-ground work, wanted to highlight both the advantages and disadvantages of planned decentralisation. The NCSS had first-hand knowledge of the social consequences of three forms of mass dispersal: the official decanting of slum dwellers to new estates between the wars, voluntary migration to the suburban new estates[93] and the wartime experience of evacuation.[94]

In 1942 the Bank of England commissioned the NCSS to undertake an enquiry into 'the lessons to be learned' from the evacuation of clerical and administrative staffs during the war. The results were to be interpreted not simply as a wartime phenomenon 'but as a permanent arrangement'. The problems of 'uprooting' were adumbrated, and so too were the advantages.[95] The NCSS study was significant for three reasons. First, some of the lessons learned from the often traumatic experiences of evacuees were recognised and adopted for the purposes of policy discussion. As the report argued, it was dangerous to generalise about the reactions of those evacuated, but whilst many had been happy to leave and had 'felt they had gained', others, especially those in makeshift accommodation, had been clearly unhappy. Many were dissatisfied at the overcrowding and poor facilities of the reception areas.[96] Second, the NCSS felt that wartime planners were overly concerned with industrial labour, and had failed to recognise the scale of white-collar staffs in London and their experiences during wartime work. This was prescient, given the coterminous growth of dispersal with the de-industrialisation of England in the postwar years. Third, the concept of dispersal, and its interwar consequences and future potential, had been taken up by professions other than those of politics and planning. The NCSS gave evidence to the Reith Committees, for example.[97]

All of this did not mean, however, that there was a cross-party and pan professional consensus in favour of dispersal. Many politicians and planners criticised the idea. Their alternative was to call for large-scale, high-density central-area and inner-urban schemes, making considerable use of blocks of flats, to be the main thrust of postwar reconstruction.[98] Yet that modernist approach, influenced in part by the Swiss architect Le Corbusier, was less influential than the Howard–Unwin–Reith lineage. The postwar residential built environment would be a largely low-density, low-level creation of etiolated garden suburb style houses. A small proportion of flats and maisonettes, however, was reserved for some of the largest new peripheral and overspill projects, and for new towns. An indication of the low relative proportion of flats to houses was evident in the fact that in Harlow, the new town where flats were most numerous, flats numbered 21 per cent of all dwellings by 1957, a figure that was subsequently revised downwards.[99] The tower block was most extensively constructed in the inner redevelopment areas.[100]

The extent of postwar dispersal

We should not interpret the postwar years in isolation from the wider historical context, because the period since the war witnessed the continuity of a number of key trends creating the momentum for dispersal. Since the industrial revolution, England has been the most extensively urbanised country in Britain, and Britain one of the most urbanised countries in Europe. By 1914, 78 per cent of English people lived in urban areas. By 1980 this had risen to 90 per cent.[101] The continuing spread of suburban housing estates, and the construction of new and expanded towns, extended the bricks and mortar of the town environment and reaffirmed England as a nation of town dwellers. More than that, as a consequence of increasing car ownership and more complex patterns of commuting, urban life became more mobile, less localised, increasingly flexible, and less polarised between the opposites of town and country.[102] This section will assess these developments.

Working-class suburbanisation occurred within both major forms of tenure, that is, the local authority rental sector and private owner-occupation. Local authority housing stocks provide perhaps the most accurate picture of the extent of the suburbanisation of the working classes. The Department of the Environment divides local authority housing developments into the following categories:

- *inner city/city centre* – the area immediately proximate to the core of large cities;
- *urban* – areas around the core of town and small cities and also older urban areas which have been swallowed up by the centre;
- *suburban* – the outer area of towns and cities, characterised by large, planned housing estates;
- *rural residential* – villages;
- *rural isolated* – isolated dwellings and small hamlets.

The extent of local authority house-building in these areas can be seen in Table 2. The borders between these classifications are problematic. For example, the urban category may contain old outer suburbs which are now inner suburbs. Yet the statistics reveal that the construction of council dwellings in suburban estates since 1919, and especially in the years since 1945, has been considerably greater in volume than in the other four categories in combination. Since 1919, 2,014,000 suburban council dwellings have been constructed, compared with a total of 1,845,000 for the remaining four categories. The years from 1945 to 1964 witnessed the high watermark of public sector housing construction generally, and suburban council house building in particular. Some of that housing replaced slums in the centre of old towns. Some 866,000 houses were erected during that period, almost double that of the preceding and subsequent twenty-year periods, and considerably more extensive than since the early 1970s. Hence for some urban sociologists, the period from 1945 to the late 1960s was the peak of what they term the 'collective provision' and 'collective consumption' of state housing.[103]

Table 2 Local authority stock: age of dwellings by location, 1991 (thousand dwellings)

	Inner city/ city centre	*Urban*	*Suburban*	*Rural residential*	*Rural isolated*	*Total*
Pre-1919	22	98	29	7	4	160
1919–44	23	241	474	68	6	812
1945–64	61	380	866	195	12	1,514
1965–80	96	400	541	122	3	1,162
Post 1980	14	73	104	21	–	212
Total	216	1,192	2,014	413	25	3,860

Source: Based on Department of the Environment, *English House Condition Survey 1991* (London, 1993). I am grateful to Sarah Fielder of the Department of the Environment for her assistance.

The type of council and development corporation accommodation provided was mostly houses, as opposed to flats. By the mid-1990s, almost two-thirds of council tenants (62 per cent) lived in a house. Of those houses, 31 per cent were semi-detached and 31 per cent were terraced. Slightly more than one-third of tenants (35 per cent) lived in a purpose-built flat. Only 3 per cent lived in non-private landlord rented accommodation built since 1984, but since that year housing associations accounted for almost all new starts, as council house construction declined.[104] As council house building tailed off after 1970, housing associations increased their operations within the rental sector. The growing contribution of housing associations was not new to the 1970s and 1980s, but a policy-led acceleration of previous trends. The Conservative government's anti-municipal housing Acts of 1981 and 1985 all but killed off council housing and placed the onus for new starts onto housing associations. A second important plank of 1980s housing policy was the promotion of owner-occupation, another pre-existing trend which was accelerated and expanded by policy.[105]

Of all owner-occupiers, nine out of ten lived in a house by 1995; 35 per cent lived in a semi-detached house, 27 per cent in a detached house, and 27 per cent in a terraced house.[106] In the twenty-five years from 1919 to 1944, 1,691,000 houses were built for owner-occupation in the English suburbs. In the period 1945–90, 4,137,000 suburban owner-occupied dwellings were built, amounting to 5,828,000 in all. In the same period, a combined total of 6,389,000 dwellings for owner-occupation were built in the other four designations of inner city, urban, rural residential and rural isolated. Moreover, since 1945 the majority of semi-detached and detached houses have been built within new housing developments in the outer wards – the local government divisions – of towns, as is evident in Table 3.

Table 3 Owner-occupied stock: age of dwellings by location, 1991 (thousand dwellings)

	Inner city/ city centre	*Urban*	*Suburban*	*Rural residential*	*Rural isolated*	*Total*
Pre-1919	237	1,605	777	554	388	3,561
1919–44	66	612	1,691	269	68	2,706
1945–64	23	301	1,579	451	59	2,413
1965–80	34	279	1,780	839	66	2,998
Post 1980	10	176	778	328	24	1,316
Total	370	2,973	6,605	2,441	605	12,994

Source: Department of the Environment, *English House Condition Survey 1991* (London, 1993).

However, there is a difficulty in giving precise estimates of working-class suburban owner-occupation in particular, and suburban growth in general. This is symptomatic of a wider problem facing government statistics. It has proved impossible to measure suburbanisation with exactitude, either in terms of ground covered or population. The Office of Population Censuses and Surveys (OPCS), for example, has highlighted the difficulty of maintaining an accurate and ongoing estimation of urban growth. Drawing the boundaries of urban areas 'has become more difficult with the spread of suburbia and the growth in the use of villages as dormitories'.[107] Furthermore, as Chris Denham of the OPCS and Bruce Wood, a political scientist, have argued, local government boundary changes complicate the problem. For example, many suburbs have been appropriated for, or pushed away from, different local authorities. And some suburban extensions to towns have been classified as 'rural' by some councils and their inhabitants who preferred the countryside *cachet* and the lower rates required by less-built-up areas.[108]

As noted, the above categories include development corporation housing schemes. It is, however, possible to separate off and quantify the specific extent of migration to the new and expanded towns. Due to the work of the development corporations in calibrating their incoming populations, and also to the efforts of academics with an interest in new towns, there is no shortage of statistical sources here.[109] In the years 1946–50, the first phase of designations, eleven new towns were designated in England, and eight of these were located in Abercrombie's outer London ring: Basildon, Bracknell, Crawley, Harlow, Hatfield, Hemel Hempstead, Stevenage (the first to be designated) and Welwyn Garden City. The latter was a symbolic reminder of the garden city idea as a progenitor of new towns.[110] Of the remaining first wave of new towns, Aycliffe and Peterlee, both situated in the North East, were intended to draw off population from the dilapidated and congested areas of the Tyne and Wear and to contribute to the revitalisation of a depressed mining area.[111] Corby in the South Midlands was designated as an overspill destination for a wide area, as its steel industry had long drawn migrants looking for work from the North East, Wales and Scotland. This was a consequence of a continuing process of migration from the declining mining and shipbuilding communities of those areas. The development corporation was appointed to ensure the continued growth of the local population and the local economy.[112]

The next major phase of new town designations was in the first half of the 1960s. Five were begun in England during these years. In the West Midlands, Redditch was intended both to relieve population from the West Midlands conurbation and to generate economic growth in a declining industrial region. Runcorn and Skelmersdale in the North West were intended to perform the same role for the South East Lancashire and North Cheshire conurbation, as was Washington in the declining coal field area of County Durham.[113]

A further wave of English new town designations was in the years 1967–70. The towns were Central Lancashire New Town, Milton Keynes, Northampton, Peterborough, Telford and Warrington. Of these Milton Keynes has become the largest, and from the late 1970s the fastest-growing urban area in Britain. In common with Peterborough and Northampton, Milton Keynes was to act as an overspill destination for London. Yet these towns were also intended both to contain growth and to act as generators of economic development in their respective regions. Furthermore, they were intended to accommodate the growing population which had resulted from the first baby boom. There was a natural increase in population, of births over deaths, of almost two million people (4.6 per cent) in England and Wales between 1951 and 1961. That first postwar generation would mature into adulthood and have children of their own. Hence the MHLG anticipated a growth of seven million in England's population between 1961 and 1981, and of this it expected at least 3.5 million new people in the London and South East region, hence the higher provision for new towns there.[114]

The new towns grew impressively, and largely in a controlled way, although there were occasional departures from, or revisions to, original targets. Table 4 provides a summary of the number of people who have moved to new towns. It also shows the greater extent of new towns in the London and South East region.

The expanded towns emanated from the Barlow Report's view that as industry and population became more mobile in the postwar years, both could be encouraged to attach to already existing urban areas in need of regeneration, thus performing a dual function of regeneration and the relief of congestion from the largest industrial centres, notably London and Birmingham.[115] The New Towns Act of 1946 allowed for the expansion of some existing towns but most emanated from the Town Development Act of 1952. Some of the largest towns designated for expansion in order to relieve London were Aylesbury, Basingstoke and Swindon, with Bury St Edmunds and Thetford typical of smaller overspill schemes.[116] Worsley in Lancashire was a large-scale town expansion scheme intended to relieve Salford.[117] By 1977 almost 89,000 houses had been completed under the provisions of the Town Development Act.[118]

A further and obviously closely related general indicator of dispersal is the decline of population from the centres of the major cities as a consequence of both policy-led and voluntary migration. In the seven largest English conurbations – Greater London, Greater Manchester, the West Midlands, West Yorkshire, Merseyside, Tyne and Wear and South Yorkshire – the outward movement of population, especially from inner city or redevelopment areas, has been considerable. Collectively, they accounted for over 19,714,000 people (42.8 per cent of the population of England and Wales) in 1961, but lost a further 1.8 million of their population between 1961 and

1981, to number 17,931,000 (36 per cent of the population of England and Wales). Greater London, by far the largest conurbation, lost 1.3 million people through dispersal in the same period.[119]

Table 4 Population of English new towns from designation to 1991

Name	*Year of designation*	*Population in year of designation*	*Population in 1991 (unless otherwise stated)*
Aycliffe	1947	16,000	24,700 (1989)
Basildon	1949	25,000	157,000
Bracknell	1949	5,150	51,350
Central Lancs	1970	234,000	255,200 (1985)
Corby	1950	15,700	47,100
Crawley	1947	9,100	87,200
Harlow	1947	4,500	73,800
Hatfield	1948	8,500	29,000 (1986)
Hemel Hempstead	1947	21,000	79,000
Milton Keynes	1967	40,000	148,000
Northampton	1968	133,000	184,000 (1989)
Peterborough	1967	81,000	137,900 (1990)
Peterlee	1948	200	22,200 (1987)
Redditch	1964	32,000	79,700
Runcorn	1964	28,500	68,900 (1989)
Skelmersdale	1961	10,000	41,800 (1985)
Stevenage	1946	6,700	81,200
Telford	1968	7,000	120,000
Warrington	1968	122,300	159,000
Washington	1964	20,000	61,900 (1989)
Welwyn G. C.	1948	18,500	41,000 (1986)

Source: *Town and Country Planning*, 60:10 (1991), p. 296.

This residential migration in Greater London was paralleled by changes in occupational location. The fastest-growing metropolitan labour markets tended to cluster around the peripheries of London's built-up area. Many people, therefore, went where the work was. But many who moved out still worked in the inner core and were prepared to commute, suggesting that an improved home and residential environment was a major factor in the decision to move, a point discussed fully in the next chapter.[120] The proportion of workers who commuted from outside the inner cities to work there rose by about 18 per cent between 1951 and 1981.[121] (By that measurement, then, dispersal did not substantially erode the journey to work phenomenon.)

As A. H. Halsey has argued, since the mid-1970s the outward movement of people from inner city areas to the suburbs and the new and expanded towns was both expanded and expedited. The drift to the South East from the declining manufacturing areas also continued.[122] These trends were maintained during the 1980s and although they began to slow down during the 1990s they have continued. The fastest-growing urban areas have remained in the South East, either within the region or on its borders. Milton Keynes grew by 37 per cent between 1981 and 1991, for example, and it was closely followed by Horsham in Sussex, Peterborough in East Anglia, and Bracknell in Berkshire.[123]

Finally, it is important to note that postwar urban expansion has been coterminous with the rise of motorised transport, a development which began on a mass scale before 1939, and which has grown considerably since. MHLG drew attention to the requirement to expand the road network in general, and in the South East in particular. This was due to the growth of private ownership of motor cars during the 1950s as a product of the increasing affluence and increasing access to personal mobility of millions more people during the years of postwar economic growth, full employment and rising real wages.[124] Between 1949 and 1966 the percentage of the population possessing at least one car rose from a little over 7 per cent to over 53 per cent.[125] More cars required more roads. In 1958 the first stretch of the M1 was opened, beginning the postwar motorway programme, and more 'A' roads were built or existing 'A' roads were widened or extended. Many new roads were built in the countryside to serve the new estates and new towns which were being developed there, and to link new developments with existing towns and with the national road network.[126] The continuation of urban dispersal, then, was accompanied by a continuation of the declining polarity of town and country. But the motor car facilitated the development of dispersal in another important way. The reduction in travelling times provided by the possession of a car enabled migrants to visit their relatives and friends often with ease. The spatial mobility offered by the motor car contributed to the widening of social networks because distance became less of a problem.

That point had important implications for the planning of towns and cities, implications whose effects can be seen most sharply in the changing design and layout of new towns. Planners were increasingly aware of the implications which rapid mobility held for the notion of closely knit and localised communities, and also for the potential of rapid communications to maintain relationships across further distances. Neighbourhood units had been designed to encourage localism, but localism was qualified by the impact of affluence and the motor car.[127] In fact, avant-garde planning theorists, notably Melvin Webber, whose ideas were to influence the planning of Milton Keynes, argued that neighbourhood and place were increasingly less important as bases for community.[128] The later phase of new towns, therefore, was undertaken in part to accommodate the increased consumption and use of cars. But it was also planned to embrace greater flexibility in the popular use of towns than the neighbourhoods had allowed for, and to move away from the determinism of the neighbourhood unit. This discussion is returned to more fully, in relation to Milton Keynes, in Chapter 6.

Who moved?

The majority of people who moved were working-class couples with children, or couples who were just about to have them. As Chapters 3 and 4 show, most people felt the new estates were good places to raise children. The slum clearance programme, the new and expanded towns programmes, and planned peripheral council estates, provided improved accommodation and living standards which were largely aimed at these households. The largest part of this migration was voluntary. For example, the Greater London Council's *Greater London Development Plan*, published in 1969, found that 'the greater part of the movement of people and jobs out of London was spontaneous ...'.[129] Within the working classes this voluntarism was most strongly located within the younger and relatively wealthier brackets, that is, young families whose 'head of household' was either a skilled, semi-skilled or to a lesser extent an unskilled manual worker.[130] Beyond the working classes, some lower-middle-class (intermediate professional) and professional households moved to the new and expanded towns, and to peripheral suburban estates, but their presence in new and expanded towns rarely exceeded one-quarter of those populations, a proportion which reflected their national percentage.[131] The middle classes were and have remained under-represented in council estates. Some 95 per cent of Dagenham, for example, was comprised of manual workers.[132] The growth of owner-occupation since 1945, and especially since 1970, has led to council estates being largely populated by households whose heads were unskilled and semi-skilled.[133]

The voluntarism of migrants requires qualification. Slum dwellers whose homes were to be demolished had a limited choice when compared to those who placed themselves on the council house waiting lists, and especially the owner-occupiers, whose housing choice was greatest. It was possible for some in the poorest redevelopment areas to apply to stay there, but it was doubtless easier to accept a house in the new peripheral council estates. As the sociologists Nicholas Deakin and Clare Ungerson argued, however, in relation to Londoners who opted to move out, even for those with restricted opportunities, choices were still being made, and those choices were meaningful.[134]

It is important to note, furthermore, that the benefits of dispersal were not enjoyed by many poorer people who were obscured from view by the images and rhetoric of affluence. In *The Affluent Society*, first published in 1958, the American economist and social commentator J. K. Galbraith argued that English slums had been largely eradicated, and that standards of cleanliness and comfort in the English home were higher than ever before.[135] This view represented something of an orthodoxy among Conservative politicians with an interest in promoting Macmillan's now famous phrase, 'most of our people have never had it so good'.[136] But Brian Abel-Smith and Peter Townsend's 'rediscovery of poverty' in the high days of postwar affluence, the later 1950s and 1960s, and Ken Coates and Richard Silburn's reminder about 'the forgotten' poor, were proof that large tracts of poor inner-urban housing and environmental deprivation stood in contrast to the smart new estate home.[137] We should keep this in mind when considering the continuing reasons for the outwards migration from the town and city centres. Millions of families took the opportunity to leave when they got the chance. Poor housing was a fate to be avoided, and it could be avoided by placing one's name on a council house waiting list, or applying for work and accommodation in a new or expanded town. Others, as Chapter 3 shows, were moved by slum clearance.

Dispersal migration, moreover, was undertaken almost solely by the white working classes, certainly before 1970. There were a number of reasons for this in relation to the ethnic minorities, which will now be demonstrated respectively in relation to Black Caribbeans, Indians, Pakistanis, Bangladeshis, the Irish and Jews. The most important factor, and one noted by a number of sociologists, was that during the phases of mass immigration in the 1950s and 1960s, Black Caribbean newcomers to London, for example, whilst they were dispersed across London, settled largely in inner metropolitan boroughs: 'comparatively few migrants live in the outer suburbs ...'.[138] Black Caribbean migrants, and also Indian and Pakistani immigrants, tended to form distinctive ethnic communities in the poorest housing areas of the cities and towns which were near to their point of arrival.[139] These were sometimes labelled the 'lodging house zones' or the 'twilight zones' or the 'zones of transition', which were situated socially and spatially within the poorest districts or between the poorest inner city and better-off suburban areas.[140] In these areas, local community and self-help networks were established which provided accommodation and employment for new arrivals, and thus helped them to settle in. Some ethnic communities settled in areas of towns and cities where populations of colour had lived since the nineteenth century.[141]

There is evidence from the 1991 census, however, that ethnic minorities in England have become increasingly represented within the peripheral projects and in the new and expanded towns as the early generations of immigrants have settled following the major phases of immigration during the 1950s and 1960s. In the technocratic language of census reporters, Black Caribbeans, for example, evince 'evidence of progressive outward diffusion' and their residential presence is increasingly prevalent beyond the centres and in new towns.[142] This process is still rather slow, however, when compared to the United States.[143]

The Indian affluent working classes and middle classes have 'paralleled the characteristics of the white population' in their movement to the suburbs and new and expanded towns.[144] Pakistanis, however, have tended to remain in non-suburban terraced housing, often poorer-quality and owner-occupied, a consequence of poverty, location of workplaces and businesses, and in many cases choice due to multi-generational household kinship patterns.[145] There are exceptions to such generalisations, however, because some Pakistani families have moved to the suburban estates and new towns.[146] Bangladeshis constitute the youngest and most rapidly growing minority ethnic group, manifesting, for example, high concentrations in inner metropolitan boroughs, but showing signs of dispersal to outer boroughs.[147] The Irish, 'invisible settlers' since the nineteenth century and before, 'are fairly dispersed and have low levels of segregation' from the English population.[148] Jewish internal migration patterns, however, have been quite specific. For example, in Greater London there has been a significant movement from the East End to the 'middle distance suburbs' of Barnet, Brent and Redbridge. Yet the Jewish presence in London's new towns has been very small, with Basildon, Crawley and Hatfield together numbering less than one hundred Jews before 1980. Harlow and Welwyn Garden City contained about 150 by that time. In Hemel Hempstead they numbered over 350, but this was due to the location of a Jewish elderly citizens' home there.[149] In sum, it would appear that dispersal away from town and city centres has not been a universal movement. However, a growing tendency is evident among ethnic groups, to greater or lesser degrees.

Conclusion

The Victorian and Edwardian years witnessed the development of train and tram suburbs, whose inhabitants were for the most part middle-class, but not wholly so. The late Victorian and Edwardian years also gave birth to the garden suburbs and garden cities. These were significant for this book in providing models of associative action and sociable life amongst their residents, a theme taken up in Chapter 6. They were also planned exemplars of the suburban styles of estate layout and house design which would find mass repetitive application in the interwar and postwar years in both municipal and owner-occupied estates. The vast majority of migrants to municipal estates were working-class. The lower middle classes were the principal inhabitants of Dunroamin, but a small minority of the affluent working classes began to move there. The 1920s and 1930s were truly decades of increased mobility, and of working-class suburban dispersal which has continued since. The period also witnessed the beginnings of the regional pattern of economic and social development which continued into the postwar period. War and the consolidation of the planning machinery enabled planners to accelerate the process of dispersal, whose rationale was both to relieve slums and poorer housing areas and to counteract uncoordinated sprawl.

The growth of the new industries and most importantly the service industries provided the structural bases to urban dispersal. England would, therefore, continue to be an increasingly dispersed urban society during the postwar years. The social experience and significance of these changes is the subject matter of the rest of this book.

Notes

1 F. M. L. Thompson, 'Introduction: the rise of suburbia', in F. M. L. Thompson (ed.), *The Rise of Suburbia* (Leicester, 1982), p. 2.

2 L. Mumford, *The City in History* (Harmondsworth, 1979), pp. 549–61.

3 A. Briggs, *Victorian Cities* (Harmondsworth, 1990), pp. 27–8; J. K. Walton, *Lancashire: A Social History, 1558–1939* (Manchester, 1987), pp. 225–6.

4 E. Royle, *Modern Britain: A Social History, 1750–1985* (London, 1991), pp. 10–11.

5 B. Weinreb and C. Hibbert (eds), *The London Encyclopaedia* (London, 1987), pp. 899–900.

6 Briggs, *Victorian Cities*, pp. 27, 288.

7 On the middle-class origins of the modern suburbs, see R. J. Morris and R. Rodger, 'Introduction', in R. J. Morris and R. Rodger (eds), *The Victorian City: A Reader in British Urban History, 1820–1914* (London, 1993), pp. 23–5; D. Reeder, *Suburbanity and the Victorian City* (Leicester, 1980), pp. 19–20.

8 H. J. Dyos, 'The slums of Victorian London', *Victorian Studies*, 11:1 (1967), p. 26.

9 See, for example, J. M. Rawcliffe 'Bromley: Kentish market town to London suburb, 1841–81', in Thompson (ed.), *The Rise of Suburbia*, pp. 27–91; M. Jahn, 'Suburban development in outer west London', in Thompson (ed.), *The Rise of Suburbia*, pp. 93–156; Walton, *Lancashire*, p. 225.

10 Reeder, *Suburbanity*, p. 20.

11 R. Lewis and A. Maude, *The English Middle Classes* (Harmondsworth, 1953), p. 36. A forceful neo-Marxist critique of suburbanisation is P. J. Ashton, 'The political economy of suburban development', in W. K. Tabb and L. Sawers (eds), *Marxism and the Metropolis: New Perspectives in Urban Political Economy* (New York, 1978), pp. 64–89.

12 A. Calder, 'Introduction' to Charles Dickens, *Great Expectations* (Harmondsworth, 1984), p. 26.

13 Reeder, *Suburbanity*, p. 20; D. Read, *The Age of Urban Democracy*,

1868–1914 (London, 1994), pp. 57–8.

14 Weinreb and Hibbert, *London Encyclopaedia*, p. 253.

15 G. S. Jones, *Outcast London: A Study in the Relationship between Classes in Victorian Society* (Harmondsworth, 1983), p. 160; J. Burnett, *A Social History of Housing, 1815–1985* (London, 1991), p. 153.

16 Burnett, *A Social History of Housing*, p. 153.

17 J. White, *The Worst Street in North London: Campbell Bunk, Islington, Between the Wars* (London, 1986), pp. 10–13.

18 Jones, *Outcast London*, p. 170.

19 M. Clapson and C. Emsley, 'Street, beat and respectability', *Criminal Justice History: An International Annual*, forthcoming.

20 Lord Morrison of Lambeth, *Herbert Morrison: An Autobiography* (London, 1960), pp. 11–12.

21 Weinreb and Hibbert, *London Encyclopaedia*, p. 455.

22 T. Burke, *Son of London* (London, n.d. 1947?), pp. 37–56.

23 D. Reeder, 'Representations of metropolis: descriptions of the social environment in *Life and Labour*', in D. Englander and R. O'Day (eds), *Retrieved Riches: Social Investigation in Britain, 1840–1914* (Aldershot, 1995), pp. 328–30.

24 J. Lewis, 'Social facts, social theory and social change: the ideas of Booth in relation to those of Beatrice Webb, Octavia Hill and Helen Bosanquet', in Englander and O'Day (eds), *Retrieved Riches*, p. 60.

25 See, for example, M. E. Rose, *The Relief of Poverty, 1834–1914* (London, 1977), pp. 42–52.

26 P. Geddes, 'City survey for town planning purposes, of municipalities and government', in R. T. Legates and F. Stout (eds), *The City Reader* (London, 1996), pp. 360–6.

27 Burnett, *A Social History of Housing*, p. 138.

28 G. Cherry, *Cities and Plans: The Shaping of Urban Britain in the Nineteenth and Twentieth Centuries* (London, 1993), p. 87.

29 Ibid., pp. 99–100.

30 See P. Hall, 'The people: where will they go?', *Planner*, 71:4 (1985); S. Bayley, 'The Garden City', unit 23, Open University third level course *A305: History of Architecture and Design, 1890–1939* (Milton Keynes, 1975), pp. 24–44.

31 G. Darley, *Villages of Vision* (London, 1975), pp. 80, 91–2.

32 W. Sarkissian, 'The idea of social mix in town planning: an historical view', *Urban Studies*, 13 (1976), p. 234.

33 J. Harris, 'Between civic virtue and Social Darwinism: the concept of the residuum', in Englander and O'Day (eds), *Retrieved Riches*, p. 68.

34 Sarkissian, 'The idea of social mix', p. 235.
35 R. M. Stern with J. M. Massengale, *The Anglo-American Suburb* (London, 1981), pp. 58–9.
36 S. M. Gaskell, '"The suburb salubrious": town planning in practice', in A. Sutcliffe (ed.), *British Town Planning: The Formative Years* (Leicester, 1981), p. 17.
37 Sarkissian, 'The idea of social mix', p. 236; Stern, *Anglo-American Suburb*, pp. 41–3.
38 Weinreb and Hibbert, *London Encyclopaedia*, pp. 356–7.
39 J. Delafons, 'Brentham estate: a new community, 1901', *Town and Country Planning* 61:11/12 (1992), pp. 317–19.
40 M. Clapson *A Bit of a Flutter: Popular Gambling and English Society, 1823–1961* (Manchester, 1992), pp. 198–9.
41 M. Harrison, 'Housing and town planning in Manchester before 1914', in Sutcliffe (ed.), *British Town Planning*, p. 125.
42 Delafons, 'Brentham estate', pp. 317–19.
43 A. A. Jackson, *The Middle Classes, 1900–1950* (Nairn, 1991), pp. 290–1; J. Stevenson, *British Social History, 1914–45* (Harmondsworth, 1990), p. 27.
44 Delafons, 'Brentham estate', p. 319.
45 Harrison, 'Housing and town planning', pp. 129–30.
46 S. M. Gaskell, 'Housing and the lower middle class, 1870–1914', in G. Crossick (ed.), *The Lower Middle Class in Britain, 1870–1914* (London, 1977), p. 178.
47 Delafons, 'Brentham estate', p. 319; Harrison, 'Housing and town planning', p. 130.
48 Gaskell, '"The suburb salubrious"', pp. 48–9.
49 Burnett, *A Social History of Housing*, pp. 220–2.
50 Ibid., pp. 222–5.
51 G. Cherry, 'Homes for heroes: semis for bypasses', *New Society*, 1 February 1979, p. 238.
52 Ibid., p. 238.
53 J. Stevenson and C. Cook, *The Slump: Society and Politics During the Depression* (London, 1979), p. 21.
54 E. Reade, *British Town and Country Planning* (Milton Keynes, 1987), p. 43; Stevenson and Cook, *The Slump*, p. 21.
55 Cherry, 'Homes for heroes', p. 239; C. L. Mowat, *Britain Between the Wars* (London, 1976), pp. 229–30.
56 P. Willmott, *The Evolution of a Community* (London, 1960), pp. 14–17; Mowat, *Britain Between the Wars*, p. 230.

57 Willmott, *Evolution of a Community*, pp. 6–7; C. Hall, 'Married women at home in Birmingham in the 1920s and 1930s', *Oral History*, 5:2 (1977), p. 76.

58 Hall, 'Married women', pp. 79–80; A. Hughes and K. Hunt, 'A culture transformed? Women's lives in Wythenshawe in the 1930s', in A. Davies and S. Fielding (eds), *Workers' Worlds: Cultures and Communities in Manchester and Salford, 1880–1939* (Manchester, 1992), pp. 84–5.

59 National Council of Social Service (NCSS), *New Housing Estates and Their Social Problems* (London, 1937), passim.

60 R. Durant, *Watling: A Survey of Social Life on a New Housing Estate* (London, 1939), pp. 27–119; T. Young, *Becontree and Dagenham: A Report Made for the Pilgrim Trust* (Becontree, 1934), pp. 88–94.

61 J. Parker and C. Mirrlees, 'Housing', in A. H. Halsey (ed.), *British Social Trends Since 1900: A Guide to the Changing Social Structure* (London, 1988), p. 377.

62 Stevenson and Cook, *The Slump*, pp. 21, 23–4.

63 Burnett, *A Social History of Housing*, pp. 255–6; I. Davis, 'A celebration of ambiguity: the synthesis of contrasting values held by builders and house purchasers', in P. Oliver, I. Davis and I. Bentley (eds), *Dunroamin: The Suburban Semi and its Enemies* (London, 1994), p. 88; R. Graves and A. Hodge, *The Long Weekend: A Social History of Great Britain, 1918–1939* (London, 1985), pp. 173–4.

64 Stevenson, *British Society, 1914–45*, p. 130.

65 A. Saint, '"Spread the people": the LCC's dispersal policy, 1889–1965', in A. Saint (ed.), *Politics and the People of London: The London County Council, 1889–1965* (London, 1989), pp. 224–8; Stevenson, *British Society, 1914–1945*, pp. 233–5.

66 I. Davis, '"One of the greatest evils..." Dunroamin and the modern movement', in Oliver, Davis and Bentley (eds), *Dunroamin*, pp. 45–6.

67 P. Vaughan, 'Linoleum, cigarette card pictures, and the glorious whiff of suburbia', *Daily Mail*, 19 February 1994.

68 Stevenson and Cook, *The Slump*, p. 15.

69 J. B. Priestley, *English Journey* (London, 1937), p. 401.

70 Parker and Mirrlees, 'Housing', p. 377.

71 M. Swenarton and S. Taylor, 'The scale and nature of the growth of owner-occupation in Britain between the wars', *Economic History Review*, 37:3 (1983), p. 386.

72 Ibid., p. 392.

73 S. Merret with F. Gray, *Owner-Occupation in Britain* (London, 1979),

pp. 5–16, 26–43.

74 S. Constantine, *Unemployment in Britain Between the Wars* (London, 1980), pp. 18–20; Stevenson and Cook, *The Slump*, p. 16.

75 E. Hopkins, *The Rise and Decline of the English Working Classes, 1918–1990: A Social History* (London, 1991), p. 33.

76 Ministry of Housing and Local Government (MHLG), *The South East Study, 1961–1981* (London, 1964), p. 1

77 Hall, 'The people', p. 8.

78 *Report of the Royal Commission on the Distribution of the Industrial Population* (London, 1940, Cmd 6153), para. 82.

79 This discussion owes much to C. Anderson, 'London government in transition: LCC to GLC, 1962–1967' (University of Luton, unpublished Ph.D. thesis, 1996), pp. 72–3.

80 Hall, 'The people', p. 8; P. Hall, *Urban and Regional Planning* (London, 1992), pp. 66–71.

81 Of relevance, but by no means central, to this discussion is the Scott Report (1942), which emphasised that high-quality agricultural land should be protected for future production purposes, and called for a planning system to embrace the countryside as well as the towns. The Uthwatt Report (1942) argued that underdeveloped rural land should be nationalised. The government should acquire it either to develop it according to official planning principles or to preserve it from *ad hoc* development. These rural goals stemmed from the inter-war concern with suburban sprawl. Hall, *Urban and Regional Planning*, pp. 71–3.

82 Burnett, *A Social History of Housing*, p. 298.

83 Ibid., pp. 298–9; Cherry, *Cities and Plans*, pp. 134–5.

84 G. Cherry, 'New towns and inner city blight', *New Society*, 8 February 1979, p. 279.

85 Ibid., p. 297.

86 K. K. Liepmann, *The Journey to Work: Its Significance for Industrial and Community Life* (London, 1944), pp. 89–92. Liepmann, however, was careful to distinguish between satellite towns and garden cities, arguing that the garden cities of Letchworth and Welwyn had been designed and laid out to overly generous low-density principles. They were, then, not properly self-contained because they had failed to halt decentralisation (p. 90.) However, see A. Smailes, 'Balanced towns: their bases and occurence in England and Wales', *Journal of the Town Planning Institute*, 32 (1945), p. 35.

87 G. Herbert, 'The neighbourhood unit principle and organic theory',

Sociological Review (New Series) 11:2 (1963), pp. 166–9.

88 In G. Cherry 'Influences on the development of town planning in Britain', *Journal of Contemporary History*, 4:3 (1969), p. 57.

89 S. Fielding, P. Thompson and N. Tiratsoo, *'England Arise': The Labour Party and Popular Politics in 1940s Britain* (Manchester, 1995), pp. 104–5.

90 N. Tiratsoo, *Reconstruction, Affluence and Labour Politics: Coventry, 1945–60* (London, 1990), p. 58; Ministry of Town and Country Planning, *Final Report of the New Towns Committee* (London, 1946, Cmd 6876), paras 43 and 44, p. 16; L. E. White, *Community or Chaos: Housing Estates and Their Social Problems* (London, 1950), p. 27.

91 P. Taylor, 'British local government and housebuilding during the second world war', *Planning History*, 17:2 (1995), pp. 17–18, 21.

92 Ministry of Town and Country Planning, *Final Report of the New Towns Committee*, para. 13, pp. 7–8.

93 White, *Community or Chaos*, pp. 7–19; NCSS, *New Housing Estates*, p. 7.

94 NCSS, *Dispersal: An Enquiry into the Advantages of the Permanent Settlement Out of London and Other Great Cities of Offices, Clerical and Administrative Staffs* (London, 1944), p. vii.

95 Ibid., pp. 3–10, 15.

96 Ibid., p. 11. For further insights into the experiences of evacuation, see B. Wicks, *No Time to Wave Goodbye: True Stories of Britain's 3,500,000 Evacuees* (London, 1988), passim.

97 Ministry of Town and Country Planning, *Final Report of the New Towns Committee*, Appendix 2, p. 71.

98 See, for example, J. Hasegawa, *Replanning the Blitzed City Centre* (Buckingham, 1992).

99 A. C. Duff, *Britain's New Towns: An Experiment in Living* (London, 1961), p. 60.

100 F. Schaffer, *The New Town Story* (London, 1972), pp. 112–13; P. Self, *Cities in Flood: The Problems of Urban Growth* (London, 1957), pp. 43–9.

101 D. Read, *The Age of Urban Democracy, 1868–1914* (London, 1994), pp. 398–9; C. Denham, 'Urban Britain', *Population Trends*, 36 (1984), p. 10

102 B. Wood, 'Urbanisation and local government', in Halsey (ed.), *British Social Trends*, pp. 322–3, 334.

103 C. Hamnett, 'Consumption and class in contemporary Britain', in C. Hamnett, L. McDowell and P. Sarre (eds), *The Changing Social Structure* (London, 1993), p. 202.

104 Department of the Environment, *Housing in England, 1994–95* (London, 1996), p. 17.
105 S. Platt, 'Goodbye council housing', *New Society*, 26 February 1988, pp. 14–16.
106 Department of the Environment, *Housing in England, 1994–95*, p. 17.
107 Office of Population Censuses and Surveys (OPCS), *Demographic Review: A Report of Population in Great Britain* (London, 1987), p. 9.
108 Denham, 'Urban Britain', pp. 10–11; Wood 'Urbanisation and local government', pp. 323–4.
109 The annual reports of the development corporations are held in *Parliamentary Publications*. The first calendar month of each year's volume of *Town and Country Planning* contains a synopsis of the pertinent facts and figures of each of the new towns. Finally, an academic debt of gratitude is owed to J. B. Cullingworth, *Town and Country Planning* (London, 1994) and Hall, *Urban and Regional Planning*, both of which present useful statistical summaries.
110 Schaffer, *New Town Story*, pp. 278–93.
111 G. Philipson, *Aycliffe and Peterlee New Towns, 1948–1988: Swords into Ploughshares and Farewell Squalor* (Cambridge, 1988), pp. 9–22, 29–35.
112 D. C. D. Pocock, 'Some features of the population of Corby new town', *Sociological Review* (New Series) 8:2 (1960), pp. 209–15.
113 Schaffer, *New Town Story*, pp. 295–302.
114 MHLG, *The South East Study*, pp. 1, 8 and 12; Schaffer, *The New Town Story*, pp. 302–10.
115 Smailes, 'Balanced towns', p. 36.
116 *Britain 1970: An Official Handbook* (London, 1970), p. 172; Self, *Cities in Flood*, pp. 72–5.
117 L. Rodwin, *The British New Towns Policy: Problems and Implications* (Harvard, 1956), pp. 135–6.
118 Hall, *Urban and Regional Planning*, p. 81.
119 Wood, 'Urbanisation and local government', p. 330.
120 See above, Chapter 3, pp. 67–72.
121 M. Savage, 'Spatial differences in modern Britain', in Hamnett, McDowell and Sarre (eds), *The Changing Social Structure*, pp. 254–6.
122 A. H. Halsey, 'Social trends since world war two', in L. McDowell, P. Sarre and C. Hamnett (eds), *Divided Nation: Social and Cultural Change in Britain* (London, 1989), p. 23.
123 T. Champion and D. Dorling, *Population Change for Britain's Functional Regions, 1951–1991* (London, 1994), p. 18.

124 MHLG, *The South East Study*, pp. 60–3.
125 A. H. Halsey 'Leisure', in A. H. Halsey (eds), *Trends in British Society Since 1900* (London, 1974), p. 551.
126 Wood, 'Urbanisation and local government', pp. 334–5.
127 See, for example, A. Ling, 'The newest towns', *New Society*, 9 July 1964, pp. 10–11; R. Llewelyn-Davies, 'Town design', *Town Planning Review*, 37:3 (1966), pp. 166–72.
128 Melvin Webber was adopted as a consultant in 1967 by Llewelyn-Davies, Weeks, Forestier-Walker and Bor, who were the planning team employed by Milton Keynes Development Corporation. This is further discussed in Chapter 6, pp. 170–1.
129 G. Rhodes, 'Research in London, 1952–1977', *London Journal*, 5:1 (1979), p. 68.
130 See, for example, N. Deakin and C. Ungerson, *Leaving London: Planned Mobility and the Inner City* (London, 1977), pp. 41–60; B. J. Heraud, 'The end of a planner's dream', *New Society*, 11 July 1968, p. 46; J. Salt and R. Flowerdew, 'Labour migration from London', *London Journal*, 6:1 (1980), pp. 40–2.
131 B. J. Heraud, 'Social class and the new towns', *Urban Studies*, 5:1 (1968), pp. 38–9; Salt and Flowerdew, 'Labour migration', p. 42.
132 Heraud, 'Social class', pp. 39–40.
133 A. H. Halsey, 'Statistics and social trends in Britain', in Halsey, *British Social Trends*, p. 31.
134 Deakin and Ungerson, *Leaving London*, p. 2.
135 J. K. Galbraith, *The Affluent Society* (Harmondsworth, 1958), pp. 211–12.
136 D. Childs, *Britain Since 1945: A Political History* (London, 1992), p. 105.
137 K. Coates and R. Silburn, *Poverty: The Forgotten Englishmen* (Harmondsworth, 1973), p. 25; D. Vincent, *Poor Citizens: The State and the Poor in the Twentieth Century* (London, 1991), pp. 149, 151–2.
138 R. Glass, *Newcomers: The West Indians in London* (London, 1960), pp. 34–5.
139 P. Hall 'Moving on', *New Society*, 24 November 1977, p. 412; A. Holmes, 'Better than no place', *New Society*, 15 April 1971, p. 635; M. Young and P. Willmott, 'The old East End', *New Society*, 18 April 1986, p. 27.
140 An important study of the urban location of immigrants and its social consequences was J. Rex and R. Moore, *Race, Community and Conflict: A Study of Sparkbrook* (Oxford, 1979), pp. 133–46, 272–85.

See also the review of Rex and Moore by S. Hall, 'Lodging house zone', *Listener*, 23 February 1967, p. 266.

141 Royle, *Modern Britain: A Social History*, pp. 76–8.

142 C. Peach, 'Black Caribbeans: class, gender and geography', in C. Peach (ed.), *Ethnicity in the 1991 Census. Vol. II: The Ethnic Minority Populations of Great Britain* (London, 1996), p 38. MKDC, *Milton Keynes* (Milton Keynes, 1988), p. 36.

143 See D. L. Kirp, J. P. Dwyer and L. A. Rosenthal, *Our Town: Race, Housing and the Soul of Suburbia* (New Jersey, 1995), passim.

144 V. Robinson, 'The Indians: onward and upward', in Peach (ed.), *Ethnicity in the 1991 Census. Vol. II: The Ethnic Minority Populations of Great Britain*, p. 119 For a summary version, see the *Independent*, 12 June 1996.

145 R. Ballard 'The Pakistanis: stability and introspection', in Peach (ed.), *Ethnicity in the 1991 Census. Vol. II: The Ethnic Minority Populations of Great Britain*, pp. 144, 149.

146 See above, Chapter 3, p. 88.

147 J. Eade, T. Vamplew and C. Peach, 'The Bangladeshis: the encapsulated community', in Peach (ed.), *Ethnicity in the 1991 Census. Vol. II: The Ethnic Minority Populations of Great Britain*, pp. 158–9

148 J. Chance, 'The Irish: invisible settlers', in Peach (ed.), *Ethnicity in the 1991 Census. Vol: II: The Ethnic Minority Populations of Great Britain*, p. 238.

149 B. A. Kosmin and D. J. de Lange, 'Conflicting urban ideologies: London's new towns and the metropolitan preference of London's Jews', *London Journal*, 6:2 (1980), p. 162.

3

Moving out

> After the war we came in our marauding hundreds, like a stream of refugees from a beleaguered city. War-weary and harassed, we forsook our damp basements, draughty attics, and our cramped quarters shared with critical in-laws ...[1]

This chapter is in two parts. First, it briefly discusses working-class life on the eve of mass postwar dispersal. The contemporary sociological debate on working-class community in the poorer inner urban areas is the focus for this discussion. Peter Willmott and Michael Young's investigations of dispersed East Londoners dominated the debate over the transition from slums to suburban new estates. A number of key sociologists in the 1960s shared their fears, and planners have since acknowledged the 'bombshell' thrown among them by Willmott and Young.[2] It was as if a noble working-class lifestyle, forged in poverty and hardship, proud and resilient, was succumbing to the worst effects of affluence, individualism and well-meaning but misguided housing policies.[3] Other sociologists, however, were optimistic about the changes taking place.

The second part of the chapter assesses why people moved out. It looks at reasons for moving to the peripheral estates from the slums and poorer housing areas, and compares these with the new and expanded towns.

The working classes on the eve of mass dispersal

Historians write of a 'traditional' working-class culture and community. This was originally forged during the industrial revolution. The majority of the industrial working classes settled into the slums and poorer tracts of housing during the urban expansion of Victorian and Edwardian society.[4] Traditional industrial working-class culture has been interpreted as being at its most mature from the later Victorian period to the 1950s.[5] This broad characterisation should not ignore local variations in working-class life, though, based upon the employment structure of an area, varying housing conditions and different regional customs.[6] Despite such differences, however, a number of fundamental social and spatial characteristics were common to working-class life across England. The extended family of three generations of kin living close-by intersected with a relatively spatially restricted community network. Sociologists used the term 'matrilocality' to describe the predominant women's support networks and 'gossip chains' which bound kin with community in traditional working-class areas.[7]

The close proximity of workplace to home was an important characteristic of many working-class areas, and in industrial districts this closeness reached its apogee in some of the distinctive occupational communities which clustered around or near to the mills, factories, shipyards, dockyards, mines and workshops. So dependent were the workers of these areas upon a single industry, that any severe depression could throw thousands out of work in many areas.[8]

Beyond work, leisure also reflected common economic and cultural characteristics. For example, the corner pub, and the open secret of the illegal yet thriving network of street betting, were intrinsic to poorer inner urban areas, although there were local variations in the nature and extent of these activities. Against such activities, moreover, a vigorous grassroots culture of Nonconformity had developed in many working-class areas. By the Second World War, however, overall attendance at the chapels of the various Nonconformist sects was in decline, as was Anglicanism and to a lesser extent Roman Catholicism.[9] Furthermore, work-based or locality-based football and rugby teams had long since flowered into town-wide and city-wide expressions of local pride and spectatorism in the highly visible local stadia. The cinema and greyhound tracks were at their peak in the 1930s and 1940s as regular weekly or twice-weekly working-class entertainments.[10]

Yet we know from a wide range of working-class autobiographies that working-class 'communities' which appeared to middle-class observers as cosy and homogenous were internally divided by status, gender, ethnic and occupational distinctions.[11] Moreover, as

Joanna Bourke has argued, the ostensible romance felt by many observers of the street life of the poor ignored a strong drive to secure privacy and personal and family space within usually cramped housing conditions.[12]

These characteristics and patterns of life in the poorer areas were to undergo changes during the 1950s and since. During the 1950s, as post wartime austerity measures were lifted, and as the postwar boom took hold, the benefits to working-class families of full employment and affluence became apparent, and have continued since. Affluence, as measured in both higher earnings and greater levels of disposable income, extended down the social scale. Rising earnings, for example, were evident in the basic average industrial earnings for the standard week for male workers, which were valued at £7.83 in 1950, but £41.52 by 1973. This occurred as the number of hours worked fell from 47.5 to 44.7 per week over the same period.[13] The clearest signs of growing working-class consumption during the 1950s and since were in the ownership of homes and consumer durables. The growth in ownership of televisions, motor cars, and domestic appliances such as washing machines and refrigerators began in earnest during the mid-1950s.[14] Moreover, during the 1950s the process of dispersal was accelerated by both government housing policies and voluntary migration.[15]

Two widely held and connected beliefs were gathering pace among sociologists and cultural critics: the working class was being dispersed to death, and privatised into atomism. According to this view, the lively street culture of the slums and the redoubtable extended kinship system, mother at the helm, was being replaced by families with 2.4 children huddled around the television set. That view appeared to receive empirical confirmation from a seminal study of London's East Enders who had moved away from the proletarian heartland of Bethnal Green to the new, raw out-county estate of 'Greenleigh', near Wanstead, in suburban Essex. In *Family and Kinship in East London*, first published in London when the capital's dispersal policy was well under way, Michael Young and Peter Willmott were explicit that 'very few people wish to leave the East End', and they stressed local attachment to 'Mum and Dad, to the markets, to the pubs' and to other well-known local institutions.[16]

And mum was more important than dad. She was the matriarchal shop steward in the informal trades union which recruited from kin and neighbours. The mother was the link between the generations of the family and the central figure in the exchange of informal services and mutual aid which underpinned community in poor areas.[17] The sociologist Norman Dennis indulged in tongue-in-cheek romanticism when he wrote of working-class women in the older terraced enclaves: 'Their neighbourliness is legendary, a folk epic, their reward for being poor and ill-endowed by nature'.[18] Preserving this time-honoured culture in an era of rehousing was the emotional and practical recommendation of Young and Willmott:

> The physical size of reconstruction is so great that the authorities have been understandably intent upon bricks and mortar. Their negative task is to demolish slums which fall below the most elementary standards of hygiene, their positive one to build new houses and new towns cleaner and more spacious than the old. Yet even when the town planners have set themselves to create communities anew as well as houses, they have still put their faith in buildings, sometimes speaking as though all that was necessary for neighbourliness was a neighbourhood unit, for community spirit a community centre. [The] sense of loyalty to each other amongst the inhabitants of a place like Bethnal Green is not due to buildings. It is due far more to ties of kinship and friendship which connect the *people* of one household to the *people* of another. In such a district community spirit does not have to be fostered, it is already there. If the authorities regard that spirit as a social asset worth preserving, they will not uproot more people, but build the new houses around the social groups to which they already belong.[19]

Young and Willmott worked for the Institute of Community Studies (ICS), itself based in Bethnal Green in 1954 under the auspices of Professor Richard Titmuss and Michael Young, both of the London School of Economics. Titmuss and Young had been involved in Political and Economic Planning (PEP), a government 'think-tank' which undertook to research into key issues raised by the effects of social policy. The rationale of the ICS was to gather information on a number of pressing social topics and to monitor the changes to family and community cohesiveness which might be engendered by the cumulative and ongoing impact of affluence and by the secondary agencies of the postwar welfare dispensation, of which rehousing was one important element. This research was undertaken, therefore, to inform the processes of policy formulation.[20]

Correspondence between Titmuss, Young and Willmott and others, and a collection of reviews of *Family and Kinship* made by the ICS, illustrate the book's impact.[21] It was, moreover, revised subsequently, and republished fourteen times by Penguin between 1961 and 1980, influencing a generation of cultural commentators, sociologists, social workers, planners, journalists and social historians. Soon after the publication of its first edition, the *Daily Telegraph* reported 'East Enders miss mum', and the *News Chronicle* lamented the 'strangers in a council paradise'.[22] Charles Madge of Mass Observation and the social psychologist W. J. H. Sprott were 'complementary' about the humanity of *Family and Kinship*. The sociologist Richard Hoggart praised the 'sensitive intelligence' of Young and Willmott. Kingsley Amis, the novelist, thought 'Messrs Young and Willmott are observant, tactful, sympathetic, humorous – and they can write'. The British Medical Association's journal *Lancet*, religious periodicals of various denominations, and a number of writers in socialist journals such as *Tribune*, *Fabian News* and *Socialist Commentary* concurred at least in part with one German-Swiss review: 'glück in slum; trübsinn in wohnparadies: sensationelle Ergebnisse englisher Soziologen': 'happiness in the slum; anxiety in residential paradise: startling findings of English sociologists'.[23]

A number of brave souls demurred from such pessimism. One irate television producer, for example, making a programme about the new towns, stated that he was 'sick of middle-class reviewers and sociologists who persist in sentimentalising the working class': 'I am delighted to be able to report that, in my investigations into the New Towns, I have found time and time again that working-class wives are happy and relieved to put thirty miles between themselves and "Mum" ... Mum is a monster, and the sooner her fangs are drawn, the better.'[24] He also argued that only a small minority longed for the pubs, fish and chip shops and 'chumminess' of the crowded streets from whence they came. A more measured note of caution was sounded by the sociologist David Donnison. Writing in the social workers' journal *Case Conference*, he did not doubt the significance of the issues raised by the Bethnal Green research, but argued that Young and Willmott were too close to their research to be dispassionate. 'It may be', he felt, 'that the cosy neighbourliness of our traditional, long-settled working-class areas has been achieved at the cost of a dangerous isolation from the outside world.'[25]

It was precisely this, the move to the outside world of the new estate, with the spatial stretching of social relationships, which exercised so many writers who adopted a romantic view of the working classes, and hence were critical of dispersal. A point of reference had been provided by Young and Willmott. But they were by no means the only sociologists to investigate the social consequences of dispersal. A number of other studies went largely ignored by the 'pop sociology' debate of the suburbs during the 1950s and 1960s.[26] These sociologies did not supply such convenient support to its preconceptions. It is noticeable that social historians, too, still take their cue most readily from Young and Willmott when discussing the qualitative changes in postwar working-class life which occurred during and since the 1950s.[27] A surprising number of other sociological studies, however, provide alternatives to the popular orthodoxy of the ICS. They illustrate nothing less than an aspiration to migrate away from the traditional working-class communities.

Moving out

The major reason for moving, whether to a peripheral estate or a new and expanded town, was the desire for better accommodation, which usually meant a new house. The pursuit of an improved residential environment was closely linked to this. That latter point was concerned not simply with material improvements but also with the distinction between rough and respectable, council and owner-occupied estates. Employment reasons were also significant, especially in the migration to new and expanded towns. Another factor, less in evidence in the sociologies of migration, was the desire for educational opportunities for children, a point which touches upon the aspiration for inter-generational upward mobility. A further important factor was follow-on migration as people moved to be near to relatives. It is important to note that whilst the primacy of the desire for better housing will be shown to be the most common reason for moving, different studies attached differing relative weights to these other reasons.

Peter Hall, synthesising popular hopes after the Second World War with the dispersal rationale of the town planning profession, emphasised the centrality of the new house in this: 'People were ready to leave the overgrown metropolis. What they wanted was a decent house with a garden, and they would as soon have it in a new town – or in a suburb attached to an old shire town, forty miles from London.'[28] There was a great deal of contemporary evidence to support the view that the desire for a better house was the main stimulus to migration. This will be discussed first in relation to suburban estates, and then to new and expanded towns.

Moving to the suburban estate

Tatsuya Tsubaki's extensive research into postwar reconstruction and the issues of popular housing provision emphasises the many opinion surveys undertaken during the war and in its immediate aftermath. They attempted to ascertain what people wanted from housing, especially working-class people, whose housing needs were greatest. National studies undertaken by a variety of organisations, for example Mass Observation and the Society of Women Housing Managers, and local studies made by local authority housing managers, found clear majorities, usually of four-fifths and above, in favour of a house as opposed to a flat. For example, a 1943 study by the Society of Women Housing Managers asked people to choose between the alternatives of a modern flat, a modern terraced house or a modern house on the outskirts. Of those already living in cottage estates, whether in inner or outer boroughs, 'an overwhelming majority plumped for a suburban house' and only 3 per cent wanted to live in a flat.[29] Other studies of working-class tenants in varying housing conditions found varying levels of preference for semi-detached houses in relation to terraced houses, but usually the semi-detached house almost always came out on top, due to its garden and its suburban position near the countryside. Many living in flats, even those in other respects content with them, wanted a garden. Levels of satisfaction with present housing, moreover, tended to be higher on council cottage housing estates, and lowest in old poor quality housing, as new houses were also preferred to old.

Women especially scrutinised aspects of the home. For example, the availability, size and condition of kitchens, bathrooms, lavatories and bedrooms, the desire for separate eating rooms from living rooms, and the need to avoid being 'squashed in', were all the subject of a wartime population who knew what they wanted from housing design.[30] Moreover, a point emphasised by Tsubaki, many people desired greater privacy than that afforded by their current accommodation, a factor strongly related to a dislike of sharing common facilities and to annoyance at noisy neighbours. This went both for those living in central London flats and for those in cottage estates. The latter, for example, did not relish the shared porch for two front doors.[31]

There is considerable evidence, therefore, that the appeal of a privacy-enhancing suburban house with a garden was by no means an unpopular choice, and was strongly in existence in working-class areas of varying conditions before the postwar years began. This view supports similar findings by the sociologists Bennet M. Berger and Herbert J. Gans for North America during the 1950s and 1960s. They emphasised that the housing values and preferences deplored as 'suburban' by many critics were endemic to poorer working-class urban cultures.[32] This was true of postwar England. Two studies of Birmingham, conducted during the 1950s, found that a majority of slum dwellers wanted to move to improved homes in the suburban rings around Birmingham, although a sizeable minority liked their old house and district. They did not have the option to stay in the slum house, however, because they were moved from those unfit dwellings under Birmingham City Council's slum clearance and redevelopment programme. Moreover, many other councils graded residents according to appearances, income and other criteria, and actively directed poorer residents away from the newest, more expensive rental estates.[33] There was, then, less choice for the poorest households.

However, it appears that even the poorest groups were mostly grateful for the move. The sociologist June Norris found that of a Birmingham sample of 166, sixty-six were 'very glad' to have moved and thirty-two were 'quite glad', which totalled 59 per cent. Thirty-six were 'very sorry' and eleven 'rather sorry' to have left (28 per cent in combination). The remaining 13 per cent had 'mixed feelings'. As Norris summarised, however, twice as many were glad to have moved than were sorry, and the aspiration towards better housing underpinned that.[34] She concluded that 'even if they have never lived in the suburbs before, they want to do so now'.[35]

The general picture of an aspiration towards the suburbs was confirmed by the government's Central Housing Advisory Committee (CHAC) in its study of Birmingham. It emphasised the distinction between rehousing for slum clearance and the provision of houses for those on the ordinary waiting list: 'the latter seek a new home voluntarily but the occupants of slums will be required to move whether they wish to or not'.[36] CHAC found, however, little evidence that most people did not want to move, because most did want to.

They 'look forward eagerly to the offer of a better house and welcome the prospect of the move'. Most, moreover, made the transition to a new house on a new estate with little difficulty.[37] Oral testimony retrospectively confirms aspirations for a better house, preferably with a garden. The following quote, for example, comes from Carl Chinn's work on Birmingham's council house tenants. One couple, married in 1946, and on the waiting list, remembered: 'When we were told we were being put in a newly built house in Sheldon we were amazed and delighted because to have a garden and a bathroom and all the other things we had done without for years, it was like a dream come true'.[38] Yet the waiting list was often less patronised by those whose housing conditions were most desperate, poor slum dwellers. In 1955 Miss D. E. Miskin of the Society of Housing Managers noted the reluctance of many slum dwellers to apply for new housing. Male workers lived near to their place of work. Some of them clocked on regularly. Others living near docks, for example, had work which was often casual and intermittent. Many women earners had part-time employment 'conveniently near'. Yet she noted that slum dwellers did want bigger, better-planned and better-equipped houses, they were just reluctant to put their names on the housing list.[39]

That a lack of applications did not mean a lack of desire for better housing was confirmed by the Kirkby study. During the later 1950s and early 1960s sociologists at the University of Liverpool monitored the mass movement of residents from 'a blighted inner residential urban zone', which they named 'Crown Street', to Kirkby, Liverpool's largest overspill development. It is important to note that Kirkby was an overspill suburb, but due to its large size and population, and because the city council relocated some employment to Kirkby, it was referred to as a 'new town', although it was never officially designated as that. Unlike most of its southern counterparts, moreover, Kirkby was constructed to higher densities due to the extreme pressure on Liverpool's inner streets and courts. Densities were raised in two senses of the term. Houses were built closely together on the ground, and large blocks of flats were constructed above it.

Kirkby was some miles away from Crown Street. It was raw and new, and possessed no intrinsic attraction for Liverpudlians. It was 'an unknown refuge in the flight from physical and social squalor'.[40] Before moving, less than half of the study's sample, 49 per cent, had wanted to go to Kirkby, 22 per cent had wanted to move out but not necessarily to Kirkby, and 29 per cent had not wanted to go there. Hence enthusiasm for dispersal was widespread but less so than in the findings for Birmingham. Once people had moved in, however, their reactions provided an interesting comparison with their prior feelings. Three-quarters wished to stay. A further finding was that, for women migrants, 'the influence of the close-knit matrilocal lifestyle is of lesser importance than the attainment of better housing'.[41] Of those who wanted to leave Kirkby, an important reason was dislike of accommodation in the flats, rather than the houses. Privacy was compromised by noise transference through ceilings, floors and walls, and the monotonous design of the large blocks of flats was noted by the observers.[42]

An early postwar study of slum dwellers in Sheffield, who had been uniquely relocated between the wars as 'groupings of neighbours', demonstrated that 70 per cent of tenants preferred their new accommodation to their old conditions.[43] Elsewhere in Yorkshire, a survey of Leeds made during the early 1960s found a resounding majority (82 per cent) in favour of relocation. Of this majority who wished to break with slum life, 'economic factors and the wish to be near relatives and friends were relatively unimportant ... Economic factors are more important as a deterrent to moving. By far the most important reasons given for wishing to move (by those in favour) concerned dissatisfaction with house and district.'[44]

In Oxford during the early to mid-1950s, the sociologist J. M. Mogey compared thirty families from a very poor area in the town centre, St Ebbes, who had moved to the new estate of Barton on the outskirts, with thirty families back in the slum. Mogey found that the desire for improved housing was the major reason for accepting relocation: 'Only 10 per cent had a good word to say about their former accommodation'. In the words of one 'typical' mover: 'It's like heaven after what we've been used to ... People today don't know of the times when we had to live in old broken down houses because we could afford nothing better. But today we are given nice little houses to live in.'[45] The use of the word 'given' could be interpreted to convey the lack of choice felt by slum dwellers, but it certainly contains an element of gratitude; it was a positive ambiguity. Yet Mogey made an important distinction between those he termed 'status assenters' and 'status dissenters'. The former were more content with their lot and more willing to stay in St Ebbes. Status dissenters, however, were more likely to be looking for an improved dwelling in a council house in order to raise their family's material and social position.[46]

H. E. Bracey's study of Bristol included thirty-nine council tenants who had been given a number of estates to choose from, and their choice was exercised according to differing criteria from those highlighted by the previous studies. Interestingly, the major reason for moving was the new house, but the choice of estate illustrated a wider set of concerns, with, for example, 54 per cent choosing a particular estate for its ease of access to the husband's place of work. They were prepared to commute, but not over long distances. Only 28 per cent were concerned their estate should be 'near to friends or relatives', a finding which militated against Young and Willmott's emphasis.[47]

The quality of residential environment was an important consideration, but not for everybody. At the very end of the 1960s and into the early 1970s, a study of three Yorkshire towns – Batley, Leeds and York – compared the perceptions and experiences of council tenants who had moved from inner slums, and relatively better-off yet still far from wealthy owner-occupiers in 'twilight housing', housing due to be condemned. Those who most wanted to stay put were the elderly owner-occupiers, the least mobile, who appeared to be satisfied with their houses, despite their poor condition. The Society of Housing Managers had made this point for elderly slum dwellers in 1955, and Norman Dennis observed the same phenomenon in Sunderland in 1970.[48] Again, it was slum dwellers with young families in particular who were most keen to move to a lower-density, accessible, greener and better-equipped environment: 'The ideal location which emerges is suburban, well provided with shops and transport, but essentially clean, quiet, and near friends with parks, open spaces and generally suitable for children'.[49] This appreciation of an improved environment is discussed further in the following chapters.

Finally, in relation to the pursuit of an improved residential context, it must be stressed that divisions within the working classes were also a stimulus to move, as Mogey's aforementioned distinction between status assenters and dissenters illustrated. Other studies inadvertently concurred. In Bracey's study of Bristol, for example, 18 per cent moved to be in a 'better residential neighbourhood', a phrase with rough/respectable overtones. One respondent justified their choice of estate: 'We had heard unpleasant things about B ... Warmley is a better district'.[50] In similar vein, Hilda Jennings's study of relocated slum families in Bristol noted that some felt themselves 'superior' to their neighbours in a poor area, and were ready to accept a new house in the outlying estate of Mossdene.[51] Dennis Chapman's study of the home in relation to status perceptions showed that many wanted to move away to be in an estate with people 'like them'. This reason was found in identical proportion (69 per cent) in both private enterprise housing and 'new working-class housing estates'. Common sentiments were expressed in relation to noise, roughness, gossip and also snobbishness.[52]

Hence, the desire for better housing was often closely connected to perceptions of social tone and residential environment. Many people moved because they felt the area in which they lived was deteriorating, not just in a physical sense, but in a social sense, too. They wanted to put distance between themselves and those they perceived as roughs or undesirables. This is not a distinctly postwar sentiment, as was illustrated in Chapter 2. Within this framework of values, it is clear that for some white residents, the growing presence of ethnic minority groups was a stimulus to move away. For example in Sparkbrook, Birmingham, the sociologists Rex and Moore found that a self-designated sense of 'respectability', based upon a conception of feeling better than those 'below' and a related fear of an influx of foreign migrants, was often a spur to moving away from the inner city areas to a more salubrious area, notably one of the suburbs surrounding Birmingham.[53]

Therefore, the desire for better housing, in a nicer environment, both of which were permeated with a notions of roughness and respectability, stimulated the move outwards of slum dwellers. These findings were pertinent for both slum dwellers and council tenants, and were similar to the values of affluent skilled manual and lower-middle-class owner-occupiers in Bristol, as evidenced in their choice of estate. Bracey also noted, however, that concern for a good school was not mentioned by English respondents, in contrast to American suburbanites. Americans placed this at the top of their list of reasons for moving.[54] This is surprising, given its implications for the 'status dissent' of many working-class householders. Its absence, it must be noted, was apparent in the other studies mentioned above. This did not mean, however, that the hope for inter-generational upward mobility via improved schooling was irrelevant to the decision to move outwards.

Early postwar studies of social mobility made crude but tangible connections between the residential location and status aspirations for children amongst the manual working class. A study of parents' preferences in secondary education, published in 1954, observed that about half of skilled manual workers had given consideration to their children's secondary education, compared to just over one-third of semi-skilled and under one-third of unskilled manual workers. This was in a prosperous area of Southern Hertfordshire whose industrial work was characterised not by heavy or traditional industries but light industries, such as engineering. Over 7 per cent of the sample lived in detached houses, 60 per cent in semi-detached houses and almost 23 per cent in terraced houses. Beyond that, it is impossible to be any more specific about the connection between social and spatial mobility in this study. Moreover, no information about tenure was supplied.[55]

A summary of 1950s and 1960s studies of education and social mobility, furthermore, came to conditional conclusions regarding that relationship:

> Working-class children who attend largely middle-class primary schools may not themselves be from 'typically' working-class families. They may belong to aspiring, ambitious families who have moved because of favourable job opportunities, or to be near a school with a good reputation for eleven-plus successes.[56]

This quote hints at *embourgeoisement*, as if ambitious 'status dissenting' working-class families were atypical, and attempting to extricate themselves from a working-class 'subculture'.[57] The *Affluent Worker* study of Luton during the 1960s, which tested the notion of *embourgeoisement* of industrial workers in the car and engineering sectors, found that half the skilled and semi-skilled manual workers studied wished for their children to undertake white-collar work, and six out of ten parents wanted their children to go to grammar school. The other half of parents were less bothered, and were simply concerned for their sons to 'get a trade'.[58] Brian Jackson and Dennis Marsden's study of Huddersfield, first published in 1963, explored the relationship between parental ambitions for their children, the occupational background of the residential area of the working-class child, and educational achievement. Huddersfield was then a prosperous industrial town. It was found that the most successful children – almost always boys at that time – came from districts where the tenure was largely 'house ownership', and where primary school catchment was mixed, taking both lower-middle-class and affluent working-class offspring. Boys from affluent workers' families in council houses sometimes did well, but those whose life chances were least tended to come from larger families, whether in poorer central areas or in interwar council estates towards the edge of town.[59]

The educational sociologist J. W. B. Douglas confirmed these general findings, noting that the move from slum to council house had a generally improving effect upon a child's chances of getting to grammar school. Moreover, better primary schools and grammar schools were rarely near to the poor central zones, but in the more salubrious areas, and some council estates benefited from being located near a greater number of available places in grammar schools and in nearby primary schools with good facilities. Douglas further observed that council-house allocation policies often favoured the better-off manual workers' families.[60] The evidence suggested that children from smaller nucleated families in owner-occupied estates, and those from smaller families in council estates, did better than those in slums or those from larger families on council estates.[61] Beyond that general finding, however, a child's educational chances were determined by many other factors, for example the material comfort of the home; pressure from parents; the educational attainment of parents; willingness of parents to teach or explain at home; size of family; peer pressure and values at school; and the quality of both teaching and the school's facilities.[62]

There does appear to have been, therefore, a relationship between education and the move from poorer areas. This may have been a consequence of the parental pursuit of better schools for their children. That, in turn, was a quest for inter-generational upward social mobility. It is a shame that more studies were not made on this relationship, however, and a recent discussion confirms the general dearth of surveys on this link. Moreover, what little does exist tends to be focused upon higher income groups, where the connection between upward social mobility and spatial mobility is assumed to be highest.[63]

A further reason for moving out to suburban council estates was the desire to reconstitute closer family networks. This was chain migration. For some, therefore, the stretching of family ties was only temporary. Norris's study of Birmingham, for example, found there was movement by relatives to be nearer to the original movers. Some families moved 'very near' for example, while in other cases friends and families moved to nearby estates.[64] In Bristol council estates, Jennings observed that as well as young couples, some elderly people accepted houses on certain estates to be near to relatives.[65] Bracey, a few years later, noted that 28 per cent of council house tenants gave proximity of relatives and friends as a reason for choice of estate.[66] In Woodford, where a majority of the working classes owned their house, Willmott and Young noted that 42 per cent had parents in the borough, although their situations were not like the close extended family model of Bethnal Green. There was a 'kinship continuum' from Woodford to Bethnal Green.[67] Kinship as a motive for moving appears to have varied from place to place, and perhaps from methodology to methodology, but the results from these three studies show that a majority were not unduly worried by the effect of outwards migration on kinship. There is, moreover, evidence of chain migration for a minority of new town migrants, discussed below.

It is safe to conclude, however, that the house and the improved environment were the priorities for working-class households on the move from poorer areas to new estates. These findings are important to understanding the general profile of most of those who moved out: the young working-class families who wanted better housing for themselves and their children, and generally an improved material environment. A similar menu of wants and needs informed the aspirants to new and expanded towns. Care is required, however, when making comparisons between suburban migration and that of new and expanded towns. This is particularly evident in relation to employment, in two ways. First, migration to council estates around towns did not usually mean a change in employment, certainly in the first instance of the move. People were still within commuting distance of their place of work. Second, many migrated to new and expanded towns via organised dispersal schemes which had no equivalent in suburban migration.

Moving to the new and expanded towns

It was noted in the previous chapter that the majority of migrants to new and expanded towns were from the skilled and semi-skilled working classes, and to a lesser extent from the unskilled. Unfortunately for historians, however, there was little official qualitative research into the aspirations and values of these new town migrants before 1970. In 1968 the sociologist John Barron Mays lamented that the 'gigantic nation-wide social experiment' involving the planned relocation of so many people had been undertaken with little accompanying systematic study and documentation of the subjectivity (that is, the feelings and values) of people in new towns.[68] Peter Willmott made a similar point,[69] and Peter Cresswell, of the New Towns Study Unit, noted that there was much material from planners and development corporations claiming to speak for those in new towns, but in contrast 'virtually none which embodied the results of a genuine enquiry into people's feelings about new towns'.[70] This state of affairs may well have resulted from the lack of centrality given to sociological research by the early postwar reports of the New Towns Committee, which recommended the establishment of a Central Advisory Committee at the outset of any new town programme, a recommendation that was not institutionalised.[71] The Reith reports, moreover, gave only a vague idea about the role of social investigation in the formulation of new town plans, a vagueness which dated back to Patrick Geddes.[72] The absence of any vision for systematic and ongoing social research was also evident in the *Report of the Committee on the Qualifications of Planners*, published in 1950, which argued that development corporations and other planning authorities 'may' want to make use of sociologists, and also economists, geographers, statisticians and other university-trained academics. The Committee stressed the need for a 'synthesis' between planning and these different professions, yet there was no prescription for a close and ongoing relationship between the gathering of social data and the 'continuing process' of planning.[73] A number of studies do exist, however, which were made independently of the new town development corporations.

Britain's first postwar new town was Stevenage in Hertfordshire, built to draw off excess population from London. Harold Orlan's study of Stevenage, made from 1948 to 1950, was primarily an investigation not into migration and early settlement, but into the relationship between the ideology of the planners and the planning machinery, and the nature and attitudes of the existing population in the designated area of South Hertfordshire. Orlans did, however, demonstrate the overriding preference for better housing and improved employment for both migrants from London and those already living in and near Stevenage old town, many of whom felt that new development would benefit them.[74] Twenty years later, these values had not significantly changed, as Valerie Karn's study of Stevenage showed. (This took place after Mays's and Willmott's observations about the dearth of social research in new towns.) She found housing and employment were the major reasons for moving to Stevenage. Moreover, she observed during the 1960s the gathering phenomenon of chain migration: 'an increasing proportion of households have moved to be near their relatives or friends'.[75] Satisfaction with housing was high, as over four-fifths were 'very satisfied' or 'fairly satisfied' with their new home. Owner-occupiers manifested higher levels of satisfaction, closely followed by development corporation tenants, who were largely incomers, and local authority tenants, who were mostly existing residents.[76] These trends were also observed by Karn for Aycliffe in North East England. Furthermore, she pointed to tenure-based migration *within* Aycliffe, noting the growing trend to owner-occupation among development corporation tenants, almost all of whom were affluent working-class households: 'virtually all the owner-occupiers who had moved had previously been development corporation tenants', and 53 per cent of all Aycliffe's owner-occupiers were ex-development corporation tenants.[77]

Karn emphasised that the structure and availability of housing for movers to new towns differed from that of the suburbs. New town development corporations held a dominant control over public housing for rent. Hence, it was 'not possible to talk about reasons for moving and choice of tenure' without considering the development corporation's influence. In Stevenage, 81 per cent of the property was owned by the development corporation, 5 per cent by the local authority, the remainder being owner-occupied. The corporation considered eligible for its houses those prepared to move to Stevenage with a relocating firm, key workers for the construction of the new town who could be relocated from London, ex-servicemen, and relatives of development corporation tenants.[78]

A similar process took place in expanded towns. J. B. Cullingworth's work on the expanded town of Swindon and that on Salford's town expansion scheme, Worsley, may be compared with each other. Cullingworth, a lecturer in planning at the University of Birmingham, was concerned to answer Young and Willmott's claims against dispersal. If they were right, it would follow that the policy of 'exporting' population to new and expanded towns and peripheral estates 'is socially undesirable'.[79] Of those moving from Salford to Worsley, 224 of the 250 families in the sample (90 per cent) had wanted to leave their cramped and insanitary dwellings for a new council house. Salford's internal housing shortage and the poor condition of most of its extant housing, however, militated against the decision to stay, and so must be given recognition in any retrospective appraisal of why people moved. Hence, 46 per cent said they *had* to move to improve their family's accommodation. When asked if they had really wanted to move to Worsley, the percentage shrank to 54 per cent.[80] Once they had moved in, however, it was found that the majority of migrants wanted to stay: only 17 per cent wished to return to central Salford. The reason for staying was the new and superior accommodation. Most had, furthermore, disliked the dirt and overcrowding of Salford. The men, moreover, were prepared to commute a few miles to work in order to be able to enjoy better living standards. Significantly, over half the women in Worsley expressed no preference for their mothers to move out when asked, because regular contacts were quickly established and maintained. There was no simple picture of 'missing mum'.[81] Pointedly, Cullingworth argued that separation from the extended family was for most a matter of no concern, and regarded as 'a minor disadvantage of suburban life'.[82]

At Swindon, Cullingworth wanted to ascertain the effect of greater distances on family relationships, because the Wiltshire town expansion scheme was seventy miles from London. Regular pop-ins of the kind valued by Young and Willmott were impossible, and there was no opportunity for regular short trips to see friends and relatives. Kinship orientations in Swindon, it was found, were mixed. Of the 149 families separated from some or all of their London relatives, 48 (32 per cent) said they disliked the separation, and of that same 32 per cent, 19 per cent said they experienced 'hardship' for themselves and their family. Hardship was felt most commonly by the less-well-off migrants who were unable to visit London frequently. Those who could afford more trips back to London accepted the separation more readily. Generally, however, Cullingworth detected 'a widespread and ill-defined feeling of guilt at having bettered themselves at the cost of the social impoverishment of the family'.[83] It was apparent, then, that greater distance heightened insecurities and misgivings about the move.

The majority of moves to Swindon were voluntary. Care is needed here, however, because voluntarism was qualified by the fact that it was quicker and easier to obtain a new house in an expansion scheme than in a redevelopment area. In the London case, moreover, the local authority, via the labour exchange, made an offer of a new house in Swindon, as in any other expanded town, on the condition that the head of household took up a job in the town. That took place through the mechanism known as the Industrial Selection Scheme (ISS) which was established in the late 1940s to encourage migration out of London to the expanded and the new towns. In the move from London to Swindon, the main motive was again 'to obtain decent housing conditions', 73 per cent of the sample giving that as their reason. Some 19 per cent moved for work-related reasons and 4 per cent 'to get out of London'. As for Worsley, Cullingworth noted that the immediate reaction of families in Swindon was 'one of intense joy at obtaining a new house', and over two-thirds of movers expressed 'unqualified satisfaction' with their houses.[84]

Cullingworth wore two hats. He was interested in social investigation into the new communities because he was an authority on town planning and a keen advocate of urban dispersal. He utilised the findings for Salford, along with Swindon, in combination with data from new town development corporations, to call for more and better-planned overspill developments.[85] Lest the current use of Cullingworth be accused of bias in favour of dispersal, further sources may be used to assess motives for moving out. A study of Bury St Edmunds in Suffolk, an expanded town scheme for Londoners, assessed the reasons for moving from the mid-1960s and into the 1970s. It found that whilst the choice for 'planned' migrants through the ISS was less than that of those who could afford to move voluntarily, for almost all migrants, regardless of housing circumstances in London, 'the dominant motive for coming was housing', and preferably for housing with a garden for children. 'The job was secondary.'[86] It must be remembered that for most of the 1950s, 1960s and the early 1970s, unemployment was a marginal problem in the metropolitan economy, and in the South East generally. It was clear that in moving to the expanded towns, the nice new home exercised a greater influence than the need or desire to be near to the extended family. This finding was also applicable to the new towns.

Some of these contemporary sociological findings gain support from retrospective oral testimony. There are many examples which demonstrate the enthusiasm with which people greeted their new homes. Ann Luhman, who moved from substandard accommodation in Tottenham, London, to Stevenage in 1953, remembers her feelings, and those of her children:

> I was thrilled with the home, it was really lovely – to think I had my own sink, my own bathroom, two toilets, one up and one down. I felt I was on holiday for months and months; the children thought it was great. There was a green dell at the side of us, and they just ran round and round. They felt free.[87]

This quote demonstrates that dispersal policies reflected the housing values of migrants from slums to new towns. The relationship between popular housing aspiration and provision concerned all new town development corporations. Milton Keynes Development Corporation (MKDC), for example, compiled process data on the formation of the new town, data which synthesised social, economic and demographic information. One reason was to ensure that housing provision, following the criticism of planners and architects for many earlier housing schemes, was more closely in tune with what the incomers wanted. A further reason was to ensure that development adhered to the social balance and mix prized by planners in the garden city tradition.

MKDC's data amounts to a valuable archive for the social historian which provides materials on most aspects of migration to the new city. Late 1980s materials on migration to Milton Keynes summarise the results of a number of studies on the motivations and conditions of those who moved since the early 1970s (see Table 5, p. 82).

It is possible to put flesh on these statistical bones. In 1973 MKDC undertook to investigate those people who had moved to the city since its beginnings. The results of this survey were published as *Four Years On: The Milton Keynes Household Survey*.[88] Some of these findings were made available to a wider audience in *New Society*, in August 1974, in the form of an article by a local community worker for MKDC, concerned with arrivals.[89] The arrivals workers personified the concern of MKDC to monitor the earliest process of settlement and to ensure things went as smoothly as possible for all concerned. This concern was most strongly directed at families in housing need. Families in housing need were encouraged to move to

Milton Keynes via the New and Expanded Towns Scheme (NETS), and, from 1975, the Direct Nominations Scheme (DNS), which replaced NETS just as NETS had replaced the Industrial Selection Scheme.[90] MKDC's definition of housing need was as follows:

> If any household in our sample used to live in overcrowded conditions or shared a dwelling with another household or lacked an indoor toilet, kitchen or bath, or when the respondent felt his previous residence was in poor physical condition, we defined that household as in housing need.[91]

As in previous decades, people in such conditions naturally wanted to escape from them. Speaking of her previous London home, one woman remembered that 'it was a terrible house':

> it was running with mice. The mice were in the beds, in the furniture, and it was making my four children's lives a misery, and mine as well 'cos I suffer badly from me nerves. It was half a house – very small, and we were paying almost £6 a week for it. It had two rooms and a kitchen; the rooms had to [be] bedrooms as well.[92]

Table 5 Milton Keynes: in-migrating households by reason for move, 1968–90 (percentages)

	1968–73	*1974–78*	*1979–83*	*1984–88*	*1990*
Employment	30.9	28.1	31.1	38.9	23
Housing	33.1	34.2	32.3	33.3	50
Kin	27.2	26.3	24.2	17.5	18
Environment	6.3	9.5	8.6	7.8	20
Other	2.5	1.9	2.8	2.5	

Source: Adapted from MKDC, *Milton Keynes Household Survey, 1983, Demographic Report* (Milton Keynes, 1985), Table XIX p. 33; MKDC, *Milton Keynes Household Survey, 1988, Demography Technical Report* (Milton Keynes, 1988) Table 26, p. 42; and Milton Keynes Borough Council, *Household Survey, 1990* (Milton Keynes, 1990), Table 2.6, p. 17.

Note: Milton Keynes Borough Council took over MKDC's household survey role in the late 1980s, prior to the winding-up of the Development Corporation in 1992, and the wording of the questions and categories appears to have changed in some instances. Moreover, in the 1990 column percentages add up to more than 100 because respondents could give more than one answer. This column is therefore not directly comparable.

Moving could certainly be a wrench, but the new house was usually the crucial factor in the decision to go. One man, working for the Post Office in London, wanted his new house but revealed his misgivings at leaving Hackney, East London, for Milton Keynes: 'My mum stood on the doorstep of 168 shedding a little tear, 'cos I think she thought we were going to the other side of the world'.[93] Yet housing could coincide with work-based reasons for moving. Another London man, a factory foreman for a sugar milling company who wanted to relocate to Milton Keynes, was put in charge of the move. He 'sounded out the men; eight of the twelve saw it as an opportunity to get their own place'. He himself was living above his parents with his wife, so they were 'looking forward to having [their] own place with a garden'. There was a link with chain migration here. Soon afterwards, his parents and other relations moved to Milton Keynes 'and didn't want to move back'. His wife said she wanted her 'own place' and spoke of 'the thrill of her own front door'. She 'wasn't homesick for London' and visited friends and family there regularly.[94] Another woman and her husband, from Watford, were among the first to move to the Greenleys estate. Again, the house was the attraction. Soon after she had moved in, her sister and brother moved up, reconstituting one whole generation of the wider family in Milton Keynes.[95]

Some migrants felt they had to leave London to get the sort of accommodation they required. The restricted level of 'choice' in a competitive housing context affected some who moved to Milton Keynes: 'It wasn't Milton Keynes, it was just what the Labour Exchange offered us was Milton Keynes'.[96] Also, the lack of choice affected those within the lower echelons of the private housing market. In one case of a teacher and his family, this was exacerbated by the age of the children, and hence the stage of the family life cycle: 'On the face of it, it was a good time [to move], the kids were young and the prospect of getting decent housing in London was virtually non-existent'.[97] However, as the sociologists Nicholas Deakin and Clare Ungerson note in their study of planned migration from London, 'even in a constrained situation, choices are still being made' and were of 'particular importance just because opportunities were so limited'.[98]

MKDC was adept at presenting the new city as a place where there was choice in housing, especially for those with such limited opportunities. Publicity materials, for example the *New City* magazines of 1974 and 1975, described, in photo-articles, the process of moving from old, overcrowded accommodation in London to the spacious, new housing on offer. The position in the family life cycle – that is, the stage of the family's development – was highlighted in these materials. In the case of one family, from Brixton, a couple with an infant son, living with the son's mother and his two brothers in a terraced house, Milton Keynes offered a new and pleasing prospect. As its policy dictated, MKDC showed them round different houses, and the couple made their choice. It was now up to the man of the prospective house to get a job in the area before they were allowed to move in. Once he had achieved this, however, the family was allowed to choose from a number of show houses, and once their own house was completed, the keys were handed over and they moved in.[99]

Not everyone who moved in during the early 1970s was from London. One man, who was living in a single room in a communal house in Luton in 1972, learned about Milton Keynes from brochures in Luton Town Hall. He was single, which he felt put him towards the bottom of the council house waiting list in Luton, although he had a pregnant girlfriend. In Milton Keynes, 'it seemed you didn't have to be married to get a house quickly'. He and his girlfriend were given a house in the radically designed Netherfield estate, and 'didn't want to go there'. They wanted 'to go to a brick house, and didn't want a three storey town house', which they felt was 'ridiculous' for a couple with a baby on the way. But that was what they got, and they felt they had little choice in the matter. He also had to get a job in Milton Keynes or nearby before they could finalise the process of gaining the house.[100] As MKDC and some of its workers noted, 'choice' had more meaning for owner-occupiers than for renters, and many people did not get the first or even second rental house of their choice.[101]

It is clear, however, that housing remained the most important reason for moving. MKDC noted in 1976 that it was 'much more important to move for a better house than for a better job for all special sample groups'.[102] Some 49 per cent of all respondents moved for a better house up to 1976, 'but of those migrating from London, 68 per cent gave this as a reason'.[103] Many of these came through the ISS and NETS. These schemes proved particularly useful to poorer aspirants in the inner London boroughs who wanted a better home. Hence, over 65 per cent of ISS migrants to all new and expanded towns before 1972 were from poorer inner London boroughs. However, many people who moved to the new and expanded towns came from outer London boroughs such as Barking, Barnet, Enfield, Harrow, Newham and Redbridge, where housing need was less, but still a tangible problem.[104]

The primacy of housing as a factor in moving was reflected in the changing trends in tenure. The postwar growth in owner-occupation was accelerated from the 1970s. This was evident with the houses built by MKDC for migrants to the city, as shown in Table 6. As MKDC noted in its 1983 survey, the changing tenure pattern can be dated from 1974, and the process speeded up in the early 1980s: 'nearly 80 per cent of households buying new town sale housing had moved to Milton Keynes since 1974', and one half of these had moved 'most recently between 1981–83'.[105] By 1990, 67 per cent of households in the new city owned their accommodation.[106]

Table 6 Tenure of households in Milton Keynes, 1967–83 (percentages)

	New town rent	*Council rent*	*Other rent*	*Sale to sitting tenants*	*Shared owner-ship*	*New town sale*	*Other sale*
Always lived in area	4.3	29.0	12.7	9.7	11.9	7.6	30.0
Moved 1967 or earlier	1.2	26.4	8.0	14.2	3.2	2.8	21.8
1968–73	6.0	22.3	13.5	16.9	5.5	10.5	15.6
1974–77	27.0	9.1	18.8	27.4	12.9	17.0	11.4
1978–80	31.3	8.4	14.5	24.2	16.7	21.7	10.6
1981–83	30.2	4.8	32.5	7.6	49.8	40.4	10.6

Source: Adapted from MKDC, *Milton Keynes Household Survey, 1983, Demographic Report* (Milton Keynes, 1983), p. 34.

The pursuit of a better, higher-paid or more secure job was a common reason for moving. It appears from Table 5 that employment as a spur to move to Milton Keynes became more important from the mid to the later 1980s. This may be a consequence of the short-lived upturn in the national and local economies from 1986. It might also reflect the diminishing number of working-class Londoners relative to the wider demographic growth of the new city. The peak of migration from London to Milton Keynes occurred during the 1970–77 period, but fell off notably thereafter. Until 1977, about 47 per cent of all incomers to the new city were from London, and their profile was largely manual working-class, due to its demand for skilled manual and construction work. By 1988, in-migration from London was about one-third of all newcomers, 'the majority moving from other parts of the South East'. 'Other United Kingdom' migration had risen from just under 17 per cent to over 25 per cent between 1973 and 1988, and 'overseas' remained constant at 3 to 4 per cent.[107]

Between 1973 and 1988 the socio-economic profile of Milton Keynes altered considerably, as shown in Table 7. It may, therefore, be suggested that the pursuit of a better job became a more important reason for moving during the 1980s for those in the higher socio-economic groups. (These are, after all, general statistics which refer to all social classes.) Some 34 per cent of the professional/managerial groups moved for this reason, compared with 28 per cent among non-manual white-collar workers and 11 per cent for manual workers, whether skilled, semi-skilled or unskilled.[108]

Table 7 Socio-economic profile of Milton Keynes households, 1973–88 (percentages)

	1973	*1976*	*1983*	*1988*
Prof/managerial	13	18	17	20
Intermediate	19	20	39	37
Skilled manual	49	44	24	22
Semi/unskilled	19	18	20	21

Source: Adapted from MKDC, *Four Years On: The Milton Keynes Household Survey, 1973, Summary* (Milton Keynes, 1973), p. 8; MKDC, *Seven Years On: The Summary Report of the 1976 Household and Employers Surveys* (Milton Keynes, 1977), Figure 1.9, p. 11; MKDC, *Milton Keynes Household Survey, 1988; Employment Technical Report* (Milton Keynes, 1989), Table 1, p. 4.

The leap in 'environment' as a reason for moving between 1988 to 1990 is tangible. However, this may also reflect the Borough Council's inclusion of 'school reasons' in that category. During the late 1980s the Borough Council had taken over the data gathering and publishing of the household survey from MKDC, in anticipation of MKDC winding up in 1992, and the Council appears to have widened the environmental category. One in five movers gave education as a factor in moving,[109] but it is doubtful it was the sole factor. It does suggest, however, that perceived better schooling as a mechanism for upward social mobility persisted as a factor in the move, a point made above in relation to the move to suburban estates. However, these 1990 statistics were not solely for working-class families, although they did incorporate them.

Environment as a factor in moving to the new towns was noted elsewhere. For example, research on working-class Liverpudlians who applied to move to Runcorn in the early 1970s found that 30 per cent living in cramped, dirty or even 'condemned' housing gave 'a nicer, cleaner, safer area' as the main reason, whilst this figure rose to 45 per cent as one 'other reason' beyond the main one, which was housing.[110]

In terms of kinship-based chain migration, Table 5 illustrates, despite a first impression, that a desire to be with or near family remained a factor for a sizeable minority of migrants. This may reflect the fact that MKDC undertook a proactive resettlement policy to encourage middle-aged and elderly people, categories which often included the parents of younger families, to move to the new city.[111] Yet a study of the largely working-class Beanhill estate, conducted in the spring of 1987, showed that the need to be near to family was still important: 'the most popular reason for moving to Milton Keynes was to be nearer grown-up children', a development which also caused the 'gradual stabilisation of the population' and the movement of other members of the family to the new city once the original migrants had settled in.[112]

Moreover, the dip in the figures for kinship as a motive for migration was probably a function of the changing origins of the migrants themselves, who from the early 1980s came increasingly from the sub-region and nearby counties, and whose family and friends were probably still nearby. They were thus moving only a relatively short distance away from established family and friends.[113] At Runcorn, however, despite a decade of settlement there, only 5 per cent gave a desire to be nearer to friends or relatives as a main reason for moving, although this rose to 20 per cent when considered as one reason among others.[114]

As noted in Chapter 2, the momentum of dispersal has been gathering pace within some ethnic minority groups since 1970. The reasons are not so very different from those of whites, as the following material from Milton Keynes shows.[115] A Pakistani couple, who ran a shop in Milton Keynes at the time of the interview, gave better housing as the key reason for their move:

> In 1980 we were living in London, in Islington. The housing wasn't very good. I would say Milton Keynes was much better than expected. We moved into Conniburrow and couldn't believe it was a council house because it was such good quality. We were used to seeing council houses in London that are dilapidated and run-down. We were quite excited by it all.[116]

A West Indian couple, interviewed by MKDC, told how they had moved to Milton Keynes from South London as a result of the obscene language and threatening behaviour from their neighbours. They did not want their children to be brought up in the area, and welcomed the 'peace and clean of the open streets': 'I like to keep an eye on the children all the time, and there was a garden here, so I could see them'.[117] These testimonies help to explain the growing presence of people of colour in the suburbs and new towns since 1970.

Conclusion

An early 1970s study of Runcorn highlighted a rather reductionist dichotomy between 'push' and 'pull' factors in migration. Push factors, they argued, were basically poor housing and slum clearance programmes. Pull criteria were the appeal of a new house, of a nicer environment, safer, greener and cleaner streets, and a desire to be nearer to family and friends. But how can push and pull be separated from each other? They were intertwined, and pull was undoubtedly a greater force than push. By no means all, but certainly the majority, of movement was voluntary, and that included very many slum tenants whose choice was limited:

> Survey evidence indicates that many slum dwellers share the general aspiration for better housing and suburban living and that most of those forced to join the outward movement because of slum clearance settle very quickly into their new way of life, and that the difficulties encountered by a minority are for the most part temporary.[118]

The working classes in general, and slum dwellers in particular, therefore, were not blithely annexed from their urban culture and community, and most settled into their new way of life. This general finding may be correlated with the findings of sociologists David Donnison and Paul Soto. During the 1970s they investigated popular ideas of 'the good city', and found that manual workers ranked the traditional industrial towns 'worst', while the residential suburbs around industrial towns ranked higher, and the new towns and the new suburbs of the South East 'consistently appear at the "best" end of these rank orders'.[119] This was the case for owner-occupiers and also for those with less choice. Workers' families enjoyed higher standards of living in new housing developments which fell within the new suburbs and towns of postwar England.

No wonder, then, working-class households moved. Their experiences of settling in are discussed in the next chapter.

Notes

1 E. Harvey, 'The post-war pioneers', *Town and Country Planning*, 41:9 (1973), p. 417.

2 C. Williams-Ellis, *Around the World in Ninety Years* (Portmeirion, 1996), p. 10.

3 B. Jackson, *Working-Class Community* (Harmondsworth, 1972), pp. 159, 186–7.

4 See, for example, C. Chinn, *They Worked All Their Lives: Women of the Urban Poor, 1880–1939* (Manchester, 1987); E. Roberts, *A Woman's Place: An Oral History of Working-Class Women, 1890–1940* (Oxford, 1984). For an outline of working-class life between the early Victorian years and the 1940s, which also draws attention to the often neglected relationship between class and space, see M. Savage and A. Miles, *The Remaking of the British Working Class, 1840–1940* (London, 1994), pp. 57–72.

5 R. McKibbin, 'Preface', in R. McKibbin, *The Ideologies of Class: Social Relations in Britain, 1880–1950* (Oxford, 1991), p. vii.

6 See, for example, the contributions on the English regions to F. M. L. Thompson (ed.), *The Cambridge Social History of Britain, 1750–1950. Vol. I: Regions and Communities* (Cambridge, 1993).

7 See, for example, Chinn, *The Worked All Their Lives*, passim; Roberts, *A Woman's Place*, passim; M. Tebbutt, 'Gossip and "women's words" in working-class communities, 1880–1939', in A. Davies and S. Fielding (eds), *Workers' Worlds: Cultures and Communities in Manchester and Salford, 1880–1939* (Manchester, 1992), pp. 49–73.

8 See, for example, C. Forman, *Industrial Town: Self Portraits of St. Hel-*

ens in the 1920s (London, 1979), pp. 1–24; D. J. Rowe, 'The North East', in Thompson (ed.), *The Cambridge Social History of Britain, 1750–1950. Vol. I: Regions and Communities*, pp. 426–33.

9 B. S. Rowntree and G. R. Lavers, *English Life and Leisure: A Social Study* (London, 1951), p. 343.

10 This discussion is based upon C. Chinn, *Better Betting With a Decent Feller: Bookmaking, Betting and the British Working Class, 1750–1990* (Hemel Hempstead, 1991), pp. 140–1; M. Clapson, *A Bit of a Flutter: Popular Gambling and English Society, 1823–1961* (Manchester, 1992), pp. 44–7; A. Davies, 'Leisure in the classic slum', in Davies and Fielding (eds), *Workers' Worlds*, pp. 102–32.

11 J. Bourke, *Working-Class Cultures in Britain, 1890–1960: Gender, Class and Ethnicity* (London, 1994), pp. 136–69.

12 Ibid., pp. 142–3.

13 P. Howlett, 'The "Golden Age", 1955–1973', in P. Johnson (ed.), *Twentieth Century Britain: Economic, Social and Cultural Change* (London, 1994), p. 321.

14 Howlett, '"Golden Age"', pp. 321–2; E. Hopkins, *The Rise and Decline of the English Working Classes, 1918–1990: A Social History* (London, 1991), pp. 159–83; J. Walvin, *Leisure and Society, 1830–1950* (London, 1978), pp. 133–4, 153.

15 See Chapter 2 above, pp. 42–8.

16 M. Young and P. Willmott, *Family and Kinship in East London* (Harmondsworth, 1979), p. 186.

17 Ibid., pp. 44–61.

18 N. Dennis, 'Who needs neighbours?', *New Society*, 25 July 1963, p. 8.

19 Young and Willmott, *Family and Kinship*, pp. 198–9.

20 J. Platt, *Social Research in Bethnal Green* (London, 1971), pp. 1–9.

21 The correspondence is held in the Richard Titmuss Collection at the British Library of Political and Economic Science. Hereafter, this is referred to as Titmuss/ICS/BLPES &c.

22 Titmuss/ICS/BLPES, 'Reception of Institute's first book', 13 February 1958.

23 Ibid. (I am grateful to Nick Bolton for translating this sentence.)

24 *Listener*, 30 May 1957.

25 Titmuss/ICS/BLPES, 'Reception'.

26 S. F. Fava, 'The pop sociology of suburbs and new towns', in I. L. Allen (ed.), *New Towns and the Suburban Dream: Ideology and Utopia in Planning and Development* (New York, 1977), pp. 106–18.

27 J. Stevenson, 'The Jerusalem that failed? The rebuilding of postwar Britain', in T. Gourvish and A. O'Day, *Britain Since 1945* (London, 1991), p. 92.
28 P. Hall, 'The people: where will they go?', *Planner*, 71:4 (1985), p. 8.
29 T. Tsubaki, 'Postwar reconstruction and the questions of popular housing provision, 1939–51' (University of Warwick, unpublished Ph.D. thesis, 1993), I, p. 240.
30 Ibid., pp. 246–79.
31 Ibid., pp. 257, 260–2.
32 A useful summary of Berger and Gans is to be found in R. J. Johnston, *Urban Residential Patterns: An Introductory Review* (London, 1971), p. 236. Also, see Chapter 7, pp. 197–8.
33 J. English, R. Madigan and P. Norman, *Slum Clearance: The Social and Administrative Context in England and Wales* (London, 1976), pp. 85–90, 105.
34 J. Norris, *Human Aspects of Redevelopment* (Birmingham, 1962), pp. 11, 27–8.
35 Ibid., p. 11.
36 Central Housing Advisory Committee (CHAC), *Moving From the Slums: Seventh Report of the Housing Sub-Committee of the Central Housing Advisory Committee* (London, 1956), p. 2.
37 Ibid., pp. 2, 19.
38 C. Chinn, *Homes for People: 100 Years of Council Housing in Birmingham* (Birmingham, 1991), p. 97.
39 The Society of Housing Managers, *Report of Conference, 'Management Problems Arising Out of the Housing Repairs and Rents Act, 1954', 28/29 January, 1955* (London, 1955), pp. 13–14.
40 N. H. Rankin, 'Social adjustment in a North-West new town', *Sociological Review* (New Series) 11:3 (1963), p. 291.
41 In B. J. Parker 'Some sociological implications of slum clearance programmes', in D. Donnison and D. Eversley (eds), *London: Urban Patterns and Problems* (London, 1973), p. 259.
42 Rankin, 'Social adjustment', pp. 292–3, 296, 301.
43 M. W. Hodges and C. S. Smith, 'The Sheffield Estate', in G. D. Mitchell, T. Lupton, M. W. Hodges and C. S. Smith (eds), *Neighbourhood and Community* (Liverpool, 1954), p. 81.
44 R. K. Wilkinson and E. M. Sigsworth, 'Slum dwellers of Leeds', *New Society*, 4 April 1963, p. 12.
45 J. M. Mogey, *Family and Neighbourhood: Two Studies of Oxford* (Oxford, 1956), p. 74.

46 Ibid., pp. 140–5.
47 H. E. Bracey, *Neighbours on New Estates and Subdivisions in England and the USA* (London, 1964), p. 53.
48 N. Dennis, *People and Planning: The Sociology of Housing in Sunderland* (London, 1970), pp. 291–3; Society of Housing Managers, *Report of Conference, 'Management Problems'*, p. 14.
49 R. K. Wilkinson and E. M. Sigsworth, 'Attitudes to the housing environment: an analysis of private and local authority households in Batley, Leeds and York', *Urban Studies*, 9 (1972), p. 208.
50 Bracey, *Neighbours on New Estates*, p. 52.
51 H. Jennings, *Societies in the Making: A Study of Development and Redevelopment Within a County Borough* (London, 1962), pp. 89–90.
52 D. Chapman, *The Home and Social Status* (London, 1955), pp. 156–7.
53 J. Rex and R. Moore, *Race, Community and Conflict: A Study of Sparkbrook* (Oxford, 1979), pp. 63, 73–5.
54 Bracey, *Neighbours on New Estates*, p. 39.
55 F. M. Martin, 'An inquiry into parent's preferences in secondary education', in D. V. Glass (ed.), *Social Mobility in Britain* (London, 1954), p. 162.
56 M. Craft (ed.), *Family, Class and Education: A Reader* (London, 1970), pp. 12–13.
57 Ibid., pp. 12, 16.
58 J. H. Goldthorpe, D. Lockwood, F. Bechhofer and J. Platt, *The Affluent Worker in the Class Structure* (Cambridge, 1971), pp. 130–6.
59 B. Jackson and D. Marsden, *Education and the Working Class* (Harmondsworth, 1976), pp. 60–96; see Fig. 1, p. 92.
60 J. W. B. Douglas, *The Home and the School: A Study of Ability and Attainment in the Primary School* (London, 1976), pp. 62–3; Jackson and Marsden, *Education and the Working Class*, pp. 92–3.
61 Douglas, *Home and the School*, pp. 12–13; Jackson and Marsden, *Education and the Working Class*, passim.
62 Douglas, *Home and the School*, pp. 60–80; G. Rose, *The Working Class* (London, 1968), pp. 40–2.
63 M. Savage, 'The missing link? The relationship between spatial mobility and social mobility', *British Journal of Sociology*, 39:4 (1988), pp. 554–5.
64 Norris, *Human Aspects*, pp. 53–4.
65 Jennings, *Societies in the Making*, p. 145.
66 Bracey, *Neighbours on New Estates*, p. 49.
67 P. Willmott and M. Young, *Family and Class in a London Suburb* (Lon-

don, 1960), p. 78. For owner-occupation, see pp. 23 and 80.

68 J. B. Mays, *The Introspective Society* (London, 1968), pp. 81–2.

69 P. Willmott, 'Social research and the new communities', *Journal of the American Institute of Planners*, 33:6 (1967), pp. 387–98. Willmott was well placed to make this point, as he was one of the few sociologists of dispersal who also studied both peripheral out-county estates and the new towns. See P. Willmott, *The Evolution of a Community* (London, 1960), passim, on Dagenham; P. Willmott, 'Housing density and town design in a new town: a pilot study at Stevenage', *Town Planning Review*, 33:2 (1962), pp. 115–27.

70 P. Cresswell, *The New Town Goal of Self Containment* (Milton Keynes, 1974), p. 2.

71 Ministry of Town and Country Planning, *Final Report of the New Towns Committee* (London, 1946, Cmd 6876), para. 294, p. 68; B. Goodey, 'Social research in the new communities', *Built Environment*, 2:4 (1973), p. 233.

72 A. Buttimer, 'Sociology and planning', *Town Planning Review*, 42:2 (1971), p. 149.

73 Ministry of Town and Country Planning, *Report of the Committee on the Qualification of Planners* (London, 1950, Cmd 8059), paras 67–9, pp. 19–20, para. 84, p. 22;

74 H. J. Orlans, *Stevenage: A Sociological Study of a New Town* (London, 1952), p. 185.

75 V. A. Karn, *Stevenage Housing Survey: A Study of Housing Development in a New Town* (Birmingham, 1970), p. 13.

76 Ibid., p. 17.

77 V. A. Karn, *Aycliffe Housing Survey: A Study of Housing in a New Town* (Birmingham, 1970), pp. 20–1.

78 Ibid., p. 12.

79 J. B. Cullingworth, 'Social implications of overspill: the Worsley social survey', *Sociological Review* (New Series) 8:1 (1960), p. 77.

80 Ibid., p. 80.

81 Ibid., pp. 80–4, 92–3.

82 Ibid., p. 93.

83 J. B. Cullingworth, 'The Swindon social survey: a second report on the social implications of overspill', *Sociological Review* (New Series) 9:2 (1961), p. 160.

84 Ibid., pp. 153, 157.

85 J. B. Cullingworth, *Housing Needs and Planning Policy: A Reassessment of the Problems of Housing Need and 'Overspill' in England and Wales*

(London, 1960), pp. 51–3, 148–50, 153–5, 161–7; see also J. B. Cullingworth, *Town and Country Planning in Britain* (London, 1974), pp. 231–54.

86 J. Husain, 'Londoners who left', *New Society*, 7 July 1977, p. 17.

87 S. Humphries and J. Taylor, *The Making of Modern London, 1945–1985* (London, 1986), p. 87. A large study was undertaken for Milton Keynes by the Living Archive Project, which is based at Wolverton in Milton Keynes. Its address is given in the bi-annual journal *Oral History*.

88 MKDC with Social and Community Planning Research, *Four Years On: The Milton Keynes Household Survey, 1973* (Milton Keynes, 1974).

89 R. Kitchen, 'Moving to Milton Keynes', *New Society*, 22 August 1974, pp. 478–80.

90 MKDC, *Seven Years On: Household Survey, 1976, Technical Report 2: The Move to Milton Keynes* (Milton Keynes, 1977), p. 3b.

91 MKDC, *Four Years On*, Summary, p. 6.

92 Kitchen, 'Moving to Milton Keynes', pp. 478–9.

93 Living Archive Project (LAP), NCY/0043, Tape 179; transcript.

94 LAP, NCY/T007, Tape 183; transcript.

95 MKDC, *New City, Milton Keynes* (Milton Keynes, 1975), pp. 2–7.

96 Kitchen, 'Moving to Milton Keynes', p. 479.

97 J. Turner and B. Jardine, *Pioneer Tales* (Milton Keynes, 1985), p. 23.

98 N. Deakin and C. Ungerson, *Leaving London: Planned Mobility and the Inner City* (London, 1977), p. 2

99 MKDC, *New City, Milton Keynes* (Milton Keynes, 1974), pp. 4–12.

100 LAP, NCY/T001, Tape 176; transcript.

101 MKDC, *Residential Design Feedback: Report of Studies* (Milton Keynes, 1975), p. 9.

102 MKDC, *Seven Years On: Household Survey, 1976, Technical Report 2*, p. 62.

103 Ibid., p. 10.

104 Deakin and Ungerson, *Leaving London*, pp. 45–50.

105 MKDC, *Milton Keynes Household Survey, 1983, Demographic Report* (Milton Keynes, 1985), p. 34.

106 Milton Keynes Borough Council, *Household Survey, 1990* (Milton Keynes, 1990), Table 2.3, p. 14.

107 MKDC, *Milton Keynes Household Survey, 1983, Demographic Report*, p. 32; MKDC, *Milton Keynes Insight* (Milton Keynes, 1989), p. 2; MKDC, *Milton Keynes Population Bulletin* (Milton Keynes, 1990), p. 31.

108 MKDC, *Milton Keynes Household Survey, 1976, Technical Supplement*

no. 2 (Milton Keynes, 1977), p. 11.

109 Milton Keynes Borough Council, *Household Survey, 1990*, p. 18.

110 R. Berthoud and R. Jowell, *Creating a Community: A Study of Runcorn New Town* (London, 1973), p. 19.

111 MKDC, *The Plan for Milton Keynes* (Milton Keynes, 1970), II, pp. 127–8.

112 P. Liddiard, *Milton Keynes Felt Needs Project: A Preliminary Study of the Felt Health Needs of People Living in Relative Poverty on a Milton Keynes Housing Estate* (Milton Keynes, 1988), p. 31. Liddiard was based at the Department of Health and Social Welfare, at the Open University.

113 See Table 2, p. 43.

114 Berthoud and Jowell, *Creating a Community*, p. 19.

115 See above, Chapter 2, pp. 50–2.

116 Turner and Jardine, *Pioneer Tales*, p. 69.

117 MKDC, *Milton Keynes* (Milton Keynes, 1988), p. 36.

118 Parker, 'Some sociological implications', p. 269.

119 D. Donnison with P. Soto, *The Good City: A Study of Urban Development and Policy in Britain* (London, 1980), pp. 102, 110–13.

4

Settling in

> Instead of the long, low railwaymen's houses, that looked like so many dusty, worn-out old carriages, there were a number of little houses surrounded by gardens. They were not luxurious [but] in comparison with our sordid dwelling they gave an impression of a gayer and easier life. First of all, each house was different; then, they were not all cracked and strained, with the plaster peeling off, an appearance which made our house and others like it seem as though their inhabitants had long neglected them through sheer indifference; and finally, the narrow, blossoming gardens which surrounded them created an impression of jealous intimacy, remote from the confusion and promiscuity of the street.[1]

> The virtue of the suburb lies in this: it is wide open to the sky, it is linked to the city, it is linked to the country, the air blows fresh, it is a cheap place for families to live in and have children and gardens: it smells of lime trees, tar, cut grass, roses ...[2]

This chapter describes and evaluates the experiences of settling into new peripheral estates and the new and expanded towns. It is concerned with the earliest days of moving. It discusses the gains which enabled people to settle happily into their new homes. One such gain was the sense of relief that many people experienced at moving away from often cramped housing conditions shared with relatives. Second, and most important, was the acquisition of the new house, and that was often also related to the improved environmental aspect offered by the new estate. Third, the ability to make friends and neighbours also facilitated adaptation to a new home.

As with the previous chapter, the experiences of suburban migrants are given careful comparison with those of new and expanded town migrants. This is because, although there were some broad similarities in the experience of moving, there were a number of differences in process. Those who moved to owner-occupied estates had no official agency to assist with settling in. However, the new and expanded towns, to varying degrees, provided social development officers for those tenants of development corporation housing. Much of their effort was aimed at helping people to settle in.[3] Moreover, the new and expanded town development corporations also employed housing managers to assist with their social development programme.[4]

The majority of the work of housing managers, however, was on council estates built and managed by local authorities. A key element of the housing manager's role was to deal with people's problems or needs when they moved. They were trained by the Society of Housing Managers and worked under both its auspices and those of the local authority or development corporation.[5] A further difference in process, as noted in the previous chapter, was that movers to new and expanded towns had to take work in order to be able to secure a house.[6]

The oral historian Stephen Caunce, referring to the major movement of working-class households to the interwar estates, has termed this move 'a crucial moment and place in working-class history'.[7] The significance of that interpretation may be extended into the postwar period. These experiences are, here, largely related either through contemporary testimony from sociologies or through retrospective oral testimony. This lends more than a little integrity to the positive and optimistic interpretation of moving home. And this is necessary to counteract the predominant tenor of academic social history, noted in Chapter 1. For example, Elizabeth Roberts, in her important and pioneering work on women and families between 1940 and 1970, has argued that 'a striking feature of the oral evidence is the great improvement which took place in housing conditions' in the period under study.[8] Yet, ultimately, she provides little testimony to illumine the sense of appreciation, and even gratitude, which many people felt as they moved for the first time away from cramped and often festering Victorian accommodation into housing which was of a decent, twentieth-century standard.

Settling in: the sense of relief at moving away from family

This little section is included simply because it presents a feeling which is not to be found in existing oral histories of moving house.

As noted in Chapter 2, the profile of the vast majority of movers was of young married couples with children, or of couples just about to have them.[9] It is not surprising that gobbets of contemporary testimony, found in sociological studies, express the sense of relief which many young couples felt as they put distance between themselves and their extended family networks. In 1947 Mass Observation had noted that working-class newly-weds were often deeply miserable because they were living with one or other of their families: 'They want to escape from intolerable home conditions, of overcrowding or unsatisfactory relationships with parents'. Mass Observation quoted one woman from a central London borough (aged 27, married at 18) who wanted to 'get out of my Mum's house more than anything ... My Mum and Dad were always squabbling; he's fond of his pint, and he used to have more than was good for him, and that used to set them off. I wanted to get married and have a home of my own and a bit of peace.'[10]

J. M. Mogey found that in some of the newly arrived families he studied in the new estate of Barton there was 'less strain than living with relatives', as had been common in the previous context,[11] and he observed a new pattern in family relations which appeared to be wholly acceptable to those who had moved. The move away from kin was often an expression of changing values which emphasised a widening of both social and material expectations:

> The social change for the family embraced, in addition to a new house, a new garden, lots of extra monetary outlay and a completely new environment, new standards of desire. For instance, one family hired a car and went off, all together, just to the sea for four days. This sort of behaviour in a family just moved into a bungalow of their own, after twelve years of sharing with the wife's parents and a brother's family in a small three bedroom house, is not to be explained in terms of economics.[12]

Yet Mogey noticed that seven out of ten families on the housing estate actively kept up, in spite of greater distances, regular contact with their relatives, and there was also a considerable level of irregular contact.[13] In common with Mogey, Elizabeth Bott and J. B. Cullingworth, sociologist and planner respectively, agreed that kinship networks were generally flexible enough to accommodate the greater geographical distances engendered by moving home.[14] In these important respects, 'settling in' may be viewed historically. In settling down to a new home further away from the wider or extended family, the English working classes were adjusting upwards to higher expectations and levels of material comfort. The home was where these material benefits were felt most fully.

Settling in: the new home

The house was the major factor which facilitated people's ability to settle down in a new suburban estate. All of the sociologies used in this chapter emphasise the pleasure and pride which the vast majority of migrants experienced on moving into their new home. It is an interesting point that many new arrivals held a common perception of their home as like a 'castle' or a 'palace', a perception which predated the postwar years, and which continued throughout them. The monarchical references owe less to any wish literally to own such a huge dwelling as a castle or a palace, and more to the appreciation of the sheer difference and improvement in domestic standards which the tenants were now enjoying. The first quote comes from a man who moved to the LCC estate of Castelnau during the 1930s. It also provides a vivid illustration of the excitement that must have been felt by children as they moved in. 'I can always remember the first night':

> it was about ten o'clock by the time we got to bed. We had three bedrooms and when I look at the rooms now they aren't that big, but when we moved in, we thought it was a castle, what with coming from a flat where us five boys had to share one room, you know. It was absolutely wonderful.[15]

A woman in Liverpool said she 'felt like the Queen' when she first moved into her new council house.[16] This language reflects the joy of both women and men who moved into new homes. The new house made the move worthwhile. Jennings's study of Bristol, for example, found that in the 'adaptation to change' the pride in the new house was paramount. A new house meant pride, and perhaps a higher level of self-esteem: 'the great majority of tenants on the postwar housing estates expressed great pleasure and pride in their houses. [Typical] comments made by the wives were "I'm thrilled with it", "It's a delight", "I shan't mind working hard to keep it nice".'[17]

Newcomers to new and expanded towns held similar expectations of their homes. As Marie Cousins, whose husband took a printing job in Stevenage in order to enable them to move there, remembered, 'on the 1st June 1957 we came to live in Stevenage New Town':

> We had four little girls aged from one year to six years old and were really pleased to be leaving our shared accommodation in Islington, to take over a three-bedroom house in Bedwell. Never before had we the luxury of a bath, hot water on tap and best of all in the children's eyes, our own stairs. They ran up and down them on that first day calling out 'these are our stairs' and they all kept flushing the toilet. This was a great improvement on our former home, where the toilet was in the back-yard.[18]

One family from London, who moved to the expanded town of Bletchley, had lived in two rooms on the second floor of a house in Islington. They had had to descend five flights of stairs to use the shared toilet. As Mrs Porter remembers, 'It wasn't very clean ... and so when we moved to Bletchley [her children] were so pleased that they'd got a toilet they could use, Linda locked herself in the first day we moved in'.[19] Another Bletchley migrant has spoken of how the house was related to the condition of obtaining employment. Alec Clifford, of London, remembers how he and his family went to Bletchley to look at the accommodation and were offered a 'little two bedroom house', a 'beautiful house': 'we went back and said "Yes we'll accept it, I'll accept the job". About a week or so later they said we could go and get the key for the house and start work at the Marston Brick Company. We thought it was magic.'[20]

The importance of feeling good about the new home was appreciated by official agencies, such as the Society of Housing Managers. The Society held an important intermediary position between the tenants of council houses and the architects departments of councils and development corporations. A great deal of its work was undertaken by women housing managers who liaised with tenants and those responsible for the design and planning of houses. Materials from the Society provide contemporary evidence of the perceptions and preferences of tenants in relation to their new homes. They found that the most popular houses had larger rooms, well-equipped kitchens, and a generous provision and arrangement of space which allowed for people to make their own impression upon it. Designs which were more rigid in character were less popular, even though people appreciated their improved housing. What were not liked, however, were departures from 'traditional' internal layouts and appearances.[21] Stephen Humphries and John Taylor's oral historical work on Londoners who moved to Stevenage confirms this retrospectively. Although Londoners were pleased with their new homes, 'there was much criticism of the modern design of many house interiors'. This criticism was directed against the experiments of development corporation architects who attempted to cultivate a taste (their taste) for 'simple, modern and functional design' within working-class families.[22]

One of the fullest sources on tenants' perceptions of their new homes, perceptions which were central to the success of settling in, was researched by MKDC. MKDC investigated what newcomers wanted for their housing and became aware of the tension between expectation from below and design from above. This was because the early pioneers of Milton Keynes had to contend with some unpopular modern designs. The *Plan for Milton Keynes* promised to 'provide for a wide range of living conditions, to attract a full range of social and economic groups'. It aimed to create 'a safe, convenient and reasonable environment at a reasonable cost'.[23] 'Reasonable cost' meant cheaper building materials.[24] Furthermore, new housing in the new town had to be built to the standards laid down in Parker Morris's *Homes for Today and Tomorrow*, published in 1961. The Parker Morris report had recommended bigger rooms and called for minimum room sizes, better fittings in kitchens and bathrooms, adequate storage space, and newer more flexible layouts of internal space to accommodate the needs of materially better-off households.[25] Its guidelines were mandatory for public housing. Thus MKDC, having to meet high standards with a lower budget than it would have liked, argued that 'rationalised' or 'industrialised' building methods were necessary for a considerable proportion of the new city's accommodation.[26] In consequence, most of the early pioneers moved into such schemes, which were designed by some of the most eminent architectural practices of the 1970s, and built by MKDC on the early estates.[27] MKDC felt that their estates exhibited a 'tremendous variety of solutions and creative approaches to design', and they wanted to give residents the opportunity to provide 'feedback' to enhance the relationship between the designer and the consumer, thus also involving new residents 'in a positive exercise in participation with the Corporation'.[28] Hence, the *Residential Design Feedback:*

Report of Studies was the summary of a consultative exercise, involving 290 households, and based upon questionnaires. These were followed up by interviews and 'theatre sessions' at the local schools, which were attended by between thirty-five and seventy residents. (MKDC felt that these meetings were 'a pleasant night out' for women.[29]) MKDC was also particularly aware of the views of some renters that they had less choice – a factor noted above – than those who could purchase. It conceded the point that 'it cannot be assumed that they have been able to select the dwelling which most closely corresponds to their priorities'.[30]

MKDC encountered a highly evaluative and often critical set of responses, which have great significance for a study of the central importance of housing for people, for at least two important reasons. First, it demonstrates the important role of housing in helping people to settle in. Second, it illustrates the centrality of housing as an item of consumption, whether as private purchase or public rental. These responses showed pleasure, and in some cases gratitude, at the spatial and material gains offered by the new housing, but considerable dissatisfaction at some perceived shortcomings in many aspects of design. For example, houses with both upstairs and downstairs washrooms or toilets were preferred to those with a single bathroom, but the absence of windows in bathrooms was disliked.[31]

Kitchens were an important functional room in the house, and all kitchens in the MKDC survey conformed to Parker Morris standards, providing the 'worktop-cooker-worktop-sink-worktop sequence'. But Parker Morris had not specified kitchen sizes, and not surprisingly larger kitchens were preferred to smaller ones. Kitchen storage space and adequate space for appliances was a primary concern, as 96 per cent of all households owned a refrigerator, 86 per cent a washing machine, and 61 per cent a tumble or spin dryer. Only 24 per cent of these working-class families had a deep-freeze by the mid-1970s. In fact, a smaller kitchen was approved of as long as the space was adequate. However, criticisms of the appearance of hot water pipes, of the non-provision of a pantry and a stated preference for sinks to be underneath windows were noted.[32]

Larger bedrooms were preferred to smaller ones, and houses with separate dining rooms were preferred to those without. There was a good deal of criticism of heating systems as many dwellings 'are not found to be well designed for warmth'.[33] Places with full-house central heating were most popular.[34] Whilst all lounges in the houses or flats conformed to Parker Morris requirements that the space should accommodate three easy chairs, a settee, a television set and room for a few other items of furniture, it was found that there was a clear preference for the largest lounges, those over fifteen metres square.[35] Another common complaint was that noise insulation between terraced and semi-detached houses was often poor, 'and most families do not feel that their houses are particularly well designed for peace and quiet'.[36] (The issue of noise transference is returned to in Chapter 5.) Lower levels of storage provision throughout the house were also criticised.[37]

External features of housing, whilst less important than interiors, were also subject to scrutiny by residents. Again, we must note the importance of the garden. It was viewed as a major asset, but in general, larger, more private back gardens were clearly favoured. Gardens which were 'overlooked' were criticised for their lack of privacy. Enclosed gardens were preferred to open frontages.[38] It is interesting to compare these findings with American studies of the suburban residential habitat which stress the non-verbal signifiers in the external environment. The appearance of trees and shrubs around gardens was a device not simply to make the gardens look pretty, but also to ensure greater privacy.[39] Moreover, a street with well-tended and cared-for gardens created a comfortable, relaxing, slowly paced, clearly demarcated, green suburban imagery. It also created a positive and respectable social tone, a feature of both owner-occupied and council estates.[40]

In this, Milton Keynes was merely heir to a long established tradition in England: the love of gardens as both an out-of-doors domestic retreat and a private domain of artistic self-expression through gardening and garden design. Hence, for the cottage estates of the 1920s and since, Stephen Constantine's historical study of gardening demonstrates convincingly its popularity and the affinity of new estates with their garden-city heritage of house and garden.[41] Hilda Jennings noted for Bristol in 1962 that the great majority of migrants were 'enthusiastic' about their garden, and it often brought the whole family together in planning, cultivation and maintenance. The garden was seen to encourage home-centredness, too: 'My husband spends all his time in the garden. He doesn't seem to want to go out in the evenings now.'[42] The garden represented the permeability and expressiveness of the suburban environment when compared to the impoverished rigidity of the slum terrace, or the limitations of the high-rise flat, a point which the contributors to the Dunroamin collection have emphasised.[43] Doreen Brace, who moved to Bletchley during the 1950s, remembered both her joy at her 'own front door' and she and her husband's appreciation of their garden, and its potential: 'I think it was about a month before they put the fences and that up, and then it was lovely 'cause your garden you started from scratch – was right up my husband's street, to start his garden from scratch'.[44] For some, moreover, a garden was simply a luxury they had not had before. The following anecdote is from Milton Keynes:

> when, according to *New Society*, the community television station, as an April Fool's joke for 1979, broadcast a message saying that the entire city (100,000 inhabitants, half the planned total, at the end of the decade) was to be ploughed back into the ground, a viewer declared that he was not going to go back to London: 'Milton Keynes had given him a garden, something he'd never had before, and he was damned if he was going to give it up now'.[45]

The garden as an external feature revealed the importance which people placed on appearances in general. Hence the outsides of the houses themselves produced strong reactions. People were conservative in their tastes, expressing a clear preference for brick and white rendering, and a 'marked dislike of cedar boarding'. One resident said that 'white paint instead of the hideous colours applied at the moment could make a world of difference'.[46] Another complained that the pink and white two-tiered exteriors of the housing 'looked like rows of false teeth'.[47]

Despite these criticisms, the MKDC's Planning Group, whose brief was to develop housing policy, concluded that 'the variety of housing in Milton Keynes seems fully justified', and claimed that four out of five liked their new homes and new life in Milton Keynes.[48] This is hardly surprising given the housing need which many had endured prior to their move. Also, the Planning Group's view may invite suspicion that MKDC petitioned its residents after the event in order to validate their early housing programme. Beatrix Campbell, for example, has pointed out that in the postwar years, residents have often been consulted on housing issues by local authorities but usually only to ratify completed plans.[49] Thus, it follows, the real wishes of the residents were not really acted upon. Many planners and social development officers working for MKDC were critical of the modernist designs of some early estates and felt that the architects had imposed their own narrow preferences upon the tenants.[50]

But it does appear that MKDC was concerned to learn from its mistakes, thus tenants' dissatisfaction with some of the early houses was the stimulus behind the decision by MKDC to commission an independent investigation whose primary concern was to gauge what people wanted in order that MKDC might adopt more populist housing policies in particular, and to help to develop a more user-friendly city in general. The research was undertaken by Jeff Bishop of Bristol University's School for Advanced Urban Studies from 1979 to 1981. One writer in the *Architect's Journal*'s special anniversary edition on Milton Keynes termed it 'a watershed in the development of the town because it offered clear guidance on the way the residents saw the place and wanted it to develop'.[51] Following Bishop, pitched roofs were placed over flat ones in a number of estates, as the tenants wished. This led one architectural purist, also writing in the same edition of *Architect's Journal*, whose inclinations were clearly minority and modernist rather than populist, to argue that such estates as Beanhill had 'suffered the indignity of added pitched roofs'.[52] But these were the types of roofs that most people appeared to want, and which they had not been given in the first place. The historical significance of the alterations to these houses goes beyond aesthetic considerations, too. These changes were in part brought about by agitation from residents' groups, a point developed further in Chapter 6.

As the earlier paragraphs illustrate, the interior of the postwar working-class home had been increasingly enhanced by a growing range of leisure items and labour-saving goods. Clearly, any discussion of suburbanisation cannot ignore growing consumption, nor can historical discussion of growing consumption ignore its relationship with suburbanisation, or with general urban dispersal. Material possessions were used to adorn the new house and make it comfortable. The consumption of labour-saving devices was growing considerably among working-class households, especially migrant working-class households, during the 1950s. For example, nationally, the access to automatic washing machines rose considerably during the 1950s, and has continued since. The refrigerator also appeared in more and more working-class homes, in common with wider increases in the consumption of household goods in the postwar period.[53]

There was also more money to spend on the television set. Many families could afford cash, but many others took out hire purchase agreements (credit) in order to obtain a television set and other consumer durables. These not only provided entertainment and more leisure time, they also reflected a widening of horizons within the increasingly affluent working classes. This was recognised by Helen Alford, a housing manager in London, who felt that televisions and cars were not simply manifestations of an inward-looking consumption and privatism. She criticised local councillors for being critical of the possession of television sets by people living in council estates, and noted how the desire for such possessions coincided with the raised expectations of the move to a new home. 'I would suggest', she argued in 1957, 'that people are entitled to have what they save up for':

> I remember a family who were so anxious to have a television set in the early days that they all gave up smoking and within a very short time had a set which cost £80. It makes one think about the cost of cigarettes. A car or a television set is, after all, an outward-looking pleasure. The family can drive off (and save railway fares), or they can enjoy the world of television (and save the price of a cinema). In either case they are taken out of their immediate world to wider horizons.[54]

Today in the 1990s the vast majority of people are used to the television set and the motor car. But the television and the car were novelties for the majority of working-class migrants during the 1950s. Yet as people watched the 'telly' with a sense of curiosity, or even wonder, Left intellectuals maligned it as a divisive symbol of status-consciousness, and castigated the silver screen for encouraging a new type of closure in working-class life, the 'keeping themselves to themselves' mentality lamented by, among others, Young and Willmott.[55] There was no attempt to evaluate the television set as a positive force for adapting to the new home.

The private world of television also fostered, for some aesthetes, an unwelcome public visual intrusion. On the new houses in the new housing developments television aerials were springing up on chimneys and gable ends. In 1963 Malcolm Muggeridge, who went on to make a career as a television-intellectual, satirised the rise of the televisions aerials – 'dreaming spires' – and the simultaneous rise of the new towns: 'how many housing estates have been built for heroes to live in!'.[56] Motor cars were also perceived as a visual as well as a practical intrusion. On the estates themselves, more and more cars were parked at the kerbside and on verges, sometimes to the extent of clogging up the estate's roads. Even the Society of Housing Managers was worried about the appearance of television aerials and cars.[57]

The focus on the subtopian aspects of the new estates obscured the fact that the majority of people moving onto them and settling down in them were pleased with their new residential and material conditions. It is important to note the importance of the residential environment in the satisfaction levels of migrants to the new and expanded towns, and these were broadly similar to those who moved to peripheral projects. These were the low-density, low-rise housing developments with generous gardens and green spaces, and with different lengths and shapes to their streets, which were attacked as irrational by modernist architects and planners such as Ivor de Wofle and Ian Nairn.[58] But it was what people moved for, and it encouraged a feeling of satisfaction when compared to the grimy streets and houses which they had left behind. Poor housing had usually been related to a poor physical environment, and the two were therefore often perceived in combination. As one middle-aged woman said in Jennings's study of Bristol: 'I've always had my "dream house", light and without the constant dirt and grime you get here from the railways'.[59]

A great many studies made at different times during the postwar decades stressed the enthusiasm with which people greeted their improved residential environment. For instance, many of those moving to council estates on the fringes of city areas in different regions of England spoke of their appreciation of the sense of space, the clean air and the greenery of the estates.[60] Margot Jeffreys emphasised how women at South Oxhey appreciated not simply the new housing, the 'fresh air' , the 'open spaces' and the 'general cleanliness' compared with their previous area, but also that this was a safer environment for their children, a point evident in other studies.[61] Strongly similar preferences persisted. During the 1980s a newcomer to Milton Keynes appreciated that he could 'see the skyline and watch the sunrise. It feels like the country compared to London.'[62] A woman resident of the new city told the *Daily Telegraph* of the 'open views, parks, and no traffic jams'.[63] As Husain argued, such comments approached 'a suburban norm' which could be identified in the value system of the postwar working-class migrant.[64] People liked the sub-rural, as much as the sub-urban, context of their new home.

Beyond the increasingly comfortable interiors of the houses, and beyond the gardens and the spacious new streets, many settled down because they made new friends and neighbours. This is the theme of the next section.

Early neighbours and friends

Ruth Durant's study of Watling during the 1930s demonstrated how, following a period of initial reticence among some new residents, the shared experience of moving in generated a kind of fellow feeling. People soon began to strike up conversation over fences, on the tube and when walking to the local school or shops. They often banded together in common identification against outside hostility or in pursuit of better facilities. Following this phase of relationship selection and establishment, which coincided with the period of settling down, the estate's social relationships shifted again to something which appeared to outsiders as 'Watlingitus', this superficial appearance of torpidity.[65] Yet it was not torpidity at all. Instead, it was a less on-the-street pattern of social interaction than the slums. The house, the pub, the club and the community centre – a centre which, as Chapter 6 demonstrates, was usually fought for by the new locals – were the indoor bases for this pattern of social interaction. A similar series of events occurred in postwar new estates. As Bracey showed for Bristol during the 1960s, and Mogey for Oxford during the mid-1950s, for example, there was sometimes great enthusiasm generated by the common experience of moving to a new estate. Friendliness was generated by a sense of 'pioneering together'.[66] Following that, neighbourly relations sometimes became more 'withdrawn'.[67]

Yet this was not true for all migrants. For the early days could establish some longer-term friendships and neighbours. Often, the very lack of local facilities drew people together, and that included new towns such as Stevenage:

> Our house was in one of the first few blocks of houses to be built in this area, and we all moved in within a few weeks of each other, and as there was nothing else here, everyone was very friendly. When each neighbour moved in, they were brought a cup of tea.[68]

This woman felt that moving to the Hertfordshire new town had provided her with considerable opportunities to make not just neighbours, but friends and acquaintances in women's groups. Moving to Stevenage also widened her social horizons. 'About the women's groups', she said, 'I suppose they really made me what I am today':

> When I first came here I was young, I lived [in London] with my in-laws, I was very shy, very retiring, never went anywhere in London without my husband, although in my youth I was connected with a political party but that did not last long. Then coming down here, because we had to make our own entertainment, getting involved in the women's clubs gave me confidence and made me really branch out in so many other things. I am sure I would not have done half the things that I have been able to do here if I had stayed in London all these years.[69]

This quote is a reminder of the freedom which some migrants felt after they had moved out. It also exemplifies a point made by Mogey for Oxford: joining clubs, groups, societies and associations was becoming more a feature of social life as migrants made the break with the traditional areas for new housing estates. Within conditions of increasing affluence, it was the social expression of an enjoyment of a wide range of hobbies and pastimes, and as a way of making new friendships should not be overlooked. Estimating the extent of associative activity is not easy. It is shown in Chapter 6 that it was actively pursued by about half of working-class migrants to new homes. But the important point is that it provided an important alternative to next-door-neighbourliness for many people, and that signified wider changes in the pattern of social and kinship relationships.[70]

The tendency for making neighbours early on has persisted. During the 1970s, a woman who moved to Milton Keynes spoke of the raw and bleak aspect of the new estate but emphasised the 'kindness of the neighbours' in helping her out.[71] And as one little girl who moved to Milton Keynes at the same time recalled, 'when we moved in the next door neighbour came out and said are you moving in and my mum said yes and he said well if theres anything you need me and my missus are only next door and my name's George'.[72] In some cases a housing manager or the social development officer responded to, and helped, people who moved to new estates. It was, after all, in their brief to do so, and had been since the pioneering work of Octavia Hill in the working-class housing developments of later Victorian London.[73] One man who moved to Milton Keynes during the 1970s remembered they had 'quite a lot to do with Roger', an arrivals worker for MKDC. They worked with him at their local meeting place 'to get things done'.[74] Yet, for Stevenage in the 1950s, one man remembered that whilst they had 'a nice home at last' they 'never had any dealings with people in authority' and so he and his neighbours formed a tenants' association to fight for the introduction of a local school, shops and buses.[75] Hence, neighbourliness was often the basis for local associative action. Housing managers noted that many associations, in both suburbs and new towns, sprang up purely on the initiative of a few keen local residents during the settling-in phase.[76] This point is returned to in Chapter 6.

Two conclusions may be drawn from these examples. First, they suggest that knowledge about social development officers and housing managers was perhaps uneven. Hence, some made use of them, whilst others did not. Second, each of these examples, whether it was the woman's kind neighbours, the little girl remembering George, the active community building with Roger, or the man who coordinated action against the lack of local facilities, can be viewed as instances of 'manifest neighbouring'. That was a term used by the sociologist Peter Mann, in his 1950s study of two municipal estates in the Wirral Peninsula, both of which had been completed in the 1920s and had matured by the early postwar years. Manifest neighbouring was characterised by overt sociable behaviour, such as mutual visiting and going out together. It was contrasted with 'latent neighbouring', which was characterised by 'favourable attitudes to neighbours' but was less active. Another sociologist, Maurice Broady, in a study of a working-class residential area in Birkenhead, which covered both established Victorian terraced streets and new housing estates, illustrated that the organisation of Coronation street parties evinced strong continuities in both areas. Both were organised largely by women, who were the mainstay of informal and manifest local neighbouring in general.[77]

The persistence of both spontaneous active neighbourliness and the more latent variety was evident in other areas. So too, within this pattern, was the contribution of women within active neighbouring during the early days of an estate's life.[78] Margaret Stacey and her research team revisited the town expansion scheme of Banbury from the later 1960s to investigate the 'Little Newton' estate which had not been built when she first studied Banbury during the 1950s.[79] It was comprised of owner-occupied semi-detached houses. Hence there was no housing manager or social development officer to encourage a spirit of community. Stacey provided a general picture of largely latent but also active neighbouring. The latter was common among young mothers who did not go out to work. Hence Stacey emphasised that the propensity to make acquaintances depended upon gender, the stage of the family life cycle, and age:

> In Little Newton the men were young and at work for the most part. Neighbouring for the men, as for the working wives, was thus largely confined to exchanges in the evening or at the weekends. The neighbour relations of working women and men were largely of the coincidental kind, superficial exchanges when working in the garden, hanging out the clothes, or cleaning the car. Without other overlapping roles, such exchanges seemed rarely to develop into any form of interaction. In contrast, those women who did not work and more particularly those who were mothers of young children (and these categories overlapped very largely) were not only available in the locality for a great many hours, but also had the mother role in common for children who played together ... For them the chances of establishing interaction with neighbours were higher because availability and overlapping roles coincided.[80]

Similarly, Lynette Carey and Roy Mapes's study of owner-occupied estates in the Potteries found that women were instrumental in meeting informally to encourage neighbourliness, whether in pubs via their husbands, or at Tupperware parties, or for tea or coffee in each other's houses. Because of such meetings, the 'initial reaction of the housewives to their new neighbours was generally a very favourable one'.[81] In general, the preferred level of neighbouring for most people was along the lines of such comments as 'People here are friendly without being intrusive' or 'The people here wouldn't push themselves, but they would help in an emergency'. However, in some cases there was concern that people were 'too friendly' at first, an over-familiarity that led to gossiping and sometimes bad feeling. Others were unsure as to the level of friendliness they should offer.[82] When trying to account for such variations, Carey and Mapes felt that personal factors such as previous location, or planning determinants such as the layout of the estate, were only minor explanations for the varying but generally encouraging propensity to settle in by making neighbours. In findings which held much in common with Margaret Stacey's, they emphasised demographic influences. It was found that women of similar age, and with children of a similar age, exhibited higher levels of house visiting.[83]

Evidence for varying and selective patterns in early neighbourliness can be found elsewhere during the 1970s and into the 1980s. For example, among women who moved to Milton Keynes from London with the relocation of their husbands' company, a closeness developed which encouraged 'a wider network of friends and also provided the social organisations where people could meet'.[84] Yet patterns varied within the new city. A MKDC study of the mixed-tenure Walnut Tree estate in Milton Keynes, made in the later 1980s, found a similar pattern to that described by Durant in 1930s Edgware and Stacey in 1960s Banbury. Despite the existence of arrivals workers, there had been an initial tentativeness and reticence on the part of many, but as the estate grew, so people began to strike up conversations, meet neighbours, and make new friends. The Walnut Tree study concluded that 'neighbourhood networks have been formed and can be identified' and that most local clubs and associations had established independence following initial encouragement and support from MKDC.[85]

The Walnut Tree study also argued that there was more neighbourliness in the housing association and cheaper owner-occupied homes than in 'the top half' of Walnut Tree.[86] That conclusion, however, may be contrasted with an early 1970s study of both council tenants and owner-occupiers in Bristol by the sociologist Bernard Ineichen. He attacked the idea that neighbouring among manual workers' households on council estates was more intimate than among manual working-class owner-occupiers. In terms of home visits, friendly cups of tea and sociable meals, 'there is less interaction between neighbours, in terms of both quality and quantity, on council estates than on owner-occupied estates'.[87]

It appeared, moreover, that council tenants were almost as concerned to maintain status and enhance their respectability as owner-occupiers, a point spectacularly confirmed by the BBC journalist James Tucker in his 1966 book *Honourable Estates*. Keeping a distance from neighbours, as well as connecting with them, was also important to settling in.[88] Maurice Broady found a similar state of affairs in the Wirral.[89] And Peter Mann emphasised how people carefully bracketed others and associated with those they felt to be mostly like themselves. Even in the estate which Mann felt to be more manifest in its local relationships – 'more of a social unit' – there was fear that some new tenants with large families might lower the tone of their 'showpiece' estate.[90] Local authority housing managers, moreover, who selected applicants for council tenancies, reported how 'the good tenant refuses a house in an area with a bad name'.[91] The reason was obvious. Newcomers wanted 'to live among the same kind of people' and this point was true for both established terraced streets and also for the new working-class housing developments in Birkenhead.[92] Dennis Chapman's study of social status and changes of residence, published during the mid-1950s, also confirmed that people aspired to live in houses and streets with those who held similar occupations and status markers as themselves. The majority of working-class movers, as Chapman stressed, had moved from a smaller dwelling to a larger one, from a poorer home to a more comfortable home, and from an area of low social status to a higher one.[93] They did not want to live next door to those whom they considered 'rough', a feeling evident amongst both council tenants and owner-occupiers.[94] Such differentiation was evident, for example, in rateable values and the size of the house. It even extended to a dislike of the age of some neighbours. Few working-class households, however, expressed any desire to live in middle-class streets. A picture emerged of a choosy cohort of migrants. They demonstrated 'the general tendency to class segregation in urban areas by voluntary movement and by the restriction of social relationships'.[95]

Hence the new estates played host to both the continuing points of communality and the continuing divisions in working-class life. Those tensions based on perceptions of superiority – the subjective basis of working-class status differentiation – which were evident in 'the classic slum' were also evident in the new housing developments.[96] As Joanna Bourke, too, has argued, both the slum and the working-class suburb shared status differences, and the idea that the former was friendlier than the latter cannot be validated.[97] Willmott and Young, however, basing their analysis upon their own value judgements, and upon a variety of disdainful quotes from their subjects, thought that women were becoming more status-conscious as a consequence of moving out. They were, moreover, allegedly more status-conscious than men. They quoted from one woman who compared the women on the new estate with conditions in Bethnal Green. Her own consciousness of difference, as measured by possessions, is evident here. Again, television features prominently:

> When I was in London I had a four roomed house on my own, but you get a few of them who come from, say, two rooms. Then they get a house. Well, they've worked hard – they've got themselves a nice home, television, and all that. So you find this type of person temporarily gets a bit to thinking that they are somebody. You do find it with some people, and I think you find it more amongst the women than amongst the men.[98]

Mitchell and Lupton, in their study of the Liverpool estate, felt that 'a tendency for [wives] to be more status conscious than their husbands was observed, this being particularly true of the wives of skilled workers ... Women also attached more importance to symbols of superior status such as the television mast, the outward appearance of respectability and the need to "keep up with the Jones's".'[99] Whether female or male inspired, such behaviour could become amusing, for example the cocktail cabinet which was displayed in the window for all to see, yet which was empty because its owners could not afford the alcohol and glasses to go into it.[100]

Two points may be made from this discussion. First, the significance of the social tone of the neighbourhood as a factor helping people to settle in cannot be denied. It was of great concern to people, many of whom had moved to gain social status. Where people on the new estates were found to be undesirable or disappointing, the ability to settle in was greatly diminished. Many people moved on because they disapproved of their neighbours. This is discussed fully in the next chapter.

Second, the sense of status superiority was intrinsically related to material possessions, and that in turn was related to pride in the new home. Status distinctions were inextricably bound up with this sense of improvement. Hence, to focus upon status in isolation would provide a rather warped perspective upon settling in. Taken together, all these considerations were important to the success of settling down in a new house in a new area. The 'house-centred' working class in the suburbs and the new and expanded towns were now enjoying the domestic fruits of their labours. Even Willmott and Young's account of Woodford accepted that 'most people seem contented enough with the result'.[101]

Conclusion

Generally, the vast majority of people who moved out wanted to move. Even the large majority of those who were relocated as part of slum clearance programmes found the move to a new home agreeable. The desire to settle down must be considered in relation to the move. People wanted to make a new life for themselves and their children. They worked hard to build upon the gains made in moving out, and were prepared to utilise credit where necessary. The new housing was appreciated, as were the gardens and the airier aspect of the suburban estate and the new and expanded town. Making neighbours was important to the experience of settling down. However, the level of neighbouring varied according to the differing needs, inclinations and status perceptions of new arrivals. It also varied according to demographic factors, and to the role of social development officers or housing managers. Hence, it is evident that any view of a qualitative decline in neighbouring during the years since 1945 is too simplistic as a means of understanding social connection on postwar new estates and in new and expanded towns.

Yet the ease with which people could settle in some housing developments was compromised by the inadequate provision of public transport, local shops and entertainments which many newcomers endured. This situation, as noted above, was to be found in some of the earliest developments in the new towns, too. It was at best inconvenient, at worst depressing. This was the structural context for the identification of problems termed 'suburban neurosis' or 'new town blues', discussed in the following chapter.

Notes

1 A. Moravia, *The Woman of Rome* (Harmondsworth, 1958), p. 14.

2 S. Smith, 'A London suburb', in S. Smith, *Me Again: The Uncollected Writings of Stevie Smith* (London, 1988), p. 104.

3 C. Christie, 'Welfare work in housing management', in R. J. Rowles (ed.), for the Society of Housing Managers, *Housing Management* (London, 1959), pp. 110–24.

4 This point is evident in the annual *Reports of Conference* of the Society of Housing Managers, which listed those local authorities and development corporations in attendance. For example, Mary Tabor, at Stevenage, was a prominent figure at these occasions.

5 M. C. Solomon, 'Public and private housing authorities', in Rowles (ed.), *Housing Management*, pp. 23–32.
6 See above, Chapter 3, pp. 81–2.
7 S. Caunce, *Oral History and the Local Historian* (London, 1994), p. 120.
8 E. Roberts, *Women and Families: An Oral History, 1940–1970* (Oxford, 1995), p. 22. See also *Oral History*, 21:2 (1993).
9 See above, Chapter 2, p. 49.
10 Mass Observation, 'Marriage and divorce in post-war Britain', in *The Changing Nation: A Contact Book* (London, 1947), p. 34.
11 J. M. Mogey, *Family and Neighbourhood: Two Studies in Oxford* (Oxford, 1956), p. 72.
12 Ibid., p. 72.
13 J. M. Mogey, 'Changes in family life experienced by English workers moving from slums to housing estates', *Marriage and Family Living*, 17:2 (1955), p. 126.
14 E. Bott, *Family and Social Network: Roles, Norms and External Relationships in Ordinary Urban Families* (London, 1968), pp. 222–5. For a useful summary of Cullingworth's findings, see G. Brooke-Taylor, 'The social effect of dispersal', *Town and Country Planning*, 2:1 (1961), pp. 37–8.
15 Age Exchange, *Just Like the Country: Memories of London Families Who Settled the New Cottage Estates 1919–1939* (London, 1991), p. 29.
16 M. McKenna, 'The suburbanisation of the working-class population of Liverpool between the wars', *Social History*, 16:2 (1991), p. 177.
17 H. Jennings, *Societies in the Making: A Study of Development and Redevelopment Within a County Borough* (London, 1962), p. 102.
18 H. and C. Rees, *The History Makers: The Story of the Early Days of Stevenage New Town* (Stevenage, 1991), p. 112.
19 M. Hill (ed.), *Bigger, Brighter, Better: The Story of Bletchley 1944–1966 Told By Its Residents* (Milton Keynes, 1996), p. 11.
20 Ibid., p. 10.
21 Society of Housing Managers, *Report of Conference 'Tomorrows Homes', 25/26 January, 1962* (London, 1962), pp. 6–7, 24–50; Society of Housing Managers, *Report of Conference, 'Housing in Towns', 28/29 January, 1965* (London, 1965), p. 76.
22 S. Humphries and J. Taylor, *The Making of Modern London: 1945–1985* (London, 1986), p. 88.
23 MKDC, *The Plan for Milton Keynes* (Milton Keynes, 1970), II, p. 91.
24 D. Walker, *The Architecture and Planning of Milton Keynes* (London, 1981), p. 39.

25 J. Burnett, *A Social History of Housing 1815–1985* (London, 1991), pp. 306–10.
26 MKDC, *The Plan for Milton Keynes*, II, p. 91.
27 J. Bishop, *Milton Keynes: The Best of Both Worlds? Public and Professional Views of a New City* (Bristol, 1986), pp. 154–8.
28 MKDC, *Residential Design Feedback: Report of Studies* (Milton Keynes, 1975), pp. 1–2.
29 Ibid., p. 3.
30 Ibid., p. 9.
31 Ibid., pp. 183–7; see also C. Ward, *Welcome Thinner City: Urban Survival in the 1990s* (London, 1989), p. 19.
32 MKDC, *Residential Design Feedback*, pp. 147–9, 161.
33 Ibid., p. 115.
34 Ibid., p. 121.
35 Ibid., p. 145.
36 Ibid., p. 97.
37 Ibid., pp. 130–1.
38 Ibid., pp. 19–22.
39 A. Rapoport, *The Meaning of the Built Environment: A Non-Verbal Communication Approach* (Beverley Hills, 1982), pp. 162–76.
40 Ibid., pp. 162–8; see also City of Sheffield Housing Management Committee, *City of Sheffield Municipal Tenant's Handbook* (Gloucester, 1964), pp. 21–7; D. White, 'Metroland', *New Society*, 1 July 1971, p. 6.
41 S. Constantine, 'Amateur gardening and popular recreation in the nineteenth and twentieth centuries', *Journal of Social History*, 14:3 (1981), pp. 398–401.
42 Jennings, *Societies in the Making*, pp. 103–4.
43 I. Bentley, 'The owner makes his mark', in P. Oliver, I. Davis and I. Bentley (eds), *Dunroamin: The Suburban Semi and its Enemies* (London, 1994), pp. 140–2.
44 Hill, *Bigger, Brighter, Better*, p. 17.
45 A. Marwick, *British Society Since 1945* (Harmondsworth, 1987), p. 198.
46 MKDC, *Residential Design Feedback*, pp. 109, 111.
47 Living Archive Project (Milton Keynes), NCY/T007 Tape 183; transcript.
48 R. MacTaggart, 'Newcomers to Milton Keynes: getting their housing priorities right', *Architectural Design*, 45 (1975), p. 766.
49 B. Campbell, *Wigan Pier Revisited: Poverty and Politics in the 80s* (London, 1984), p. 53.

50 M. Clapson, M. Dobbin and P. Waterman (eds), *The Best Laid Plans ... Milton Keynes Since 1967* (Luton, 1997).

51 T. Mars, 'Little Los Angeles in North Bucks'. *Architect's Journal*, 15 April 1992, p. 26.

52 R. Owens, 'The Great Experiment', *Architect's Journal*, 15 April 1993, p. 32.

53 P. Howlett, 'The "Golden Age", 1955–1973', in P. Johnson (ed.), *Twentieth Century Britain: Economic, Social and Cultural Change* (London, 1994), pp. 321–2.

54 Society of Housing Managers, *Report of Conference, 'Housing Management', 10/11 January, 1957* (London, 1957), p. 17.

55 M. Young and P. Willmott, *Family and Kinship in East London* (Harmondsworth, 1979), pp. 147–69.

56 M. Muggeridge, 'England, whose England?', *Encounter*, 118 (July 1963), pp. 15–17. T. Vahimagi, *British Television: An Illustrated Guide* (Oxford, 1994), pp. 134, 146.

57 Society of Housing Managers, *Report of Conference, 'Housing Management, 10, 11 January, 1957*, p. 17.

58 See above, Chapter 1, pp. 6–8.

59 Jennings, *Societies in the Making*, p. 90.

60 See, for example, A. Blowers, 'London's out-county estates: a reappraisal', *Town and Country Planning*, 41:9 (1973), pp. 409–14; H. E. Bracey, *Neighbours on New Estates and Subdivisions in England and the USA* (London, 1964), pp. 29, 56–7; A. Holmes, 'Better than no place', *New Society*, 15 April, 1971, p. 635; M. Jeffreys, 'Londoners in Hertfordshire: the South Oxhey estate', in R. Glass, E. Hobsbawm et al., *London: Aspects of Change* (London, 1964), pp. 239–40; N. H. Rankin, 'Social adjustment in a North-West newtown', *Sociological Review* (New Series) 11:3 (1963), p. 291; R. K. Wilkinson and E. M. Sigsworth, 'Attitudes to the housing environment: an analysis of private and local authority households in Batley, Leeds and York', *Urban Studies*, 9 (1972), p. 206

61 Jeffreys, 'Londoners in Hertfordshire', p. 239; Hill, *Bigger, Brighter, Better*, p. 20.

62 Bishop, *Milton Keynes: The Best of Both Worlds*, p. 77.

63 *Daily Telegraph*, 20 January 1992.

64 J. Husain, 'Londoners who left', *New Society*, 7 July 1977, p. 17.

65 R. Durant, *Watling: A Survey of Social Life on a New Housing Estate* (London, 1939), pp. 21–8.

66 Bracey, *Neighbours on New Estates*, p. 58.

67 J. M. Mogey, 'The climate of opinion on housing estates', *Sociological Review* (New Series) 4:1 (1956), p. 63.
68 Rees, *History Makers*, p. 94.
69 Ibid., p. 100.
70 See below, Chapter 6, passim.
71 J. Turner and B. Jardine, *Pioneer Tales: A New Life in Milton Keynes* (Milton Keynes, 1985), p. 108.
72 The People's Press, *This Place Has Its Ups and Downs, Or Kids Could Have Done It Better* (Milton Keynes, 1977), Toni, aged nine. This book has no page numbers.
73 H. Alford, 'Historical background', in Rowles (ed.), *Housing Management*, p. 4; Christie, 'Welfare work', pp. 110–25.
74 Living Archive Project, NCY/T007 Tape 183; transcript.
75 Humphries and Taylor, *Making of Modern London*, p. 90.
76 E. M. B. Hamilton, 'On living in a new town', *Society of Housing Managers' Quarterly Review*, 4:4 (1956), p. 7; Society of Housing Managers, *Report of Conference, 'Housing Management, 10, 11 January, 1957*, p. 17.
77 M. Broady, 'The organisation of Coronation street parties', *Sociological Review* (New Series) 4:2 (1956), p. 229.
78 L. Kuper, 'Blueprint for living together', in L. Kuper (ed.), *Living in Towns* (London, 1953), pp. 55–6.
79 M. Stacey, *Tradition and Change: A Study of Banbury* (Oxford, 1960), passim.
80 M. Stacey, E. Batstone, C. Bell and A. Murcott, *Power, Persistence and Change: A Second Study of Banbury* (London, 1975), p. 94.
81 L. Carey and R. Mapes, *The Sociology of Planning: A Study of Social Activity on New Housing Estates* (London, 1972), p. 55.
82 Ibid., pp. 56–7.
83 Ibid., pp. 97–8.
84 N. Deakin and C. Ungerson, *Leaving London: Planned Mobility and the Inner City* (London, 1977), p. 176.
85 MKDC, *Walnut Tree Neighbourhood Review, July Through December 1990: A Report on the Community Development Programme Undertaken by Milton Keynes Development Corporation Between 1987 and 1990* (Milton Keynes, 1991), p. 14.
86 Ibid., p. 29.
87 B. Ineichen, 'Home ownership and manual workers' lifestyles', *Sociological Review* (New Series) 20:3 (1972), pp. 400–1.
88 Ibid., pp. 401–2; J. Tucker, *Honourable Estates* (London, 1966), passim.

This is discussed below, Chapter 5, pp. 132–4.

89 Broady, 'Coronation street parties', p. 240.

90 P. Mann 'The concept of neighbourliness', *American Journal of Sociology*, 60:2 (1954), p. 164.

91 H. Clark, 'Problems of the housing manager today', *Society of Housing Managers' Quarterly Bulletin*, 4:7 (1957), p. 4.

92 Mann, 'Concept of neighbourliness', pp. 166–7.

93 D. Chapman, *The Home and Social Status* (London, 1955), pp. 165–6.

94 Bracey, *Neighbours on New Estates*, pp. 58, 62.

95 Chapman, *Home and Social Status*, pp. 160–5. Also, see below, Chapter 5, pp. 133–4.

96 See also, for example, S. Fielding, P. Thompson and N. Tiratsoo, *'England Arise': The Labour Party and Popular Politics in 1940s Britain* (Manchester, 1995), pp. 104–6. See also Robert Roberts, *The Classic Slum: Salford Life in the First Quarter of the Twentieth Century* (Harmondsworth, 1983), pp. 13–31.

97 J. Bourke, *Working-Class Cultures in Britain, 1890–1960: Gender, Class and Ethncity* (London, 1994), p. 157.

98 Young and Willmott, *Family and Kinship*, p. 156.

99 G. D. Mitchell and T. Lupton, 'The Liverpool estate', in G. D. Mitchell, T. Lupton, M. W. Hodges and C. S. Smith, *Neighbourhood and Community: An Enquiry into Social Relationships on Housing Estates in Liverpool and Sheffield* (Liverpool, 1954), p. 49. This quote is referred to by Young and Willmott, *Family and Kinship*, p. 156.

100 Humphries and Taylor, *Making of Modern London*, p. 88.

101 P. Willmott and M. Young, *Family and Class in a London Suburb* (London, 1960), p. 132.

5

Suburban neurosis and new town blues

> We rolled into the new territory in old vans, our furniture tied on with string, or in ancient pantechnicons which looked altogether too large for our few pathetic bits brought from furnished rooms or cast off by relatives. The new territory was bright, clean, cold, and hostile.[1]

> Loneliness pressed on the women much harder than on the men.[2]

The previous chapters explored the positive experiences of moving out and settling in. This chapter focuses upon the problems encountered during and immediately after the move. For some, these became insurmountable. In their extreme form, these problems were bracketed under the terms 'suburban neurosis' and 'new town blues' by a number of medical experts, sociologists, social psychologists and neurologists. Suburban neurosis was a term originally coined by the general practitioner Dr Stephen Taylor, writing in the *Lancet* during the 1930s. As Jane Lewis and Barbara Brookes demonstrate, in their historical study of Peckham Health Centre, in South London, suburban neurosis referred to the psychological problems of the suburban and lower-middle-class 'Mrs Everywoman'. She had backache, loss of breath, weight loss, and complained of insomnia. These symptoms were blamed upon two major factors. First, isolation and loneliness caused by the absence of community and kin. Second, suburban women were presented as victims of 'false values', of the advertisement of labour-saving devices such as Hoovers, gas stoves and ready-made clothes which left them with too much time on their hands and inculcated a sense of worthlessness which undermined good health and welfare.[3]

This debate was revisited during the 1950s and afterwards. A number of studies of women settlers in new towns and on suburban new estates investigated the incidence and symptoms of neurosis. In 1958 the *Lancet* felt that the earlier interwar problems had to some extent been solved by the war, which, argued the journal, had engendered a new sense of pulling together and of community life among women who had worked on the Home Front.[4] But as the years since 1945 elapsed, and as 'great working-class populations were translated into new homes in country suburbs', the big new out-county estates of London, it argued, were 'partly repeating the story of the prewar speculative estates'. Male wage earners continued to commute back into the centres of employment, as working-class women apparently began to follow 'the obsolescent middle-class pattern of social isolation as a measure of respectability'.[5]

Problems of loneliness, of physical and psychological disorders, of spiritual poverty in conditions of increasing material well-being, underpinned the notion of 'suburban sadness'. This term was devised by David Reisman, and he also felt that women suffered most from it. He emphasised the 'captivity of the housewives tied down in their suburbs' by their young children, by the lack of a car, and by the absence of nearby parents to act as baby-sitters. These factors were consequences of the move away from the extended family and the heightened emphasis upon the materially enriched interior of the new suburban home. Reisman was 'struck by the eagerness of the housewives to talk to somebody', and noted that 'the visiting intellectual [finds] the lives of these women empty ...'.[6] Reisman was writing about American women, but his analysis, as illustrated in Chapter 1, was eagerly received by cultural critics in England. Many articles and novels have been written, television programmes made, and songs sung, about suburban sadness.[7]

This chapter assesses the major problems raised for female working-class migrants by the move to a new home. It is in three sections. First, it assesses the causes of the difficulties and crises which brought about the notions of suburban neurosis and new town blues. It shows that usually there was an interconnected pattern of problems and irritations. Second, it illustrates how such feelings stimulated some migrants to move on because they could not settle. Third, it evaluates the debates about the psychological problems of women in the suburbs and new towns. The general aim of this chapter is to demonstrate that the new estates and neighbourhoods were only partly responsible for the problems encountered in the move, throwing into relief, as they did, wider processes in English society which made life difficult for women, especially poorer women.

The interconnected pattern of problems

In its 1967 overview of migration to new towns, expanded towns and peripheral suburban housing estates, the MHLG summarised the major problems of 'settling in' which had been faced by migrants since 1946. These were as follows. First, there were the social problems caused when wider family and older community networks were left behind. They could be compounded by problems with making friends or neighbours straight after the move out had been made. A second issue was the lack of services and amenities in the earliest phase of an estate. Many studies highlighted the initial difficulties which the lack of local services caused, although this was of lesser magnitude in new towns.[8] It was clear that new estates could not compete with older areas for variety of entertainment and amenities, a point which Young and Willmott had spared no effort in emphasising.[9] A third cause of difficulties was money, or, more accurately, the lack of it. These problems were connected, for many women migrants, with a fourth factor: the difficulties of mobility. A fifth cause of much anxiety, and one which was ignored by MHLG, was the social tone of the estate, something which was related to judgements about roughness and respectability in working-class life. The rough/respectable distinction was related to residential standards. These difficulties and hardships, it will be shown, were sometimes exacerbated by planning itself. The layout of some estates, and the poor design and construction of some houses, must also be considered as causes of discontent. Each issue will now be explored.

The increasing distance between movers and their relatives and the earlier community networks was, as shown in the previous chapters, mostly the concern of Young and Willmott. Other studies felt that the issue of 'missing mum' had been exaggerated.[10] The extent of this phenomenon is impossible to measure, yet some did suffer from it. For example, during H. E. Bracey's interview with a married couple, the husband was praising the new estate as 'lovely' when his wife interrupted 'No it's not!'. After eighteen months, she was still missing the nearness of her mother, and also of older friends and acquaintances. The only thing that was right about her new life was the house itself, which she could not bring herself to leave.[11] 'Missing mum', however, was symptomatic of a wider problem of adjustment to new estates with no established family or friends close by. Josephine Klein argued that the young housewife on the new estate, 'coming from a close-knit network of the Bethnal Green type', was forced into loneliness once she had moved. Klein provided an example from Young and Willmott – which was similar to that of Bracey – of a husband who was 'congratulating himself' on the new house, garden, bathroom and television set when his wife interrupted: 'It's all right for you. What about the time I have to spend here on my own?'[12] With a similar emphasis to Young and Willmott, the writers Trevor Blackwell and Jeremy Seabrook placed this apparent emiseration at the crux of their analysis of what was wrong with the migration of the working classes to the suburbs. They have written evocatively of 'the inner emptiness of the young woman' in a new house in the deserted streets of the new estate, who 'felt the absence of mam and burst into tears for no reason'.[13]

Children, so often neglected in historical accounts of social change, were of course affected by the move too. They could sense or see that things were going wrong for their mothers after their family had moved in. During the mid-1970s, for example, eight-year-old Julie of Bletchley in Milton Keynes wrote of the tension between her parents caused by moving home: 'the people started to come here then they started to go back where they yust to live most homes are emtey mum wants to move but dad dus not want to move dad likes it here'.[14] This child's eye view of the new life in a new city hints at the marital problems which many migrants no doubt experienced.

As a number of social studies noted, once couples moved to a new town they were pushed more closely together in their new home, without long-standing neighbours or friends to give support to their new life.[15] People living in areas characterised by migration also observed this phenomenon. As Madame Morgana, a white witch in Wolverton, Milton Keynes, put it: 'There is great unrest with the overspills from London. We have a mixed community here, [there are] break-ups of marriages like it's going out of fashion. So people have to learn to find themselves ...'.[16] 'Learning to find themselves' was a consequence of the couple being pushed more closely together in their new home. It was further away from 'mum' and the informal support networks of their original extended family and community. As Elizabeth Bott argued, in her study of families in their social networks, the kinship and community networks of a family that moved away from their old area to a new housing estate 'will rapidly become less connected and for a time at least husband and wife will develop a more joint relationship with each other'.[17] Josephine Klein made the same point.[18] Such greater reliance upon each other must have caused problems for some migrants. In 1975 a spokeswoman for a tenants' group, speaking on Anglia Television's documentary-and-debate programme on Milton Keynes, blamed many marriage break-ups upon the move to the city.[19] The interconnection between marital problems and the 'new town blues' cannot be ignored. Nor, however, can it be accurately measured. But it does require some historical context. Nationally, the Divorce Act of 1969 had resulted in a considerable rise in the divorce rate.[20] Milton Keynes must have shared in this. Moreover, as a new town Milton Keynes was composed of a higher proportion of younger people than the national average. Divorce statistics published by the Registrar General showed that whilst the divorce rate was increasing among all age groups during the 1970s, it has was higher amongst younger married couples than older couples.[21]

Marital problems were related to another important point. There was no substantive and permanent reconstruction of male identity, nor did working-class men revise their household roles to any significant degree, as a consequence of moving house. Clearly, the blissful domestic role convergence between the suburban 'new man' and 'the modern housewife' predicted by Mark Abrams in 1959, a view strongly endorsed by the sociologist Ferdynand Zweig in 1961, was failing to materialise.[22] Fiona Devine's 1980s study of affluent workers in Luton, therefore, illustrated how task-sharing in the home was also accompanied by the continuity of 'traditional' roles for men and women, and this included segregation in a number of child-rearing, housework and leisure activities.[23]

The move to a new house encapsulated wider changes occurring in the size and composition of the working-class family as the more displaced nuclear family grew to replace the more proximate extended family. These changes, which had begun between the wars,[24] became much more widespread in the 1950s and since, as both planned and voluntary dispersal widened distances between and within generations of family members. The network of the family itself was geographically stretched. Yet this was only one element, a spatial one, of the growing preference for smaller nuclear families.

Easier access to birth-control had ceased to become the almost exclusive monopoly of middle-class women, and it is a compelling point that at roughly the same time that this was occurring, suburban living was ceasing to become a mostly bourgeois monopoly. Increasing numbers of working-class women sought birth-control during the interwar period, a pursuit which was continued after 1945.[25]

In the initial separation from kin and friends, loneliness could undoubtedly result. The early problems of loneliness were also part cause and part effect of the difficulty of connecting with neighbours. Oral testimony lends support to Ruth Durant's view of Watling, that many people were intimidated by their position as strangers on a new estate, and reticent to meet people.[26] Looking back on the move to suburban new estates, those who have talked of the problems they encountered have tended to focus upon a lack of immediate neighbourliness in the early days. One woman who moved within Yorkshire during the 1960s remembered: 'At the time we first moved in everyone seemed to keep themselves to themselves. People come and go.' But she added, 'I don't think Windybank's a bad place to live, people rally round if someone needs help'.[27] Experiences differed, however. Writing of the demise of 'effortless sociability' in terraced streets of the North Lancashire towns of Barrow and Lancaster when compared with new estates there, Elizabeth Roberts showed how making new acquaintances could be a slow experience and, once it had happened, could be intrusive. It was sometimes difficult to avoid over-familiarity:

> Well to be quite honest it was the neighbour across the road. I had befriended her as she was lonely. I said 'If you get lonely just come across for a chat'. It turned out that she was in nearly as much as I was. I didn't want to offend her so I thought if I could get a little job just to get out of the way for a little while. She was coming across as soon as the kiddies went to school at nine and she didn't go until they came home in the afternoon.[28]

Lest the impression be given that entire generations of working-class families were distanced from kin or neighbouring for evermore, it is pertinent here to point out that initial problems were, for the most part, temporary. The majority of new migrants soon established a pattern of regular visiting with relatives.[29] In many cases, chain migration brought about a measure of spatial reconciliation between different generations of families, as was illustrated in Chapters 3 and 4.[30] And new neighbours and new social relationships were usually formed, sooner or later, as was illustrated in Chapter 4, and is more fully developed in Chapter 6.[31]

Beyond the family, more instrumental problems hampered adaptation to new estates and encouraged disenchantment, namely the inadequate provision of shops, recreational facilities, public transport and welfare services. Again, this was not simply a new problem of postwar dispersal. A number of historians have noted similar conditions on the large interwar estates around England's cities. In Catherine Hall's study of Birmingham, both private owner-occupied estates built to house the better-off industrial workers and lower-middle-class clerks, and municipal housing estates built for slum clearance, lacked many basic facilities. These shortcomings were greater on the interwar council estates. The lack of adequate shops, places of worship, libraries, meeting halls and parks caused the bus conductor to call out 'Siberia' when the bus reached its suburban terminus.[32] Furthermore, Wythenshawe, near Manchester, was 'notorious for its lack of the most basic facilities', with ill-situated and infrequent shops, its one pub, and single cinema.[33] Durant was scathing in her criticism of the local authorities for failing to ensure adequate social facilities on the Edgware estates.[34]

Postwar surveys came to similar conclusions. Hilda Jennings's study of Bristol noted that complaints about the lack of shops, telephones, street lighting and other services 'were frequent, and continued over a long period of time'.[35] Other studies made at different times in different peripheral projects came to similar conclusions.[36] The problem of women's mobility was also noted in the expanded and new towns. J. B. Cullingworth found that the new estates in Swindon could not compete with London for easy access to a wide variety of shops, parks, cinemas, theatres, schools and public transport, and this was a cause of extensive criticism.[37] A later study of Swindon made a similar point about the inadequacy of public transport. It made many women feel 'cut off'.[38] During the 1970s, work by the New Towns Study Unit, based at the Open University in Milton Keynes, showed that the greater level of self-containment of the first two phases of new towns when compared with the suburbs was gained in no small part at the expense of women, who became if anything less able to travel around and commute to work. Men had first ownership of the household car for commuting and leisure purposes, whereas women were less mobile because they were more dependent on 'the slow growth of public transport' in new towns.[39]

Mobility cannot be viewed in isolation from other problems, which were usually financial. For example, the social psychologist Bernard Ineichen, in his study of the working-class new estate of 'Southover' in Bristol during the early part of the 1970s, found that lack of practical convenient access to shops and services for women in general was connected with money problems. The Bristol estate was comprised largely of affluent manual workers' families and some less-well-off households. The majority of houses in Southover were owner-occupied, but a 'substantial minority' were rented from the local authority and included the poorer families.[40] For the wives of poorer manual workers, especially, there was a 'strong association between neurotic symptoms and the admission of financial problems'.[41]

Interestingly, however, when Ineichen compared his findings for the suburban estate with a local authority central redevelopment area, he revealed relatively good mental and physical health among women in the former, and 'high level of neuroses' among wives in the latter. In central redevelopment areas problems were compounded by the behavioural problems of children in high flats, which were worse than those of children living in council terraced houses of three or four bedrooms in the outlying estate.[42] The presence of young children decreased a woman's ability to get out of the house alone or with friends. In both the central redevelopment area and the suburban estate that problem was exacerbated by the relative lack of female access to a car as the most convenient means of personal mobility, and to the telephone as a mechanism of instant communication over distance. Affluence, however, made a difference:

> The commuter families are much more mobile in their daily life and during their lifetime. All own at least one car, and 63 per cent have a telephone. In the central area, 50 per cent have a car and 6 per cent a telephone. Carless central area families find that contact with their relatives in the outer suburbs is particularly difficult.[43]

But families on outer estates who could afford neither cars nor telephones also had problems. In her participant observer's study of Wellington Road, Margaret Lassell noted the pathetic state of affairs for those who could not afford a car or a telephone: 'Joe had bought a car for twenty pounds, he said. It was outside the door, but broken down. They had had a telephone installed, but it was not working because they had not paid the bill.'[44] Such findings demonstrated that lack of money sharpened the impact of problems brought about by the move to a working-class estate, as the mechanisms of instant communication across distances probably eased the transition. The inequality of access to telephones and, more recently, to electronic communications, notably computers, has been noted elsewhere.[45]

Other studies, made of different places at differing times, came to similar conclusions about financial hardship, and they chose to emphasise, from the weight of their evidence, how the consequences were felt more heavily by women. A mid-1950s study of a council estate some fifteen miles away from London, made by the London School of Hygiene and Tropical Medicine, noted that once families had moved out, the average daily fares to work increased by 8d. a day for most. Male workers tended to stay on in their former jobs, but 75 per cent of working housewives changed their employment in order to work locally.[46] At the South Oxhey estate in South Hertfordshire, Margot Jeffreys also found that the majority of women who had worked in London found employment nearer to the estate once they had moved. She also observed that many women who had not worked before now took jobs near to home, although there were few jobs actually on the estate. Some 40 per cent of married women were in employment a short while after moving, 'just under half of them in full-time work', the rest in part-time.[47] Different figures were supplied by June Norris for Birmingham during the early 1950s. There, 27 per cent of male heads of households had changed their jobs, but only 21 per cent of those wives who had worked throughout the period of transition had done the same. Furthermore, while six wives had given up work, ten had taken it up since the move. In all, 34 per cent of working women had made a major change in employment.[48] It is difficult to explain with total sureness these differences between London's out-county estates and Birmingham's suburban rings. Both groups were for the most part decanted from slums. Yet the Birmingham sample was closer to its older area than the London sample, and thus within easier reach than was the case for the London sample. The restrictions on women's mobility mentioned in this chapter may have discouraged London women from commuting to work as frequently as their husbands. Women earned less than men, of course, so regular longer-distance commuting costs might make such employment only marginally worthwhile, if at all.[49]

Difficulties with access to work could exacerbate economic problems at home. Norris noted that in some moves the loss of a wife's job due to mobility problems or other factors could hit the family exchequer hard. In general, this was one factor making for a considerable degree of anxiety about costs. The change to suburban living involved increased rents, dearer food at shops or in mobile vans, as these traders often held a near monopoly on new estates, and the expense of new furnishings for a new home.[50] A number of local council housing managers concurred with this and found that some of the unhappiest households suffered from a critical mass of higher rent, travel costs and difficulties.[51] In Milton Keynes, during the early 1970s, strongly similar difficulties continued to cause hardship, and they fell most heavily upon the families of unskilled workers. For example, almost 67 per cent of unskilled manual workers and just over 61 per cent of semi-skilled manual workers felt 'it's a struggle' to make ends meet, compared with 27 per cent of non-manual heads of household.[52]

The costs of making a new start in a new city required the expense of new furnishings for the house. Planners were aware of this and some emphasised the anxieties brought about by the financial commitments of the new house.[53] These were particularly expensive for those moving from furnished, rented accommodation, and this led to a continuation of the cycle of debt and credit, of 'making ends meet', which encouraged the use of hire purchase to underpin many of the material improvements gained by moving to a new house:

> We bought a table, four chairs – that was £48 – a stair carpet, we got that on HP – we paid £40 deposit – that cost £178. As you will understand, the time we had the flat in London we only had the one bedroom and when we were in there we had fitted wardrobes. But before we left London we bought some wardrobes and things second hand which cost us £35. We had to buy a single bed for the little girl. We bought a gas cooker, too.[54]

As Melanie Tebbutt has argued, hire purchase arrangements did in fact indicate a rising standard of living among the growing numbers of affluent working-class families.[55] The poorest were still the unemployed and casually employed unskilled manual workers living in the slums, unable to gain credit, and hence reliant upon informal self-help schemes and clubs which had evolved in the poorest areas during and since the Victorian years.

Yet it cannot be said that finding the money was always easy on the new estates. On top of major items involving considerable sums, there were the daily and weekly costs, a factor emphasised by Deakin and Ungerson's study in Milton Keynes. Many worried about greater transport costs, higher rents and bills. One man expressed concern about the rent rise to £10.00: 'and I'm paying £8.00 a week for food, who's going to pay the electric bill?'.[56] Moreover, MKDC's stipulation that the provision of a house would only follow the full employment of the head of household often meant that many were forced to commute up to Milton Keynes to work for a while prior to moving in. This placed increased financial burdens on the new movers.[57] Whilst the costs of new furnishings and transportation affected both renters and owner-occupiers, it was those in the rented sector who exhibited higher levels of dissatisfaction, based on higher levels of financial difficulty. Many financial problems were subsumed under the term 'temporary arrangements': 26 per cent of all households who had moved to Milton Keynes since 1967 had required temporary accommodation; 16 per cent had been forced to commute on a temporary basis; 4 per cent had had to do both.[58] Moreover, employees from the professional and managerial categories, and those better-paid workers from the service occupations, were more likely to receive financial assistance from their employers in defraying their expenses. Those workers earning less than £50 per week, who needed such assistance most, were more likely to have to pay the costs of temporary arrangements themselves.[59]

Table 8 Most frequently mentioned practical problems facing arrival households in Milton Keynes in the early 1970s (percentages)

Poor public transport to shops	24
Local shops expensive and inadequate	18
Poor public transport to work	17
Lack of hospital	17
Mud and rubbish left over from construction	16
Poor workmanship of house	12

Source: MKDC, *Four Years On: The Milton Keynes Household Survey, 1973, Summary* (Milton Keynes, 1973), p. 23. Presumably these figures exceed 100 because some households mentioned more than one problem.

Hence problems with expenses made practical difficulties worse. MKDC found that once households had moved in, three-quarters of them encountered one or more of a variety of practical problems, summed up in Table 8. Again, difficulties of access and mobility crystallised these issues. The physical layout and incomplete facilities of the immature city did not help. The inadequate public transport system impeded women's access to shops or the Meeting Places, and was compounded by many women's reluctance to use the redways. These innovative routes, free of cars and designed for pedestrians and cyclists only,[60] were perceived as dangerous and ill-lit by women.[61] Clearly, the poorer and less mobile were at the highest level of disadvantage and perceived risk.

Such problems persisted into the 1980s. A study of the new housing development of Thamesmead noted that it was 'at least two miles and a tedious bus journey away to the nearest shopping centre' and this was one factor among many which led to depression. So too did the increased costs of transport and the expensive rents.[62]

A significant cause of further dissatisfaction lay in the design of the house and its alleged lack of privacy. The Thamesmead study, moreover, reveals the expectations of the new house and the resulting disappointment if that house was out of kilter with the tenant's wishes. The aforementioned study of Bristol by Ineichen also emphasised the general dislike of three-storey houses; 73 per cent of women were critical of them and complained of 'too many stairs'.[63] At Thamesmead, the quasi-Corbusian designs of the houses and flats, which were intended to create a sort of 'St Tropez on Thames', were a failure in the eyes of its residents: 'the futurist design made Thamesmead a formidable and unfamiliar environment to the early residents'.[64]

Complaints about the houses were often related to the social tone of the new estate. The construction and design standards of the housing and the physical layout of the estate could combine with the rough/respectable continuum to produce considerable disquiet among many new arrivals. For example Leo Kuper's study of a 1950s Coventry housing estate explored the effects of housing design and the degree of separation between houses on the pattern of privacy and sociability. He found that most people aimed for a measure of sociability within an overriding concern for unqualified privacy. Tension between neighbours resulted when privacy was compromised, and it could be compromised in many ways. Thus, for example, noise transference between party walls in semi-detached and terraced houses was the cause of many complaints:

It's noises from other people that distress us.

You can even hear them use the pot, that's how bad it is.

You sometimes hear them say rather private things as, for example, a man telling his wife that her feet are cold. It makes you feel that *you* must say private things in a whisper.[65]

In his report on Swindon, J. B. Cullingworth argued that in contrast to Young and Willmott's emphasis on unfriendliness in the Greenleigh survey, Londoners in Wiltshire 'complained of the difficulties of securing privacy: the neighbours were not aloof; on the contrary they were too "nosy"'.[66] Such concern for privacy extended to the garden, a point noted in the previous chapter.[67] As many as 80 per cent of migrants to Swindon felt their gardens were 'overlooked'.[68] It was not surprising that lack of privacy could cause annoyance, as many had left older, cramped and poorly constructed housing, often with little more than a back-yard. As noted in the previous chapter, the pursuit of privacy was an important stimulus to leave the traditional areas.[69]

Privacy was highly valued in itself, but it was also inextricably linked with an appraisal of the desirability or otherwise of associating with neighbours. That desirability depended to a considerable extent upon notions of respectability. Having one's privacy intruded upon was worse if the intruders were deemed to be unrespectable. It was also noted in the previous chapter that a further stimulus to move was the social ambition to increase the spatial distance from 'roughs', and when the roughs appeared on the new estate, tensions resulted. The BBC journalist James Tucker, for example, found during the mid-1960s that such tensions were rife in council estates. He concluded that 'some of the bitterest class denunciation of council house living comes from those who have one'.[70] Ineichen's study of Bristol found that a major general cause of insecurity and associated physical symptoms identified by Ineichen were status considerations. For the wives of affluent workers especially there was dissatisfaction at the perceived low social status of the estate. Poorer women, however, thought the area was too 'superior' and had felt more comfortable where they had lived previously.[71]

The sociologist Bernice Martin, discussing Muriel Spark's acerbic short story on working-class respectability ('You should have seen the mess'), has argued that perceived roughness and the fear of bad behaviour was defined as a lack of respect for boundaries and hence privacy: 'cursed is he that removeth his neighbour's landmark'.[72] As Kuper found, the good neighbour was 'someone who keeps his weeds down', whilst a bad one 'lets his kids wander over your garden'.[73] Loud, ostensibly threatening behaviour, bad language, scruffy clothes and scruffy children symbolised a lack of 'control, order and respect for the proper boundaries' upon which demarcations of status and respectability were constructed.[74]

J. H. Nicholson, in his review of the survey literature on new communities in Britain, published in 1961, noted the feeling in some new towns – he gave the example of Basildon – that there was 'a low tone in part of the town', and resentment in overspill estates when so-called 'difficult' or 'problem' families were placed by the development corporation into 'respectable streets'. A study of 'difficult' families on 'difficult housing estates' argued that such families tended to be low-status, low-income and 'poor managers' of the household budget. They were 'almost always families with low occupational status' and displayed behaviour 'which society does not like and cannot ignore'.[75] These tensions were to some extent produced by local authority policies which attempted to disperse 'problem' or 'anti-social' families around the new housing developments. Nicholson further observed how, in such circumstances, there was a tendency for those with 'like standards and interests to group themselves together anyhow, wherever they are housed'.[76] Yet the policy alternative to mixing through spreading thinly was to concentrate difficult families into single estates. It was a strategy which could create estates with large numbers of such families, and thus hasten the onset of economic and social decline, which necessitated higher levels of social service intervention. It also fostered the local reputation of some housing developments as 'problem estates'.[77]

The role of the local newspapers, moreover, often worsened the problem. Press coverage amplified the negative reputation of some estates by repeatedly labelling them as rough and dangerous, fostering juvenile delinquency among dislocated slum children and a host of other unwelcome intrusions into established communities. This point was germane, for example, to Edgware in the 1930s, to South Oxhey and the new estates of Coventry during the 1950s, and to the Greater London overspill estate at Bletchley during the 1970s and since, which is now part of the Borough of Milton Keynes.[78] The

Bletchley estate, for example, was attacked by the press almost as soon as it was built, as an unwanted intrusion into both quiet Bletchley and rural North Buckinghamshire. During the 1980s, Milton Keynes newspapers were still targeting the estate. The following is a selection of five alarmist headlines out of many more:

GRAFFITI SPELLS OUT MESSAGE OF DESPAIR (13.1.1982)

TEENAGE SEX IN ALLEYWAY HORROR (7.12.1984)

FEAR THAT ESTATE IS ON THE BRINK OF A RIOT (11.10.1985)

CALL FOR TIGHTER SECURITY AFTER SUICIDE (19.2.1987)

MUGGERS' HAVEN IS ATTACKED (6.6.1986)[79]

As a study by the Joseph Rowntree Foundation found, the stereotyping of an estate could lead to a sense of being personally slighted, and led many to feel unhappy at their estate's reputation. It also reinforced a sense of isolation or 'social exclusion' from mainstream and more affluent society. Moreover, living on an estate with a bad reputation made it difficult to get jobs, as employers tended to assume the worst of applicants. This exacerbated low self-esteem, added further hardship to the household economy and compounded the collective problems of the estate.[80] Many wished, therefore, to get out, and this has remained a motivation throughout the postwar years. During the 1960s, for example, one worried mother told James Tucker, 'we are all being branded', while another stated, 'It's not our fault we are here. [I] could never get a transfer say to somewhere else now.'[81]

Moving on again

It is feasible to argue, then, that problems of adaptation, whether caused by loneliness, financial constraints, difficulties in mobility, or disappointment at the housing and social tone of the area, could lead people to move on. It is also clear that the propensity to pack the bags once more varied considerably from suburb to suburb, and from new town to new town. Jennings found for the Bristol estates that as many as 31 per cent of the 407 families in her study were 'unsettled' and transferred or applied to transfer to other areas. The reasons she identified were loneliness experienced by women, separation from relatives, financial problems, more difficult access to the place of employment of the householder and a widespread feeling that the estate was not good enough, hence applications for 'better' estates. A desire to move on was also related to aspirations for owner-occupation. Twenty-one families had moved within less than three years and half of those took privately owned accommodation.[82]

Cullingworth found that twenty-three of 161 families (14 per cent) wished to leave Swindon. The distance of the move from London – over sixty miles – had meant that separation from relatives was a hardship for some, especially the poorer, less mobile families. Financial problems were compounded by 'unreasonable' rents, and weekly hire purchase payments were high.[83] Yet only eleven of the twenty-four were 'adamant' about leaving, and the remainder saw their initial difficulties as 'teething troubles'.[84] Financial problems with rents may have been responsible for lapsed tenancies in Hemel Hempstead, noted in 1961, which amounted to 4–5 per cent of all tenancies there. Some 19 per cent of lapsed tenancies were those of professional people, who accounted for only 9 per cent of all tenancies. But almost 52 per cent of lapses were skilled and semi-skilled manual workers' households, an occupational stratum which held 58 per cent of all tenancies.[85] In Kirkby during the early 1960s, Rankin found that a third of residents wanted to move on, but he stressed design and construction factors, especially in flats, which were in turn linked to the opinion of the neighbours. Over half the households 'expressed some reservation about the "kinds of people" they preferred to mix with in Kirkby'.[86] Other studies were clear that it was harder to achieve the desired levels of quietness and personal private space in flats than in houses.[87]

It can be suggested that poorer people on rental estates had the most difficulty settling in because they had to face at least one of the problems given here. During the 1970s in Milton Keynes, MKDC ascertained a dissatisfaction rate of one in five arrival households. This, moreover, appeared 'greater on rent estates than on sale estates'. A small but significant minority, a little over one in twenty households, wanted to go back, and most, but by no means all, were from the rental estates.[88] Any decision to go back was not made lightly. Testimony is sparse for this area of experience, but we may read from the following quote that the gains made by the poor in a new city were welcomed, but they could be extremely fragile. An unemployed husband, who had recently applied for a job in the forthcoming department store in the as yet unfinished shopping building in Central Milton Keynes, told the magazine *Over 21* in 1978:

> we've been here eighteen months, and *in spite of all the problems here* it's better than what we had before we came. We feel we owe the place a chance. If the shopping centre is successful, Milton Keynes will really get on its feet. If it isn't ... well, then we'll start looking around elsewhere.[89]

This quote suggests that one problem could be compounded by others. It also hints at the disappointment felt at aspirations which might yet be denied. In similar cases, therefore, any decision to move was probably made in misery. It was also, sometimes, made in haste, as problems mounted up and became too much. An examination of some findings for Milton Keynes demonstrates the continuity of the types of problems experienced by migrants, despite the arrivals programme of MKDC. This was a mechanism for arrivals workers to provide vital information for newcomers and to encourage people to come together within their estates. In the early 1970s an arrivals worker for MKDC wrote a piece on the phenomenon of 'doing a moonlight'. This was a secretive, nocturnal flight away from Milton Keynes back to the place of departure, or on to a new destination. The seemingly romantic and exciting image of 'doing a moonlight' obscured the usually tragic or difficult circumstances which caused people to leave secretly and in haste.[90] A number of local causes were identified for the reported problems of adaptation experienced by women, problems which stimulated them to move on. First was the often bleak environment of the new estate. In Milton Keynes in 1975, an assistant housing manager wrote in similar terms to earlier surveys of life on new estates. As well as a lack of leisure and social facilities, 'outside their back door is a long stretch of open space with no view, no neighbours, nothing – they're isolated'. Then, of course, there were oppressive financial difficulties. A combination of such factors clearly dissipated the hopes of the new migrants.[91]

A number of important issues must be raised here, however. Were these problems specific to migrants to the suburbs and new and expanded towns, or were they general to the experience of internal migration – of moving house – in any circumstances, for example from village to village or major city centre to major city centre? In other words, were there wider 'transitional' difficulties?

'Transitional neurosis', suburban neurosis and new town blues

This section will demonstrate that, once all the evidence was in, it was unfair to blame the suburbs and the new towns for a specifically suburban or new town malaise. Hence, for instance, the allegedly higher incidence of 'nerves' on north London out-county estates in comparison with the national average was noted by the *Lancet* in the 1950s. But the *Lancet* qualified that view with two considerations: the problem got better over time; and, significantly, rehousing for many women and men was in itself partly determined by the possession of a medical certificate.[92]

Three studies, which were begun at the turn of the 1950s and 1960s, and published in 1966, attempted to discern whether neurotic behaviour was a problem caused by moving to the suburbs or a symptom that perhaps reflected *a priori* problems which the move had exposed. In Sheffield the problems of an 'uprooted' working-class population rehoused from a slum to a big new estate appeared to demonstrate that moving house was no more a cause of complaints such as loneliness, neglect and boredom than other known causes, such as 'poverty, wealth, idleness, overwork, lack of love, excess of love' and so on. The study did concede, however, that the obliteration of the home and of familiar slum streets, and the move away to a less well known or unknown area, bore strong similarities to the phenomenon reported for relocated slum dwellers in the 1930s, termed 'demolition melancholia'.[93] Demolition melancholia had been defined in 1939 as the sense of dislocation and loss which resulted from the destruction of well known areas and removal from them. It ranged from minor apprehension through to 'a tendency to seize upon a slight incident as symbolical of a dire calamity'.[94]

In Crawley New Town, by the late 1950s, hospital psychiatrists were investigating the nature of 'Crawley neurosis', an 'emotional disturbance' allegedly caused by the difficulties of adjusting to life after London. This was one study noticeable for the involvement of a woman psychiatric worker. Some 80 per cent of Crawley's new inhabitants were from the capital. Crawley was a markedly young town comprised mostly of young couples, the majority of whom were raising children.[95] This study divided its subjects into patients and controls, the former being those who were undergoing treatment at the town's out-patients' clinic. Three-quarters of both male patients and controls preferred Crawley to their previous London place of residence, compared to less than two-thirds of women patients and controls. Hence the women patients were more likely to express dissatisfaction with Crawley and manifested higher degrees of loneliness: 40 per cent of women patients complained of boredom and other symptoms of anti-social behaviour such as indifference or a sense of superiority to their neighbours. In qualification, though, the authors could not and therefore would not state whether these were consequences of moving house generally or of the specific move to Crawley.[96] A later study of a psychiatric practice in the same new town of Crawley, published in 1967, came to the uncomfortable conclusion that the problem of 'new town blues' and also of the blues in established towns was felt most miserably by women of childbearing age, 44 per cent of whom were diagnosed as neurotic in Crawley, as opposed to 43 per cent in a compared old town.[97]

A study of Harlow New Town attempted to discover whether there was any evidence to support a view that neighbourhood provision there lessened the incidence of transitional neuroses when compared with the move to the less well planned suburbs. Harlow, like Crawley, was a predominantly young town, a veritable 'pram town', whose average age was twenty-seven years. The study concluded that any neurotic symptoms manifested by the newcomers could not accurately be ascribed to the new town, but to the general experience of moving house and district. It found that the peak prevalence of neurosis was to be found in menopausal women aged between forty-five and fifty-four years. Any apparent high levels of neurosis in women of younger age groups in the new towns could be explained by their prevalence in the local population. The study did not find evidence of a specifically 'suburban' or 'new town' neurosis, and argued that the new towns manifested lower levels of reported 'nerves' than in less well designed and planned suburban developments.[98] In Croydon, a comparative study of the mental health of the populations in an established part of town and in a new estate found that there was no difference at all between the two areas.[99]

The emphasis upon existing factors which predisposed women to suburban neurosis or the new town blues is an important one. A review of the literature on suburban neurosis and new town blues concluded that both these alleged conditions had little to do with moving to suburbs or new towns. There was, it argued, 'no significant difference in the prevalence of neurotic ill-health under widely differing conditions of urban life'.[100] Another study concluded that rather than a concentration upon the notion of suburban neurosis, a more apposite focus for debate might be 'transitional neurosis'.[101] The difficulty of specifically blaming new town or suburban environments as distinct from the general phenomenon of moving home was noted by five of the psychological studies discussed here.[102] Jeffreys's study came to similar conclusions, observing that women in the South Oxhey council estate 'showed no definite symptoms of a higher incidence of a psycho-neurotic illness than women of the same age elsewhere'.[103] Perhaps the most telling synopsis of all was that of Dr Stephen Taylor and his colleague Sidney Chave, in their study of mental health in 'newtown':

> We found no real evidence of what one of us (Taylor) twenty five years ago described as 'the suburban neurosis', nor of what has more recently been described as 'new town blues'. [Some] people do indeed show loneliness, boredom, discontent with environment and worries, particularly over money. It is easy enough for enterprising enquirers to find such people, and to attribute these symptoms to the new town. But a similar group of similar size can be found in any community, new or old, if it is sought.[104]

The discovery that new towns were not to blame for the blues was, not surprisingly, seized upon by the advocates of new towns, and of dispersal policies in general.[105]

There were certainly problems, then, for women on new estates. But there were deeper causes of symptoms which became manifest in the move. An important historical issue may be raised here. In what ways is it possible, with no archive of detailed retrospective cradle-to-grave life histories of suburban migrants, to explore the predisposing factors – personal factors – and their relationship to transitional neurosis? One possible solution is provided by fiction. To argue that, however, does not mean we have to treat uncritically the view that in fiction we find 'real history'.[106] But the literary imagination and empathy can open up areas of experience at which other sources merely hint. A contemporary historian has argued that fictive *genres* 'can give an insight into the manners, mores and ways of thinking of a particular period' and they may 'stimulate imaginative insight into a period and so be of help to the contemporary historian'.[107] That is true, but it is a limited view of literature. Whilst many historians might balk at the problems of verification with literature, few would deny that fiction provides 'imaginative insights' not simply into a particular period, but also into areas of personal feelings and experiences where the empirical archive is lacking. And that is pertinent not just to the novel, but also to screenplays.

In 1965, by which time the media debate about new town blues was well known, the BBC launched *The Newcomers*, a television series which became popular and was screened regularly until 1969. The newcomers were the Cooper family from London, decanted to the expanded town of 'Angleton'. It appears that they moved in accordance with the Industrial Selection Scheme. The reactions and experiences of Mrs Cooper must have rung true for many women who encountered misgivings at the thought of the move:

> Ellis Cooper, shop superintendent of a firm making components for computers, tells his wife Vivienne that his factory is moving to a sleepy country town in East Anglia and he has been offered promotion to works manager. Vivienne, city born and bred, a modern woman, marriage counsellor, content with her home and social circle, quails ...[108]

The Coopers had to 'grapple in a dazed way' when preparing to move, and once they had arrived in Angleton they faced transitional difficulties in an alien environment. But they also enjoyed the compensations of the nearby countryside and the nice new home.[109] According to one historian of television: 'All the pains and pleasures of living on a new housing estate were brought into focus, from the loneliness and boredom that such existence brings, to comprehending the local, rural lifestyle'.[110] Or as the *Radio Times* put it in 1965, for the 'strangers on new housing estates there is loneliness, fear and boredom' but also new friends and new social opportunities, 'copious material for the twice weekly serial on Tuesday and Fridays'.[111]

The Newcomers worked within the traditions of documentary realism and soap opera fiction. The series aimed to reflect in dramatic form the everyday experiences of newcomers to new towns, and to be entertaining enough to be accessible to a television audience which would tune in regularly. The written word in novels worked within very different conventions, but the concern for people's feelings within the context of their daily lives was strongly similar to that of television playwrights. There is, as was elaborated upon in the first chapter, a rich seam of anti-suburban literature, much of it risible and superficial in its mockery of its subject.[112] With this in mind, two (male) writers deserve to be discussed for their treatment of suburban misery and new town claustrophobia, namely Keith Waterhouse and Angus Wilson.

Waterhouse is a journalist, playwright and novelist. His autobiography tells us that after a childhood and an early marriage spent in Yorkshire, he moved to Harlow new town *en route* to his eventual destination, London. His experience in Harlow and his perception of the new town were quite favourable. On visiting Harlow, Waterhouse felt it would be a good place for his children to grow up.[113] A similar route from northern town to southern new town was followed by Waterhouse's most famous fictional creation, Billy Liar, in two novels which deserve to be treated together. In the first, Billy lived a life of unfulfilled dreams in his parent's semi 'Hill Crest' in the suburbs of Stradhoughton during the later 1950s. His way out of a stultifying suburbia was through dreaming. Billy also met girls from 'cold new houses' in a dance hall where the new estate petered out onto the moors. He dreamed of London – and presumably of a properly vital metropolitan life – but never made it. Instead of eloping to the Metropolis with Liz, whom he most fancied, he contrived to miss the train, and walked back home to his other girlfriend, 'the Witch', and to subtopia.[114] In the trans-textual step from the novel to the feature film of 1963, the pathetic farce of the railway station was given extra bathos. Billy, played by Tom Courtney, also missed the train to London which Liz, played by Julie Christie, had already boarded.[115]

The train station as a terminus of Billy's dreams represented, within English fiction feature film, the closing-off of an obvious and potential escape route from suburbia. Those very points of connection which had once made Victorian suburban life possible had been reinterpreted as the first point of escape from the suburbs. The 1945 film *Brief Encounter*, for example, is best described by Leslie Halliwell's unromantic film criticism:

> A suburban housewife on her weekly shopping visits develops a love affair with a local doctor but he gets a job and they agree not to see each other again. [Even] those bored by the theme must be riveted by the treatment, especially the use of a dismal railway station and its trains.[116]

In 1966, within a different film medium, Ken Loach's documentary drama *Cathy Come Home* ended tragically in a station, with the destruction of Cathy's family, and of her motherhood, when the officials from the Social Services forcefully removed her children from her, leaving her homeless and weeping on a station bench.[117] Cathy had travelled from the comfortable parental home, to new council flat, to dilapidated terraced house, to squat, to local authority hostel, and to no home at all, a bitter reversal of the life path from slum to new house which many millions of working-class women had pursued.

To return to Billy Liar: a worse fate awaited Billy than the disappointed dreams of his existence in Stradhoughton. In the sequel novel, *Billy Liar on the Moon*, first published in 1975, Waterhouse placed his anti-hero in 'the concrete and motor way hell' of Shepford New Town.[118] Just off the M1, Shepford was portrayed as a bleak, soulless, alien place. Billy sometimes reflects miserably that he lives in 'a suburb of the moon'. He is unhappily married to Jeanette, and having an affair with Helen, who is very much a novelist's stereotype of the promiscuous suburban woman. His mother, who like Jeanette has a secondary role to Billy, has moved to Shepford with them and is unhappy there. Billy, Jeanette and his mother live in a council flat, but they want, eventually, to move to a private house which Billy sardonically labels 'Mortgagedene'. Billy is also unhappy, working in the town council offices with selfish, ineffectual and unprepossessing people like himself. He wants to break free with his mistress Helen and leave Shepford. So, after deciding he is missing something in life, he decides unequivocally to leave Jeanette and run away with Helen. The novel draws to its conclusion, however, with Billy realising the futility of his dreaming and the reality of his life in Shepford. The narrative ends with his wife Jeanette phoning him about golf clubs from their new mortgaged bungalow. It is possible to summarise, therefore, that Billy's contempt for Stradhoughton and Shepford reflected his slowly painful journey from immature anomie into maturity. At the end of the novel, Billy reflects how he had 'grown up'.[119] On another level, it simply made for hilarious reading.

The Penguin edition of Angus Wilson's *Late Call*, first published in 1964, was unoriginal and inaccurate in describing the Midlands new town of Carshall as a 'concrete jungle'.[120] New towns were rarely concrete jungles: the dangerous, high-density and untamed urban wilderness which this implies was an inappropriate blurb-writer's shorthand for social novels about life in new towns. The negativity of the imagery, moreover, persisted. In a rather narrow interpretation of Wilson's novel, the literary critic Bernard Bergonzi argued that Wilson's aim was to explore 'the spiritual desolation of life in a new town in the Midlands, where the gimmickry of affluence has become a way of life rather than an aid to living'.[121] Unlike Waterhouse's novels, the central character of *Late Call* is an elderly woman, Sylvia Calvert. She has just retired as a seaside hotel manageress, and moves with her elderly and ailing husband Arthur to live with her recently bereaved son Harold and his family in the new town.

Harold clearly personifies aspects of new town life and culture which Wilson hated as social engineering. He is living to the progressive ideology of the new town 'experiment' which he also wills others to live to. He is presented as inflexible and doctrinaire, even more rigid than the development corporation's representative at cultural events, Jock Parsons. He and his family is, moreover, a suburban family in a new town context. They had moved from a house near the centre of Carshall to a larger ranch-style house on the outskirts called 'The Sycamores'. The Sycamores contained all mod cons, and Sylvia and her husband found it difficult, embarrassing and often time-wasting to get to grips with these so-called labour-saving devices.

Writers who are in sympathy with the new towns movement have been defensive about *Late Call*, yet they need not be.[122] A reading of the book which emphasised Carshall as a subtopia for the superannuated would obscure some important insights, and thus some alternative interpretations, about new town life and the so-called problems of neurosis. Sylvia Calvert took with her the depredations of her marriage and the personal legacy of her unhappy childhood. She was, moreover, treated by her son in a 'progressive' manner which, whilst fulfilling the writer Wilson's desire to satirise the pretensions of 'sixties' radicals, also ignored the long-established needs and problems of his character of Sylvia. Hence, the aforementioned agreement among many socio-psychologists of the suburbs and new towns, that the causes of neuroses went deeper than the social determinism of the new towns or of suburban life, and stemmed from individual as well as environmental causes, was inadvertently confirmed by Wilson. This was painfully evident in the way he described Sylvia's reaction to the play *Look Back in Anger*.[123] Most importantly of all, 'late call' is a metaphor for the late morning calls Sylvia had enjoyed as a hotel manageress, when she would lay on for a few precious moments in bed before work. She finds a belated new life for herself through her own self-realisation, by making new friends and by becoming active in the social life of the new town. In *The Newcomers*, too, Vivienne Cooper took the initiative in calling for a new community centre, a children's playground, a Citizen's Advice Bureau and better medical facilities.[124] It is worth emphasising, then, that Sylvia Calvert, Vivienne Cooper, Billy Liar and his wife Jeanette, in common with the vast majority of those who moved out to a new town after 1945, did not go back.[125]

Finally, both Waterhouse and Wilson presented women in the background of politics and planning in the new towns. This was not wholly true. A number of women had occupied key positions in the postwar movement for new towns, notably, for example, Evelyn Denington, the chair of Stevenage Development Corporation and a former chair of the LCC's New and Expanding Town's Committee, Mary Tabor, the Housing Manager in Stevenage from 1951, Evelyn Jones at Redditch, and Elizabeth Mitchell, a pioneer of Scottish new towns. One chapter in the *Town and Country Planning* journal's special issue on new towns, published in 1968, was called 'The ladies join in'. It gave space to female planners, notably Evelyn Denington, Elizabeth Mitchell and two women residents, one from Stevenage and one from Crawley.[126] The idea of 'ladies joining in' was unwitting testimony to the fact that what has been termed 'second wave feminism' was in its earliest stages, in social politics generally, and within the context of planning theory in particular, and had not yet begun to influence the language and to question the preconceptions of a predominantly male profession.[127]

To be fair, some male planners, notably L. E. White, who was active in the Community Associations movement, which had a strong presence on new estates, argued in *Town and Country Planning* that 'housewives, whose influence has transformed the kitchen, should now turn their attention to bettering the neighbourhood and the town'.[128] It is doubtful, however, that any women beyond the readership of that professional journal had ever heard of him.

Hence Clara Greed has argued that, in general, planning has relegated women to second-class citizens both in its view of women and in terms of their problems of mobility as consumers of services. It was, after all, women who spent most of their time on the estate, especially married women with children, the majority of whom stayed at home for most of the day, took the children to school and did the shopping. Many were inconvenienced by the spatial design of estates, by the relative lack of mobility due to male ownership of motor cars, and most were economically dependent upon their husbands.[129] However, planners prescribed a largely marginal and consultative role to women's organisations, and only then within institutional contexts laid down from above. Some annual reports of development corporations, for example, praise the role of the Women's Advisory Committees in new towns, for their recommendations on improved heating or kitchen design, for example.[130] Yet, as any investigation into the annual reports for most new towns will show, little or no mention of women's groups tended to be the norm. This was one-sided. Women's participation, both organised and informal, on the new estates and in new and expanded towns was tangible and growing in the postwar years, and is discussed in the following chapter.[131]

Conclusion

By the mid-1960s, the debate about suburban neurosis and the new town blues had moved between professional annals, popular fiction, the television and the daily newspapers. In so doing that debate widened, and there is little doubt that planners were forced to take notice of it. Thus the MHLG felt that the popular impact of these depictions of suburban and new town life had encouraged a rather critical and unfair perception of the new towns which was articulated in a new and popular lexicon of urban pathology:

> 'new town blues', 'suburban neurosis', 'social ghettos', 'prairie planning', 'cultural deserts', and the like. These melodramatic terms are frequently exaggerations; certainly problems do exist, but where the necessary thought and social provision has been made, they can be dealt with before they become serious.[132]

The idea that suburban neurosis or new town blues were 'melodramatic' probably reflected the popular influence of *The Newcomers*. Proponents of new towns and the MHLG felt that the phrase 'new town blues' was a convenient catch-phrase for social critics of new development.[133] Yet it would be inaccurate to argue that the MHLG, or the planning profession generally, were guilty of any sustained complacency about the problems of urban dispersal policies. Development corporations did maintain a surveillance to highlight the problems of those in need. It must be noted, however, that the institutional commitment to monitoring for dysfunctional symptoms probably varied with the different commitment to social development from town to town.[134]

Within central government, moreover, there was little point in pretending everything was running smoothly when it was not, as this would have stored up problems for the future, and destroyed the intentions and reputation of the Ministry and its policies for population dispersal. The MHLG's survey of facilities in expanded towns, *The First Hundred Families*, published in 1965, argued that adequate services and facilities in the earliest days of migration and settlement were crucial to adaptation. It further argued that arrivals workers and the social development programmes had tended to solve the 'inevitable problems which arise in the first few months after moving ...'.[135] This was not an inaccurate assessment. Looking back on the postwar slum clearance programmes, one sociologist agreed that 'the break-up of working-class communities [has] no more than a minor and short term effect on people'.[136] Even Peter Willmott came to such conclusions. As a singular social investigator – in contrast with his partnership with Michael Young – Willmott's study of Dagenham found that the nature of working-class life had evolved with the maturation of the estate, and that many, but not all, of the social and cultural characteristics of pre-suburban working-class life were to be found in Dagenham. He further pointed out that many of the more pessimistic positions taken on working-class dispersal stemmed from studies which had been undertaken very early on in the life of an estate which was rapidly filling with very recent movers. The temporary nature of many of the early problems had not been sufficiently emphasised.[137]

A historical perspective on the dispersal phenomenon, moreover, manifests the truth in Norman Dennis's observation that 'housing estates represent that exaggerated result of processes that are common to our society'.[138] Such processes included the changes within family life, the demise of the spatially proximate extended family and the rise of the nuclear family. The smaller size of families as a consequence of increased demand for contraception was certainly concomitant with dispersal, but not totally restricted to it.[139] Dennis's observation may be applied to the planning process: poor provision and the 'lack of integration of other supporting land uses and amenities' do appear to have affected women more than men.[140]

That final point reminds us that the social experience of urban dispersal should be interpreted as a learning process. In the official and popular pursuit of improved housing and residential environments, mistakes were made from above, and that led to hardships below. Advocates of new and expanded towns liked to point to what they saw as the superior provision of services in new and expanded towns when compared to council estates as proof that the new towns were better at helping people to settle in.[141] Yet as this chapter has shown, there were often difficulties for migrants to the new and expanded towns, and some planners felt that many aspects of planned provision might have been handled more effectively.[142] A final conclusion must be, therefore, that although the case for suburban neurosis and new town blues is largely not proven, it would be impossible to deny, from the vantage point of the later 1990s, that some neighbourhood units and new estates could have been better built, and that supporting facilities were lacking. This made life unnecessarily difficult for many migrants, given the personal and financial problems which many carried with them. At a time of continuing dispersal from the city and town centres to suburbs and new towns,[143] the lessons from their earlier experiences should not be forgotten.

Notes

1 E. Harvey, 'The post-war pioneers', *Town and Country Planning*, 41:9 (1973), p. 417.

2 R. Durant, *Watling: A Survey of Social Life on a New Housing Estate* (London, 1939), pp. 26–7.

3 J. Lewis and B. Brookes, 'A reassessment of the work of the Peckham Health Centre, 1926–1951', *Milbank Memorial Quarterly; Health and Society*, 61:2 (1983), pp. 330–2; see also A. A. Jackson, *Semi Detached London: Suburban Development, Life and Transport, 1900–1939* (London, 1991), pp. 137–8.

4 *Lancet*, 'Suburban neurosis up to date', I, 18 January 1958, p. 146.

5 Ibid., p. 146.

6 D. Reisman, 'The suburban sadness', in W. M. Dobriner (ed.), *The Suburban Community* (New York, 1958), p. 388.

7 See above, Chapter 1, pp. 11–13.

8 Ministry of Housing and Local Government (MHLG), *The Needs of New Communities: A Report on Social Provision in New and Expanding Communities* (London, 1967), p. 21–3.

9 M. Young and P. Willmott, *Family and Kinship in East London* (Lon-

don, 1979), pp. 142–4, 167, for example.

10 See above, Chapter 3, p. 79.

11 H. E. Bracey, *Neighbours on New Estates and Subdivisions in England and the USA* (London, 1964), p. 63.

12 J. Klein, *Samples From English Cultures* (London, 1965), I, p. 226.

13 T. Blackwell and J. Seabrook, *A World Still to Win: The Reconstruction of the Postwar Working Class* (London, 1985), p. 110.

14 The People's Press, *This Place Has Its Ups and Downs, or Kids Could Have Done It Better* (Milton Keynes, 1977). This book has no page numbers.

15 E. Bott, *Family and Social Network: Roles, Norms and External Relationships in Ordinary Urban Families* (London, 1968), pp. 109–10; H. Gavron, *The Captive Wife: Conflicts of Housebound Mothers* (London, 1983), pp. xix–xxiv; M. Young and P. Willmott, *The Symmetrical Family: A Study of Work and Leisure in the London Region* (London, 1973), pp. 278–9.

16 J. Turner and B. Jardine, *Pioneer Tales: A New Life in Milton Keynes* (Milton Keynes, 1985), p. 76.

17 Bott, *Family and Social Network*, p. 109.

18 Klein, *Samples From English Cultures*, p. 227.

19 Anglia Television programme, originally transmitted December 1975. This is now available on video at the Living Archive Project, Wolverton, Milton Keynes.

20 J. Lewis, *Women in Britain Since 1945* (Oxford, 1993), pp. 51–6.

21 In 1976, the *Milton Keynes Household Survey* found that 56 per cent of employed workers in Milton Keynes were aged between twenty and thirty-nine years of age, compared with 41 per cent nationally: MKDC, *Seven Years On: Household Survey, 1976; Technical Report 3: Employment* (Milton Keynes, 1976), p. 6. On postwar divorce rates into the 1970s generally, and their age breakdown, see R. Fletcher, *The Family and Marriage in Modern Britain* (Harmondsworth, 1974), pp. 146–50.

22 M. Abrams, 'The home-centred society', *Listener*, 26 November 1959, p. 915; F. Zweig, *The Worker in an Affluent Society* (London, 1961), pp. 207–9.

23 F. Devine, *Affluent Workers Revisited: Privatism and the Working Class* (Edinburgh, 1992), pp. 113–33.

24 C. Hall, 'Married women at home in Birmingham in the 1920s and 1930s', *Oral History*, 5:2 (1977), p. 67.

25 J. Lewis, *Women in England: 1870–1950* (Hemel Hempstead, 1984),

p. 223.

26 Durant, *Watling*, p. 21.

27 S. Caunce, *Oral History and the Local Historian* (London, 1994), p. 188.

28 E. Roberts, 'Neighbours: North West England 1940–70', *Oral History*, 21:2 (1993), p. 41.

29 See above, Chapter 3, p. 83.

30 See above, Chapter 3, pp. 75–6, 78.

31 Durant, *Watling*, pp. 27–8, and see above, Chapter 4, pp. 108–14.

32 Hall, 'Married women', p. 65.

33 A. Hughes and K. Hunt, 'A culture transformed? Women's lives in Wythenshawe in the 1930s', in A. Davies and S. Fielding (eds), *Workers' Worlds: Cultures and Communities in Manchester and Salford, 1880–1939* (Manchester, 1992), p. 85.

34 Durant, *Watling*, p. 20.

35 H. Jennings, *Societies in the Making: A Study of Development and Redevelopment Within a County Borough* (London, 1962), p. 160.

36 B. Ineichen, 'Neurotic wives in a modern residential suburb', *Social Science and Medicine*, 9 (1975), pp. 485–6; M. Jeffreys, 'Londoners in Hertfordshire: the South Oxhey estate', in R. Glass, E. J. Hobsbawm et al., *London: Aspects of Change* (London, 1964), pp. 239–40; J. Salt and R. Flowerdew 'Labour migration from London', *London Journal*, 6:1 (1980), p. 47.

37 J. B. Cullingworth, 'The Swindon social survey: a second report on the social implications of overspill', *Sociological Review* (New Series) 9:2 (1961), p. 157.

38 M. Harloe, *Swindon: A Town in Transition. A Study in Urban Development and Overspill Policy* (London, 1975), pp. 124–5.

39 R. Thomas, *London's New Towns: A Study of Self-Contained and Balanced Communities* (London, 1969), p. 399.

40 Ineichen, 'Neurotic wives', p. 482.

41 Ibid., p. 485.

42 B. Ineichen and D. Hooper, 'Wives' mental health and children's behaviour problems in contrasting residential estates', *Social Science and Medicine*, 8 (1974), pp. 369–71.

43 Ibid., p. 373.

44 M. Lassell, *Wellington Road* (London, 1962), p. 159.

45 S. Graham and S. Marvin, *Telecommunications and the City: Electronic Spaces, Urban Places* (London, 1996), pp. 193–6, 232.

46 H. G. Maule and F. M. Martin, 'Social and psychological aspects of rehousing', *Advancement of Science*, 12:48 (1956), pp. 444–5.

47 Jeffreys, 'Londoners in Hertfordshire', p. 225.

48 J. Norris, *Human Aspects of Redevelopment* (Birmingham, 1962), p. 48.

49 On the lower level of women's earnings, see J. Lewis, *Women in Britain: Women, Family, Work and the State in the Postwar Years* (Oxford, 1993), pp. 81, 117–20.

50 Norris, *Human Aspects*, pp. 50–1.

51 H. Clark, 'Problems of the housing manager today', *Society of Housing Managers' Quarterly Bulletin*, 4:7 (1957), pp. 2–3.

52 N. Deakin and C. Ungerson, *Leaving London: Planned Mobility and the Inner City* (London, 1977), p. 133.

53 J. F. Beatson-Hird, 'Case history of "newstate"', *Town and Country Planning*, 25:8 (1967), p. 381.

54 R. Kitchen 'Moving to Milton Keynes', *New Society*, 22 August 1974, p. 480.

55 M. Tebbutt, *Making Ends Meet: Pawnbroking and Working Class Credit* (London, 1984), p. 195.

56 Deakin and Ungerson, *Leaving London*, pp. 131–2.

57 Kitchen, 'Moving to Milton Keynes', p. 480.

58 This discussion is based upon MKDC, *Four Years On: The Milton Keynes Household Survey, 1973: Summary* (Milton Keynes, 1974), pp. 21–5. Kitchen's article in *New Society* was based largely on these findings.

59 MKDC, *Four Years On: The Milton Keynes Household Survey, 1973: Summary*, p. 22.

60 T. Bendixson and J. Platt, *Milton Keynes: Image and Reality* (Cambridge, 1992), pp. 176–8.

61 R. Deem, *All Work and No Play: The Sociology of Women and Leisure* (Milton Keynes, 1986), pp. 27, 29 and 32.

62 D. Danaher and J. D. Williamson, '"New town blues": planning versus mutual', *International Journal of Social Psychiatry*, 29:2 (1983), pp. 148–9.

63 Ineichen and Hooper, 'Wives' mental health', p. 371.

64 Danaher and Williamson, 'New town blues', pp. 148–9.

65 L. Kuper, 'Blueprint for living together', in L. Kuper (ed.), *Living in Towns* (London, 1953), pp. 14–15.

66 Cullingworth, 'The Swindon social survey', p. 162.

67 See above, Chapter 4, p. 103.

68 Cullingworth, 'Swindon social survey', p. 154.

69 See above, Chapter 4, pp. 96, 103.

70 J. Tucker, *Honourable Estates* (London, 1966), p. 11.

71 Ineichen, 'Neurotic wives', p. 485.

72 Cited in B. Martin, *A Sociology of Contemporary Cultural Change* (Oxford, 1985), p. 53.
73 Kuper, 'Blueprint for living together', p. 61.
74 Martin, *A Sociology*, p. 55.
75 R. Wilson, 'Difficult housing estates', *Human Relations*, 16:1 (1963), p. 18.
76 J. H. Nicholson, *New Communities in Britain: Achievements and Problems* (London, 1961), p. 133.
77 Wilson, 'Difficult housing estates', pp. 41–2.
78 Durant, *Watling*, p. 31; Jeffreys, 'Londoners in Hertfordshire', pp. 213–14; Kuper, 'Blueprint for living together', pp. 61–2; C. Brooks, 'The Lakes Estate, Bletchley: a case study of a GLC overspill development designed on Radburn principles' (Oxford Polytechnic, unpublished Diploma in Urban Planning dissertation, 1990), pp. 22–32.
79 Brooks, 'Lakes Estate', p. 26.
80 M. Taylor, *Unleashing the Potential: Bringing Residents to the Centre of Regeneration* (York, 1995), pp. 9–11.
81 Tucker, *Honourable Estates*, p. 70.
82 Jennings, *Societies in the Making*, pp. 151–4.
83 Cullingworth, 'Swindon social survey', p. 162.
84 Ibid., p. 164.
85 G. Brooke-Taylor, 'Social problems of new towns', in P. Kuenstler (ed.), *Community Organisation in Great Britain* (London, 1961), p. 75.
86 N. H. Rankin, 'Social adjustment in a North-West newtown', *Sociological Review* (New Series) 11:3 (1963), p. 296.
87 Beatson-Hird, 'Newstate', p. 383.
88 MKDC, *Four Years On*, pp. 24–5.
89 D. Brinig, 'What it's really like to live in Milton Keynes', *Over 21*, July 1978, p. 115 (emphasis added).
90 R. Kitchen, 'Doing a moonlight' (Milton Keynes, unpublished manuscript, 1975, held at the Living Archive Project), p. 1.
91 Ibid., p. 1.
92 *Lancet*, 'Suburban neurosis up to date', p. 146.
93 P. Hall, 'Some clinical aspects of moving house as an apparent precipitant', *Journal of Psychomatic Research*, 10:1 (1966), pp. 68–9.
94 *British Medical Journal*, 'Demolition melancholia', 15 July 1939, p. 129.
95 P. Sainsbury and J. Collins, 'Some factors relating to mental illness in a new town', *Journal of Psychomatic Research*, 10:1 (1966), pp. 45, 48.

96 Ibid., pp. 50–1.
97 *Lancet*, 'Psychiatric illness in a new town practice', 31 March 1967.
98 S. P. W. Chave, 'Mental health in Harlow new town', *Journal of Psychomatic Research*, 10:1 (1966), pp. 38, 40–3.
99 E. H. Hare and G. K. Shaw, *Mental Health on a New Housing Estate: A Comparative Study of Health in Two Districts of Croydon* (London, 1965), pp. 101–2.
100 E. H. Hare, 'Mental health in new towns: what next?', *Journal of Psychosomatic Research*, 10:1 (1966), pp. 54–5, 58.
101 S. D. Coleman, *Mental Health and Social Adjustment in a New Town* (Glasgow, n.d.), cited in Ineichen, 'Neurotic wives', p. 481.
102 Chave, 'Mental health in Harlow', p. 43; Hall, 'Some clinical aspects', pp. 68–9; Hare, 'Mental health in new towns', p. 58; Ineichen, 'Neurotic wives', p. 481; Sainsbury and Collins, 'Some factors', p. 51.
103 Jeffreys, 'Londoners in Hertfordshire', pp. 245–6.
104 Lord Taylor and S. Chave, *Mental Health and Environment* (London, 1964), p. 175.
105 F. Schaffer, *The New Town Story* (London, 1972), pp. 192–4.
106 See above, Chapter 1, p. 5.
107 J. Barnes 'Books and journals', in A. Seldon (ed.), *Contemporary History: Practice and Method* (Oxford, 1988), p. 50.
108 *Radio Times*, 30 September 1965, p. 35.
109 *Radio Times*, 7 October 1965, p. 37; 14 October 1965, p. 39.
110 T. Vahimagi for the British Film Institute, *British Television: An Illustrated Guide* (Oxford, 1994), p. 139.
111 *Radio Times*, 30 September 1965, p. 35.
112 See above, Chapter 1, pp. 5–6.
113 K. Waterhouse, *Streets Ahead: Life After City Lights* (London, 1995), pp. 6, 95.
114 Back cover of K. Waterhouse, *Billy Liar* (Harmondsworth, 1985).
115 L. Halliwell, *Halliwell's Film Guide* (London, 1986), p. 98.
116 Ibid., p. 133.
117 *Cathy Come Home* was shown by the BBC in November 1966. See the *Listener*, 24 November 1966, p. 783.
118 Back cover, K. Waterhouse, *The Billy Liar Novels* (Harmondsworth, 1993).
119 Waterhouse, *The Billy Liar Novels*, p. 388.
120 Back cover, A. Wilson, *Late Call* (Harmondsworth, 1992).
121 B. Bergonzi, *The Situation of the Novel* (Harmondsworth, 1972), p. 185.
122 C. Ward, *New Town, Home Town* (London, 1993), p. 11.

123 J. Brannigan, 'Literature's poor relation: history and identity in the writing and criticism of 1950s literature' (University of Luton, unpublished Ph.D. thesis, 1996), pp. 127–8.
124 *Radio Times*, 14 October 1965, p. 39.
125 See above, Chapter 2, pp. 46–8.
126 E. B. Mitchell, E. Denington, G. Pitt and K. Baker were joint contributors, in that order, to 'The ladies join in', in H. Evans and P. Self (eds), *New Towns Come of Age* (London, 1968), pp. 92–8. On Evelyn Jones at Redditch, see G. Anstis, *Redditch: Success in the Heart of England. The History of Redditch New Town* (Stevenage, 1985), pp. 117, 161. On Mary Tabor, see H. and C. Rees, *The History Makers: The Story of the Early Days of Stevenage New Town* (Stevenage, 1991), pp. 6–13.
127 On late 1960s feminism and planning, see A. Ravetz, *The Government of Space: Town Planning in Modern Society* (London, 1986), pp. 120–1. A useful introduction to 'second wave' feminism from the late 1960s is K. Sayer 'Feminism and history', *Modern History Review*, November 1994, p. 5.
128 L. E. White, 'Good kitchens and bad towns', *Town and Country Planning*, 19:89 (1951), p. 396.
129 C. Greed, *Women and Planning: Creating Gendered Realities* (London, 1994), pp. 47–9.
130 See for example, Hemel Hempstead Development Corporation, *Eighth Annual Report for the Period Ended March 31, 1955* (*Parliamentary Papers*, 1955–56 (91) Vol. XXV, p. 273); Hemel Hempstead Development Corporation, *Ninth Annual Report for the Period Ended March 31, 1956* (*Parliamentary Papers*, 1955–56 (365) Vol. XXV, p. 282).
131 See below, Chapter 6, pp. 176–80.
132 MHLG, *Needs of New Communities*, p. 21.
133 Schaffer, *New Town Story*, pp. 192–3.
134 See above, Chapter 3, p. 77. This point is also evident from study of the *Annual Reports of the Development Corporations* in the *Parliamentary Papers*.
135 MHLG, *The First Hundred Families* (London, 1965), pp. iii, 1.
136 B. J. Parker, 'Some sociological implications of slum clearance programmes', in D. Donnison and D. Eversley (eds), *London: Urban Patterns, Problems and Policies* (London, 1973), p. 249.
137 P. Willmott, 'Social research in the new communities', *Journal of the American Institute of Planners*, 33:6 (1967), p. 388.
138 N. Dennis, 'The popularity of the neighbourhood community idea',

in R. E. Pahl (ed.), *Readings in Urban Sociology* (Oxford, 1969), p. 84.

139 On contraception, see D. A. Coleman, 'Population', in A. H. Halsey (ed.), *British Social Trends Since 1900: A Guide to the Changing Social Structure of Britain* (London, 1988), pp. 57–9.

140 Greed, *Women and Planning*, p. 47.

141 Schaffer, *New Town Story*, p. 179.

142 P. McGovern, 'Social facilities in new and expanded towns', *Town and Country Planning*, 35:8 (1967), p. 395.

143 A. H. Halsey, 'Social trends since world war two', in L. McDowell, P. Sarre and C. Hamnett (eds), *Divided Nation: Social and Cultural Change in Britain* (London, 1989), pp. 22–3; J. Herington, *The Outer City* (London, 1984), p. 18.

6

Suburban solidarities: social life on the postwar new estate

This chapter looks at how people have come together in postwar housing developments during a period of growing affluence. It demonstrates that 'community' as neighbourliness, as a local formation of similarly placed and like-minded people, is only one element, and deserves to be treated as only one element, in our understanding of the evolution of postwar working-class social life. As Joanna Bourke has argued, historians are especially vague in their definition of community, which is taken for granted to include 'identification with a particular neighbourhood or street, a sense of shared perspectives, and reciprocal dependency'.[1] However, as this chapter aims to show, neighbourhood was but one context which brought people together. In addition, people formed groups and associations and made social connections around interests which had little to do with local identification. To demonstrate this, the first part of the chapter assesses the fortunes of the Community Associations movement and its emphasis upon neighbourhood.

The second section of this chapter discusses the pattern of active social relations in Milton Keynes since the end of the 'golden age' of the postwar period from 1973.[2] For as A. H. Halsey has written, after the oil crisis of the mid-1970s:

> a new phase of economic and social transformation appeared. The shift away from nineteenth-century urban industrial manufacturing was accelerated, unemployment rose, and population movement away from the inner cities towards suburbia, the South East, and the new towns was discernible.[3]

Milton Keynes is an apposite city to assess the social impact of these trends. It was designated as a new town by an Act of Parliament in

1967, and after a three-year planning period was pitched into life, its construction and in-migration taking off in earnest from 1970. It is in the South East. It is a new city of 'grand suburban design'[4] which was not planned to neighbourhood unit principles as were earlier new towns. Economically, it has witnessed the considerable growth of service sector employment, the relative decline of manufacturing and the increasing trend to home ownership. There is nothing new in historians focusing upon one area to assess the nature and significance of wider trends. A. J. P. Taylor, for example, did it for Victorian Manchester as an industrial and trading city, and American writers have treated postwar Los Angeles as a paradigm of suburban life in the United States.[5]

Third, leisure interests and pursuits in Milton Keynes will also be explored in order to assess their role as mechanisms of sociability in a late-twentieth-century city, a city designed to be less localised than the urban-industrial communities.

The fourth part of the chapter concludes by arguing for a flexible and nuanced interpretation of working-class social life within suburban new estates and new towns, which takes the term 'associative culture'. It recognises the richness and diversity of interests and activities which are evidenced in both the private and associative worlds of working-class life. Yet the chapter argues that an associative culture may not just reflect these differences, it may also transcend them in a common interest, if and when the need arises.

The rise and reorientation of the Community Associations movement

The Community Associations movement was born in both Britain and America between the wars. In Britain, it was largely a suburban phenomenon. Those large new housing estates, both council and private, stimulated people to come together due to their very lack of community facilities. In this, they were supported by statutory organisations, notably the National Council of Social Service (NCSS) via its Community Centres and Associations Committee. As the NCSS annual report for 1932–33 noted, 'on most new estates there is now some form of community association'.[6]

Many other voluntary groups, religious, political, sporting and recreational, joined in the calls and campaigns for community centres and for new facilities on these suburban developments. For example, the YMCA, the YWCA, trades unions, the Conservative, Labour, Liberal and Communist Parties, and the Workers' Educational Association (WEA) lobbied local authorities and supported residents' groups. Moreover, the British Association of Residential Settlements and the Educational Settlements' Association, which had been active in the poorer parts of the cities since the later Victorian years, also supported the Community Associations movement. For Left groups, this was a logical extension of local campaigning on behalf of culturally improving rational recreational facilities for the unemployed. In these important respects earlier strategies for improving the social and cultural life of the poor working-class districts fed forward into the new estates.[7] Such campaigning led to moves to standardise community facilities nationally on the new estates, and the Housing Act of 1936 permitted local authorities to build facilities which would provide 'a beneficial service' to their tenants. The following year, the Physical Training and Recreation Act allowed – but did not enforce the promotion of – new facilities to be built into new council estates.[8]

The NCSS saw new estates as playing a central role in the social as well as the physical renewal of Britain in the aftermath of the tragedy of the Great War. It was adamant that the development of new communities 'in the stirring and creative years since the conclusion of peace in 1919' was 'one of the greatest developments in England'.[9] But the NCSS was also aware that many of the new estates which housed the new communities remained inadequately equipped by local authorities. Many of the estates, it argued, were dormitories, with few social amenities of their own. The report described the costs and distances of public transport to workplaces, to former neighbourhoods, and to faraway cultural institutions such as the cinema or concert halls, problems which continued into the postwar years.[10] The continuing urgency of the problem from the point of view of local authorities, moreover, was seemingly evident in the rapid growth of their attendance, during the later 1930s, at the Community Associations Annual Conference. Only six local authorities attended the 1935 event, but this had risen dramatically to 170 by 1939. The reason was clear. As the number of community associations expanded greatly, local authorities were increasingly disposed to liaise with them. The number of community associations rose from below sixty to 110 over the same period.[11]

Social investigators provided vivid contemporary detail on the experiences of residents who fought for the community centre, for better shops, schools, pubs, churches or chapels. In Dagenham, a LCC estate of 120,000 people, built in large part to house the families of industrial workers at the new Ford plant, Terence Young's survey for the Pilgrim Trust identified the 'local patriotism' stimulated by the new estate. This was promoted in the development of institutions, organisations and societies for mutual aid and for shared leisure, such as the tenants' associations, horticultural societies, loan clubs, the Dagenham Girls' Pipers Band, the Boys' and Girls' Club, and the numerous sports clubs.[12]

At Edgware, Ruth Durant noted similar processes, but she paid more attention to their social and historical significance. Durant noted the inculcation of local patriotism among newly arrived Watlingites as a result of both the hostility or indifference of nearby rural or established suburban communities and a determination to do something about the lack of social and practical facilities. A community association was formed to campaign for a community centre, the Watling Association, which by 1939 was supported by the wealthy charities the Pilgrim Trust and the Carnegie Trust.[13] As a result of the association's actions and well-attended meetings often amounting to over 250 people, the public case for the centre was strongly made. Once it was built, it provided a focal point which spawned other associations and groups: a District Nursing Association, a Loans Club, a horticultural society, sports and athletics clubs, political party meetings, religious groups, a Women's Co-operative Guild, and a host of other fund-raising self-help groups. As Political and Economic Planning (PEP), revisiting Watling soon after the end of the Second World War, argued, 'this new one-class community of 20,000 "strangers" has brought into existence about seventy self-governing associations'.[14] They stressed the particular contribution made by women's societies and associations which had persisted into the new era: 'women became the mainstay of local corporate life'.[15] Similar developments were observed in other suburban areas between the wars.[16]

The community association was but one force which had brought together many people in the achievement of a community centre. But subsequently, the community centre did not mobilise everyone from all walks of local life. Rather, it was a meeting place for specific groups. Durant stressed that this diversity was an expression of the different areas from which Watlingites came, their varying levels of income, various stages of the life cycle, and the myriad interests and activities of a suburban population. Such diversity militated against 'community' because 'one can hardly speak of a common mode of living where there is considerable social differentiation as measured by origin, size, income, occupations and ages of the population'.[17]

In 1944–46 Durant (now Ruth Glass, due to her marriage to the demographer D. V. Glass) carried this analysis forward in her work on the reconstruction of Middlesbrough, a town which was already characterised by a considerable degree of cross-town movement between estates and between different districts for a wide range of social, recreational and practical purposes. She found that these wider patterns of movement meant that growing mobility conflicted with pure localism, a localism implied by the neighbourhood unit concept. She emphasised that the attempts to mix different occupational classes militated against the already residentially differentiated areas of Middlesbrough. It was to say the least 'difficult to find neighbourhoods which are not only distinct territorial groups but the inhabitants of which are also in close social contact with each other'. And it was difficult 'chiefly because such neighbourhoods rarely exist'.[18]

These important findings were obscured from the view of the Community Association movement and the NCSS during the conflict of 1939–45. The collective effort required to defeat Nazism led to a growing faith in the concept of the neighbourhood unit as the organic basis for social reconstruction at the micro level. Indeed, the NCSS explicitly linked the social health of postwar community with the neighbourhood idea and argued that 'every planning scheme' should aim at producing socially balanced and mixed neighbourhood units.[19] Moreover, at the 1943 Communities and Associations Conference A. C. Richmond, the Vice Chairman of the affiliated Land Settlement Association, argued that the forthcoming freedom from war would provide new opportunities to create a revitalised community life. Individuals could be made more community-minded and thus become more culturally elevated.[20] This individual, a similar creature to T. H. Marshall's notion of the active citizen, was to be fostered within neighbourhood conditions. Sir Robert Wood, the Deputy Secretary of the Board of Education, argued to the same conference that the country required a 'defined community' operating as a social entity within the framework of the neighbourhood unit. The neighbourhood was to be organised around the school or local college. These would serve social needs first and educational needs second.[21] The NCSS argued that such neighbourhoods should number between 5,000 and 10,000 people.[22] Leading planners were advocating neighbourhood units of such size, for example Sir Patrick Abercrombie in the *County of London Plan* (1943) and the *Greater London Plan* (1945).[23] Abercrombie was but one planner whose belief in the neighbourhood stemmed from an established tradition of urban and social reform which was initiated by the Settlements Movements in the later Victorian and Edwardian city in both Britain and America. The ideas of Ebenezer Howard in England and Clarence Perry in the United States, with their emphasis upon self-sufficient and active urban dwellers, fed directly into the neighbourhood unit idea.[24] These were to be institutionalised by planners and politicians via the New Towns Act of 1946, and in the design recommendations for urban overspill estates recommended in the *Design of Dwellings* manual (1944).[25]

There was, then, broad agreement between members of the NCSS, the Department of Education, and town planners, that neighbourhoods were going to be important. A new co-ordinating body, the National Federation of Community Organisations (NFCO), was formed in 1945, with Sir Wyndham Deedes of the NCSS, and Sir Ernest Barker, at its head.[26] Hence historians of the Community Associations movement have looked back to the wartime and early postwar projects as a golden era of both the neighbourhood unit idea and the principles of community association.[27] Its influence can perhaps be seen at its rhetorical apogee in Lewis Silkin's second reading to Parliament of the New Town's Bill, in 1946:

> The towns will be divided into neighbourhood units, each unit with its own shops, schools, open spaces, community halls and other amenities. [I] am most anxious that the planning should be such that the different income groups living in the new towns will not be segregated. No doubt they may enjoy common recreational facilities, and take part in amateur theatricals, or each play their part in a health centre or a community centre. But when they leave to go home I do not want the better off people to go to the right, and the less well off to go to the left. I want them to ask each other 'are you going my way?'[28]

The master plans of the first phase of new towns institutionalised these ideas.[29] But such hopes were to be disappointed. As Ruth Glass had emphasised, the neighbourhood unit was deterministic because it attempted to delimit people's area of movement and sociability, and thus proved limited in relation to choices engendered by affluence and greater personal mobility. The geographical boundaries of the neighbourhood were restricted. They were defined in relation to a walking distance or pram-pushing distance from shops or schools, a distance measured by whether it was still comfortable for people living in houses furthest away within the neighbourhood. These good intentions, however, were undone by the motor car, which speeded up travel times and allowed for a greater level of privatised, personal mobility than did walking or the public transport system. Ownership of cars among the skilled and to a lesser extent the semi-skilled and unskilled working class grew rapidly throughout the 1950s and 1960s, and that exposed an unanticipated trend in the early post-war planning of new towns. For example, in 1955 Basildon Development Corporation noted with alarm the rise in requests for garages on estates where existing provision was insufficient, and the growing number of cars parked along the sides of neighbourhood roads 'which cause difficulties with the police'.[30] People wanted to travel further to utilise a wider range of shops and facilities.[31]

Nor was there an overriding neighbourhood camaraderie. As Peter Willmott observed for Stevenage in 1962, the 'friendship map' he plotted demonstrated that neighbourhood was no major influence on friendships. Although some people drew friends from a more localised area, many had friends elsewhere.[32] A later 1960s study of a very large neighbourhood unit in Stoke-on-Trent found that in some areas, some three-quarters of residents 'claimed to have friends off the estate and to have little involvement in the social life of the community'.[33]

Moreover, Silkin's dream of cross-class neighbouring on new estates, both in new towns and in expanded or peripheral estates, rarely occurred. Instead, people gravitated to groups according to status and subjective perceptions of rough and respectable. Cross-class mixing was 'to be fixed in the procrustean bed of neighbourhood units'.[34] As was abundantly clear soon after the war, however, these planning principles were far from synchronous with neighbouring behaviour from below, whether working- or middle-class. For example, Mass Observation discovered that among its own panel of voluntary observers, who were 'a predominantly middle-class group' and 'more than usually socially conscious', about one-fifth held a conscious disinclination to neighbourliness. Not uncommon statements were along the following lines: 'I don't know my next door neighbours at all. On one side I don't even know his name (retired man).'[35] Most people were on friendly but casual terms, for example: 'I know my neighbours by name, profession, and those habits which one can observe over the garden wall. My relations with them are purely casual and limited to meetings around the houses.'[36] A study of a two neighbourhoods in the university city of Cambridge, made during the early 1950s, demonstrated the persistence of residential segregation by class. 'Area A' was a well-endowed and spacious area of academics and wealthy business types. 'Area B' was more mixed, with properties ranging from the best Grade 1 to the worst Grade 5. It was in fact difficult to say how far social mixing was encouraged or even hindered by a balance and mix of housing. People were seeking to reside in housing districts with like status and occupational backgrounds. Equally significantly, their range of choice fulfilment, for example shopping beyond the neighbourhood or choosing a school elsewhere in town, illustrated that such choices usually transcended the limitations of locality.[37]

There were other examples. A woman at Edgware told the social anthropologist Geoffrey Gorer that she felt educationally inferior to her neighbours and 'know my neighbours think they are superior to me'.[38] Similar statements were found in new towns. A 31-year-old 'worker' from Crawley complained his neighbours spoke with 'an *Oxford* accent but work, perhaps in a better job, but have to live to work as I do, but make you think that they are just that bit above you'.[39]

Feelings and expressions of superiority and inferiority were equally strong *within* the working classes. For example, J. M. Mogey's study of Oxford, undertaken from the early to mid-1950s, demonstrated that a measured and highly selective neighbouring was evident in both the 'traditional' area of St Ebbe's and the new estate of Barton. This was evident in a number of ways, for example in the women's 'gossip chain' – gossip was automatically deemed to be a women's trait – and in the fact that 'next-door-neighbouring' was a misnomer, because the best neighbours did not always live next door. In St Ebbe's, not untypical statements were 'you must talk to the neighbours but you mustn't say too much' or 'you have to be careful what you say'.[40] Fear of over-familiarity was evident, and was accompanied by a feeling of 'I like to keep myself to myself'. This was evident in Barton, too: 'I believe in keeping the family very much to themselves; I dislike women who spend two or three hours chatting in one house'. Another said: 'there's a lot of rough customers in this area'.[41]

It was demonstrated in Chapters 4 and 5 that social gradations in the slums or poorer areas were cast forwards into the estates.[42] This militated against neighbourliness between those who perceived others as different from themselves. A number of examples may serve to demonstrate this. Elizabeth Roberts, for example, has shown how in traditional working-class districts donkey-stoning the doorstep of the terraced house was a mark of cleanliness and respectability.[43] In 1950s Dagenham, the quest for cleanliness and difference at the doorstep had moved to the porch:

> 'I don't like sharing the porch', said one wife. 'This morning I was scrubbing my side of the porch and I thought I'd better scrub hers as well to make it look all the same, and she came out and said "Why do you have to scrub my half?" [I] suppose it made her angry because she banged me on the top of the head with a broom. Well, I thought, I'm not going to put up with that, [so] I hit her back.'[44]

James Tucker's 'self-portraits' of working-class council tenants emphasised similar feelings which militated against the notion of social balance, for example: 'People living here are such a terrible mixture. You get all kinds of people living together.' He observed derision among aspirant owner-occupiers for council estates, too.[45] And as Peter Collison found in his investigation into the infamous Cutteslowe Walls saga in Oxford, a débâcle that continued from the 1930s to the 1960s, some private owner-occupiers were ready and willing to fight against the attempt to mix social classes by building brick barriers across streets to keep out the council tenants.[46]

Three conclusions may be drawn from these examples. First, this represented an evolution of working-class life onto the new estates which, even before the Second World War had broken out, let alone finished, had *a priori* defeated the intentions of the transcendent neighbourliness implied in the language of wartime reconstruction. As Willmott and Young admitted, Woodford came from Bethnal Green (but they gave considerably more attention to the social divisions in the former than in the latter).[47] Second, these were gobbets of working-class consciousness from the 1950s and 1960s, an era which sociologists term as 'collective consumption' in housing, a term which hints at the shared and common experience of tenants in council estates . However, the above quotes warn against the danger in looking back on the unprecedented state provision of postwar council housing in those decades as fostering a social consensus implied in the notion 'collective consumption'. Third, ideas of rough and respectable were in their ways mechanisms not just of division but of solidarity with like.

The idea of neighbourliness was also held to be under threat from an alleged decline in the capacity of the working classes for organisation from below. The NCSS, for example, argued that 'traditional' working class culture was 'dead' as soon as it encountered the new estate, and that the new working-class required 'leadership from elsewhere': 'On the municipal estates there [is] a tendency for the residents to be drawn exclusively from those groups who do not throw up national leaders to organise community life'.[48] This judgement is somewhat puzzling, given the earlier conversion of many so-called dormitory estates into living estates by local action, action which was often initiated by leaders such as those identified by Ruth Durant and others, whose contribution had been recognised by the NCSS itself. It was the sociologist Norman Dennis, however, who made studies of both 'traditional' working-class life in the mining town of 'Ashton' and the process of social organisation on new estates, who really got to grips with the leadership question in new estates and neighbourhoods.[49] In a study of local leaders in the Community Associations movement, Dennis pointed to the changes in both leadership recruitment and leadership roles on new estates as consequential upon the phases of an estate's evolution. He examined the postwar estate of 'Boltwood', wherein a community association had been formed in 1948, very early in the estate's history, when the estate was a mud site, with no shops, no doctor's surgery or post office, and no bus service. Roads on the estate were unfinished. The first estate group was called 'the tenants' association', which was affiliated to the more militant Central Tenants' Association, a communist organisation. A number of 'leading spirits' in the tenants' association were skilled and semi-skilled manual workers, and a few were members of the Communist Party. Elsewhere, in early postwar Liverpool for example, Mitchell and Lupton noted the contribution of politically motivated individuals, trades unionists and 'housewives' in the formation of the residents' association there.[50] They agitated for local facilities, and in the early years of the tenants' association attendances at meetings were high, though often hectic. The new community centre which was eventually built was soon hosting well-attended weekly or fortnightly social evenings, sports events, shows and children's entertainments.[51]

The civic functions and the problem-solving role of Boltwood Community Centre, however, soon began to decline, as did numbers at the tenants' association meetings. The rooms of the centre were increasingly used for leisure activities by people who were unconnected with the community association. Furthermore, as the estate began to mature, and as the local groups achieved the facilities and resources they had campaigned for, or which they secured through subscription, there was an attenuation of the function of the initial leaders, who began to argue amongst themselves and to resign. The most salient point, however, lay in the fact that organisations followed a similar pattern to that observed by Durant at Edgware. They grew less concerned with activities of general interest to the estate and became geared towards activities which appealed to distinct sections of the local population. These organisations reflected a number of organising principles, notably age, gender and specific interests. For example, in Boltwood by April 1954 there was a Ladies' Section, comprised of 'twenty young respectable women', and an Old Age Pensioners' Association came into existence in 1955. Increasingly, any general activity on the estate which was promoted by the community association 'became hinged on two gambling activities', namely the football pools and the estate's tombola.[52] Elsewhere, for example in Barton, Oxford, local members of the WEA had been instrumental in bringing together residents in the early days of the estate.[53] As the estate matured, however, people became less interested in estate-based activities. A significant proportion of the estate's population – 40 per cent – eventually joined voluntary associations, whether religious, political, charitable or, more usually, sporting and recreational clubs and teams, which were usually located in facilities off the estate. This compared to 10 per cent in St Ebbe's. Similar developments were strongly in evidence in many other new suburban council estates.[54] And at roughly the same time as Mogey, a housing manager at Newton Aycliffe, who had worked with the community association, observed the same process there, too.[55]

A pattern emerged, then, of estate-wide sociability among many tenants at first, following which a more varied sociability developed, based upon distinct memberships or shared interests, or on specific issues, which displaced the estate-wide basis. Mogey's analysis, which went to the heart of the changes in working-class life engendered by the move to a new estate, was not a pessimistic one. 'The signs of a different social outlook in Barton', as opposed to St Ebbe's, he argued, were evident in increased privatism (discussed above) but also in 'the ability and willingness to form friendships and to join voluntary associations':

> [Barton] is in fact not a localised society nor do its inhabitants feel loyal to an isolating set of social customs. The inhabitants of Barton have lost their ties to a neighbourhood and gained in return citizenship in the wider and freer atmosphere of *the varied associational life* of a city.[56]

Such changes did not rule out neighbourliness, but they undermined the viability of the community association as a constantly mobilised neighbourhood movement. In addition to Dennis and Mogey, and to varying degrees of emphasis and enthusiasm, the sociologists Frank Bechhoffer, Maurice Broady, David Donnison, Ronald Frankenberg, Ruth Glass, John Goldthorpe, Josephine Klein, David Lockwood, T. Lupton, G. D. Mitchell, J. H. Nicholson, Jennifer Platt, Margaret Stacey and the singular Peter Willmott were all clear that wider social networks due to migration, the ability to enjoy more diverse interests as a happy consequence of affluence, and the adaptive role of both formal and informal associations focused on specific concerns or interests, were supplying alternatives to neighbourliness as a mechanism for bringing people together in postwar working-class housing developments.[57] For example, John H. Goldthorpe and the Luton team in the later 1960s noted, with conscious reference to Mogey, the more flexible and associative pattern of working-class social integration in a rapidly expanding boom town. They observed that membership of one or more voluntary associations amounted to 48 per cent of male manual workers, a figure which was apart from membership of trades unions. Of the wives of these men, 37 per cent belonged to one or more formal voluntary association.[58] The Luton team identified residential mobility as the source for these changes, and argued that privatism was now the 'major concern of the industrial worker'. Neighbours, moreover, still mattered, but they were not to be overestimated.[59]

The character of the associations observed by Goldthorpe and his team fell into two kinds. First were those which were likely to be almost wholly working-class in membership, such as working men's clubs, angling clubs, allotment societies, British Legion clubs, pigeon clubs, football clubs, weightlifting and body-building clubs, and council tenants' associations.[60] However, and this resonated strongly with the Luton survey's findings against *embourgeoisement*, few of these associations were comprised of lower-middle-class white-collar workers. The latter tended to belong to the second type of association: Freemasons, Conservative clubs, golf clubs, flying clubs, sailing clubs and school parent/teacher associations.[61] There was a little class mixing, but not much, in such associations as the cricket club, secondary modern parent/teacher associations, the Townswomen's Guild, gardening clubs and the residents' – as opposed to the tenants' – association.[62]

Interest-based associations thus undermined the neighbourhood unit and the community association as a neighbourhood formation. They could and did co-exist with neighbourliness in many areas,[63] but the important point is that they demonstrated that 'community' was alive at other points of social connection. For Norman Dennis, then, the neighbourhood as a basis for community had been overestimated in postwar planning. Instead, Dennis highlighted the significance of what he termed 'interaction communities' based around common interests, tastes and goals, as distinct from the more traditional 'social system' communities of the established working class. The decline of the latter and the rise of the former led Dennis to his fundamental proposition that 'housing estates represent that exaggerated result of processes that are common to our society' and this implied that inner urban areas would also eventually become more associative in their social life.[64] The reduction of localism as one variable amongst many in sociability and interaction meant that 'the Community Association movement as a device for making housing estates into communities is moribund'. It also raised serious issues for the ICS and its insistence upon primary group care as the basis for community.[65] Ruth Glass characteristically argued for a sociological paradigm shift away from a focus on 'all the trivial aspects of living together' for studies which focused upon associations and common interests.[66] Peter Mann's study of neighbourliness came to similar conclusions: 'In many cases all the people have in common is the fact they happen to live near one another. Community centres, clubs, and other such groups cater largely to special interests; they rarely attract the whole population of a neighbourhood.'[67]

It is interesting to note that a strongly similar development was occurring in the expanded towns[68] and new towns. Development corporations reported the successful actions of community associations in producing halls and centres which supplied the meeting spaces for a great many groups, clubs and societies. During the 1950s, a number of new town development corporations tended to view the campaigns for community centres, their instigation and the subsequent proliferation of groups who used them as healthy signifiers of neighbourhood life. Hence, many corporations offered support to members of the Community Associations movement who were working for their estates. At Bracknell in Berkshire, for example, the community association was praised for its role in searching for better facilities for a growing range of associations and societies, of which there were fifty-four by 1955.[69] Other development corporations observed similar patterns. But estate-wide action was only a short-term phenomenon, followed by a more varied culture of sociability.[70]

A number of other important points, which are related to each other, deserve recognition. Campaigns for new premises rarely included all or even a majority of the estate's tenants, a point which was applicable to the Community Associations movement in its early postwar heyday.[71] However, a few committed individuals could mobilise enough support to move enough local people to act. This was why some planners stressed the role of the 'critical minority' and their associational role in town development.[72] Equally as important, they could foster co-operation between local councils, non-local government organisations such as new town development corporations, and other institutions with a desire to promote an active social life on the new estates, notably the NCSS and its local councils of social service. For example, the Hemel Hempstead Council of Social Service had representatives on a number of neighbourhood councils.[73] When actions failed, as they sometimes did, this was a consequence not simply of disinterest from below, but of the failure of local agencies to co-ordinate properly. As Basildon Development Corporation lamented in 1956, for example, the scheme to provide a permanent community centre in the Fryern's Neighbourhood Centre had been 'delayed, despite all the Corporations' efforts to assist the County Council to start this project this year'.[74] That admission obscured the perspective, and the conditions, of the tenants at Fryerns. According to one Basildon stalwart, the first tenants were 'marooned' in 1952. Their estate was some way off from shops and they faced a journey of two miles to the nearest shop by an 'unreliable bus service'. It was thanks to the efforts of 'local leaders' such as the carpenter Ted Parsons, Bill Ferrier, a trades unionist and an active member of the Labour Party, and Alf Dove, 'born in a slum in Shoreditch', that a tenants' association was formed which 'stirred the Development Corporation into action in 1953'.[75]

This section concludes with the following three connected points. First, leadership was not wanting, but it was the preserve of a few. Second, the reasons for the decline of the Community Associations movement was connected with the demise of the neighbourhood unit concept. Third, the original notion of the neighbourhood had failed to anticipate wider changes in working-class sociability. As David Donnison has argued, looking back to the history of the Community Associations movement in the 1950s and 1960s, it was 'a questionable assumption that people want to spend their time making friends with neighbours by accidents of proximity rather than because they have shared interests ...'.[76]

Donnison is a link into the next section on Milton Keynes. During the 1960s he was Director of the planning and sociology think-tank the Centre for Environmental Studies (CES). The CES aimed to encourage a synthesis between social investigation and social policy. It also made a number of studies of the consequences of social and housing policies. Donnison was appointed as a consultant to Llewelyn-Davies, Weeks, Forestier-Walker and Bor, who were the planning team appointed by MKDC to draw up the master plan for Milton Keynes. His role was to inform the Llewelyn-Davies team of ideas about social patterns in the near future of urban society. To this end, Donnison, in his turn, appointed Melvin Webber, a professor of urban theory at the University of California, Los Angeles, to discuss his ideas about, and anticipations of, social relationships in the future urban context.

Webber is important because he understood that locality and neighbourhood were becoming less important to the interpretation of the changing nature of social relations in the city. For example, technology, notably the motor car, the telephone and the computer screen, were enabling people to communicate beyond the locality and to maintain kinship and friendship across considerable distances. Webber also stressed the significance of 'interest communities', people who came together not on the basis of proximity, but because they shared common interests and values, whether in their leisure time or as political and economic animals pursuing particular programmes or organisational goals. People formed clubs, societies and associations, and their memberships were recruited widely, usually beyond the basis of next-door-neighbourliness. Yet, just to be clear, Webber did not predict the imminent or ultimate death of localism. It was simply one basis for social connection, but by no means the only one. However, as society moved 'beyond the industrial age', it moved away from the more close-knit spatial environments of poor urban-industrial communities towards more flexible and diverse forms of social interaction.[77] Many English planners shared this broad view that England was becoming less a society of urban-industrial communities and more of an 'associatory society'.[78]

The Plan for Milton Keynes was redolent with such thinking. It contained a far more rigorously thought-out set of ideas and approaches for social development than the earlier new towns had produced. Social development in Milton Keynes meant two things. First, there were to be arrivals workers to supply information and assistance to newcomers to facilitate their settling-in. A major aim of these workers was to help offset the new town blues. Second, the *Plan* aimed to provide financial assistance and facilities to any societies or associations which, it anticipated, would be formed in the new city. However, it did not attempt to lay down any definitions or guidelines on the structure of social interaction in Milton Keynes. It was intended to be flexible, responsive and enabling rather than, as the neighbourhood units had been, deterministic.[79] In moving beyond localism as a key factor in social organisation, the new city of Milton Keynes may reveal much about the nature of social action in the final third of the twentieth century. It is not claimed here that the experience of Milton Keynes is exactly the same as other towns. However, broad trends can be identified in this new city, trends which can be observed elsewhere in English society.

Suburban solidarities in a new city: Milton Keynes in an era of 'fragmentation'

The growth of Milton Keynes coincided with significant social and economic trends in England since 1970. These changes have been viewed in a pessimistic way, as 'fragmentation'. As Eric Hopkins has argued, since the peak of trades union activity in the later 1970s, a new image of the working classes, said to mirror their increasing selfishness, came into focus. Sociologists writing about the better-off sections of the working classes 'drew attention to their self-centredness, at the same time referring to "sectionalism", "privatism", "instrumentalism" and even to "consumption cleavages" with reference to different social outlooks based on different consumption levels'.[80] This sociological perspective is particularly evident in interpretations of the accelerated growth in private tenure and a decline in council house renting. It has been argued that owner-occupiers form a distinct and growing housing sector whose 'objective conditions' result in a schism between their interests and those of non-owners. It has been further claimed that their 'lifestyle (e.g. suburbanism) leads them to claim a superior status to non owners ...'.[81] Given the findings of this book, the idea that suburbanism is the sole pursuit or possession of owner-occupiers is a misleading one. Anything that agitates people in the domain of consumption, that is, beyond workplace issues to do with pay and working conditions, will, it is alleged, reflect specific 'consumption sites' and residential particularism.[82]

Moreover, the changing occupational system and the more diverse post-industrial employment structure, with a greater proportion of smaller workplaces, have been seen to have led to increased divisions within the working classes. Together, these developments might constitute the alleged 'fragmentation' of urban social relations. Then again, they might not.[83]

Any examination of the impact of these trends on the nature of social life in Milton Keynes deserves a contextual framework which illustrates the linkages between these social developments and economic (that is, structural) changes in order to demonstrate what Milton Keynes reveals about them. As noted at the beginning of this section, Milton Keynes may be interpreted as a city moving beyond the industrial age, whose development throws into relief a number of wider changes in the economic and social organisation of late-twentieth-century England.

Economically, Milton Keynes's growth was based upon a growing service sector and manufacturing industry, both major planks of a successful strategy by MKDC to attract investment from within Britain and from overseas. Between 1967 and 1990 the service sector increased considerably from 32 per cent of the employment structure of Milton Keynes to 70 per cent.[84] This took place within a context of rapid growth, and by the mid-1980s Milton Keynes was a boom town. There was a problem here, however. Its rate of immigration outstripped its rate of job creation. A study of Britain's booming towns in 1985 found that most high growth towns in the South East shared an extremely low unemployment rate by comparison with the national figure of 13.2 per cent. However:

> The exception is Milton Keynes, where apparently the exceptionally fast growth rate in population has outrun its rate of job growth, rapid though the latter has been. The next highest levels of unemployment [found] at Basingstoke and Bracknell, are also associated with rapid population growth.[85]

The unemployed in Milton Keynes during the 1980s may, therefore, be seen as victims of the city's success in attracting people as well as jobs. Alongside the growth of unemployment, the nature of Milton Keynes's employment structure and its increasing dependence upon the service sector were creating problems of low pay and anti-social hours for many workers in Milton Keynes. This, on one level, was a by-product of an otherwise sound MKDC policy to encourage a mixture of sectors and companies, and especially smaller companies, that Milton Keynes now possesses. MKDC's reasoning was based upon a desire to avoid the legacy of over-dependence upon one or two huge large employers, where any mass redundancies or closure, as the earlier example of Corby's dependence on steelworks had illustrated, could seriously destabilise a new town's economy.[86] These policies must, furthermore, be set within the national trend of de-industrialisation, and the growing proportion of the service sector industries as the manufacturing sector diminished in size in proportion to the service sector from the early 1970s.[87]

The service sector has traditionally been associated with smaller workplaces and workforces than manufacturing. By 1976, only 10 per cent of firms in the service sector employed more than thirty-five employees, and most retail outlets had less than eight workers on their books.[88] The considerable widening of Milton Keynes's retail base from 1979, with the opening of the shopping building in Central Milton Keynes, and the accelerated growth of office space during the 1980s, assisted the trend to smaller workplaces. By the mid-1980s, two-thirds of all establishments employed ten or less people, about half the city's workforce.[89] The pattern persisted: MKDC's employers' survey for 1990 noted 'an increased proportion of establishments employing ten or less people'. By then, 64 per cent of the workforce worked in establishments of this size, despite the fact that the number of companies employing over 100 workers had increased.[90]

This is the wider context for a discussion of the downside of Milton Keynes's employment record. At the wealthier end of the service sector range of jobs, the growth of middle-class and lower-middle-class professional, managerial and intermediate occupations was paralleled by an increase in low-paid, part-time jobs which were concentrated in the service sectors of retail, distribution, education and 'other services'. In hotels and catering, furthermore, a majority of the workforce have been part-time.[91]

By the mid-1980s 'the vast majority of part-time jobs' were held by females and 90 per cent of all Milton Keynes's part-time occupied jobs were 'found in the service industries compared with 63 per cent of full-time occupied jobs'.[92] Women hairdressers, waitresses, shop assistants and checkout operators, kitchen hands, barmaids, receptionists and cleaners have, historically, remained among the worst paid in Britain.[93] This reflected wider inequalities in the local and national labour markets. As MKDC's employment survey for 1988 noted, 'the majority of females (60 per cent)' worked in the 'intermediate/junior non manual category', compared to 21 per cent of males. However, only 10 per cent of females compared with 26 per cent of males belonged to the 'professional/employer-manager' categories.[94] Higher levels of unemployment and part-time work among women were symptomatic of this wider structural inequality.

Small workplaces have also militated against trade union formation in Milton Keynes, due to the absence of an extensive personnel base. Both MKDC employers' surveys and materials from the Labour Party's Regional Business Centre in Luton illustrate clearly that whilst the larger manufacturing companies and older institutions such as British Rail Engineering Limited at Wolverton have trades unions, most of the small workplaces have not.[95] In the late 1970s MKDC, basing its findings on information from the Department of Employment and on regular bi-annual censuses of local employers, and placing these within the context of a local economy dominated by small units, emphasised 'the low level of unionisation' and the almost complete absence of notified industrial disputes in the city's history. One of its last glossy brochures extolling the virtues of business relocation to Milton Keynes argued that a major 'secret of success' was the city's workplace staff and the low level of trades unionisation:

> The workforce is young and adaptable and the level of skill is high. Industrial relations are excellent – there have been no notified disputes in the manufacturing and service sectors in the past ten years. Some companies have employees represented by one union, others by more than one while many firms run non-union plants.[96]

Milton Keynes thus reflects the national decline in trades union numbers since the later 1970s.[97]

It is also pertinent to note that the new estates of Milton Keynes have no geographically concentrated occupational working-class communities where houses were close to factories and mills. For Milton Keynes was planned as a zoned city, wherein residential and employment gridsquares have been kept separate. The majority of the 'economically active' population in Milton Keynes has travelled to work from home. By 1988, of the 65,000 who lived in Milton Keynes and went out to work, 46,000 commuted to work by bus, car or on foot; 18,900 commuted outside the city to work in the sub-region or further afield.[98] More men than women in Milton Keynes have commuted to work, and low income explains that among unskilled workers. Inequalities between the sexes in access to cars had marked consequences: 55 per cent of male unskilled workers commuted to work by car, compared with 19 per cent of females; 46 per cent of women who commuted walked to work, compared with 8 per cent of men.[99]

However, social organisation and action existed where trades unionism was of no great magnitude. Collective action consists not only in trades unionism but in non-workplace societies and associations. The relative demise of trades unions since the later 1970s has been paralleled by an increase in non-workplace associations, both nationally and within Milton Keynes. The sociologist David C. Thorns has asserted the importance of these associations as responses to broader social, economic and political processes. He argues that associations do not refute the variables of class, localism and gender. However, he continues, they do reflect a greater level of individualism born of affluence, and the demise of older forms of solidarities such as trades unionism and the working-class residential community. A more eclectic range of associations have, for Thorns, assumed the mantle of local action to confront key issues, but these associations were usually, although not always, short-term.[100] A number of important examples of associative action in Milton Keynes since 1970 validate Thorns's general approach.

One of the earliest campaigns, and certainly one of the most successful and long-running, was the agitation for a local hospital in Milton Keynes. In 1973 the Oxfordshire Regional Health Authority postponed plans for a new hospital. In response, a woman teacher, Margaret Jones, formed the Hospital Action Group with another woman friend. Their tactics were simple and effective, and drew upon common techniques of local agitation: a slogan was devised, 'Milton Keynes is dying for a hospital'; letters were written to the local press and to local councillors; a delegation visited Bill Benyon, Milton Keynes's Conservative MP; and a number of demonstrations to the Houses of Parliament in Westminster were arranged. The Health Minister Sir Keith Joseph and Geoffrey Rippon at the Department of the Environment received over 1,400 letters mobilised by the Hospital Action Group. Despite these actions, the health authorities appeared disinclined to respond, so the campaign was stepped up from the mid-1970s. Labour's Health Minister, Dr David Owen, was handed an 18,000-strong petition when he met with the protesters. The Group also registered itself as a charity as the hospital plans began to take shape in the later 1970s, and it used charitable status to win funding to fight on with its campaign. By 1980 it possessed over £5,000 to help the hospital with any early financial difficulties it might face.

In 1980, as the first piece of turf was cut out of the earth to mark the construction of the new hospital, the local press paid tribute to the initial organisers in their 'Our Hospital' special editions.[101] With much justification, Milton Keynes Urban Studies Centre, which was linked with the Open University, argued that the hospital group was 'an extremely effective protest movement'.[102]

That campaign united many people across class and tenure lines. The following example, however, is more pertinent to a specifically working-class campaign. The socio-economic profile of the estate of Beanhill has been characterised by the predominance of manual workers, and in terms of tenure three-quarters of all dwellings were rented from the local authority.[103] This campaign, then, mostly took place within the domain of 'collective consumption' in a period when the collective *provision* of housing has certainly been undermined by the Tory attack on council housing.

In 1992 a writer for the *Architect's Journal* lamented the 'indignity of pitched roofs' on the once flat-roofed, metal-clad dwellings of Beanhill and other estates.[104] If only this aesthete had known of the struggle the residents had engaged in to get those pitched roofs placed upon their Norman Foster Associates-designed houses. The first phase of Beanhill was completed by 1972.[105] As early as spring 1977, the Beanhill Residents' Association was holding one hundred-strong meetings to discuss, with MKDC officials, the condensation and general disrepair of their accommodation.[106] As the problems persisted, despite expenditure on them, tenants met regularly, often manifesting anger at the damp and mould and expense of fuel bills and repairs. The Beanhill Tenants' Action Group (BTAG) was formed, whose tactics included meetings, letters to the local press, letters to the local MP and the petitioning of MKDC and the Department of the Environment.[107] BTAG demanded new pitched roofs with loft insulation, general repairs to exteriors, and an upgrading of heating and insulation. This was unsurprising, really, given the emphasis which people have placed on traditional-looking, comfortable and permeable houses since the war.[108] By spring 1982, partly as a result of their actions, and partly as a result of MKDC's recent commitment to respond more practically to residents' needs and aspirations, the new roofs were begun. There were, however, to be delays and further inconveniences, about which the residents were keen to articulate their concerns, but by 1986 the roofs were completed.[109]

Unfortunately, the residents of Beanhill had a further problem awaiting them in the 1990s: the decision by Bucks County Council to close the Moorlands Community Centre in 1993, as part of a package of £2 million cuts proposed by the County Council's Social Services Department. There was a considerable reaction from local people against the cuts, and Beanhill's action must to some extent be viewed as an element of that.[110] They argued that the Centre was a meeting place for a wide variety of groups, including Job Search, Money Advice, a child abuse clinic, a 'budget lunch' club, holiday play schemes, youth and senior citizens' clubs, and other local groups which met there morning, afternoon and evening. The users' group organised a petition, and a coach load of protesters was mobilised. The leader of the users' group pointed out to the press that the Centre was the 'heartbeat' not just of Beanhill but of the nearby estate of Netherfield, which, she emphasised, had no such centre.[111]

The majority of users protesting against the cuts were women, as the local newspaper articles illustrate. The role of women in residents' and community associations' relations with local services in Milton Keynes has been demonstrated in many other episodes. For example, in the early 1980s the appearance of barriers and shrubbery at the ends of alleyways and redways which stopped at the road's edge was partly the result of local councillors responding to action by mothers on the estate of Fishermead whose children on bicycles had suffered accidents or near fatal collisions with cars.[112] What was the tenurial and occupational context of this action? We know from the slightly later 1991 census that Fishermead was at that time developing as an estate of mixed tenure. By 1991, 41 per cent of dwellings (including shared ownership with a housing association) were owner-occupied, 48 per cent were rented from local authorities, and the remainder were rented from private landlords or a housing association. Half of those in work were doing manual work, with professional and managerial residents numbering 15 per cent by the time of the 1991 census, and intermediate and clerical/administrative residents amounting to 33 per cent. ('Armed forces' and 'Inadequately described' accounted for the other percentages in these estates.[113])

Later, from the mid-1980s, women in Fishermead and the adjacent estate of Oldbrook were instrumental in the successful campaign to gain a chemist's shop and a general practitioner's surgery. Oldbrook's tenure was weighted more towards owner-occupation, with a figure approaching 60 per cent owner-occupation and 22 per cent public rental by the end of the decade. Oldbrook's socio-economic profile was largely white-collar, with intermediate/clerical and administrative jobs accounting for 43 per cent of employed people by the 1991 census, professional/managerial for 23 per cent, and manual for 34 per cent of Oldbrook's breadwinners.[114]

In the October 1985 edition of *Oggie Post*, the residents' newspaper for the Fishermead and Oldbrook estates, the Fishermead and Oldbrook Residents' Association noted the lack of medical facilities on the estates. A 'Doctor and Chemist Action Group' was formed by four women, one of whom also pointed out to the local press and its readers the continuing interface between public transport problems and access, as there were many pensioners on the estates 'hamstrung without a car'.[115] A door-to-door survey of people's requirements for a surgery and a chemist was carried out by the Group, and a petition of over 400 signatures was presented to the Family Practitioner's Committee in that year. The organisers had solicited the support of the Community Health Council to lend weight to it: 'The Family Practitioner's Committee, who had previously stated that there were not enough patients for a new surgery, finally wilted on seeing the results of the survey, and agreed to advertise the new post'.[116]

These campaigns and issues reflected two fundamental and continuing aspects of social change in postwar England. These were continuities pertinent to towns with or without neighbourhood units. One was the key organising role of women in these successful local struggles, demonstrating a strength of commitment to getting or improving local facilities. This commitment was articulated and fought for within the realm of 'informal politics'.[117] Local informal political action is often based upon the collective networks of women who are dependant on local centres. Centres and networks substitute for family and community, provide safe female environments and enable women to go out to work.[118] It is notoriously difficult to measure the extent of women's involvement in informal politics, but their predominance within it is undoubted.[119] We should be reminded here of Milton Keynes's economic context of restructuring, which decommissioned women from manufacturing employment for a greater range of service sector occupations, many of which were part-time, low-paid and required flexible hours in non-unionised working environments. Furthermore, the very existence of such networks and local facilities reflects the still primary role of most women as unpaid houseworkers and carers, and as the key co-ordinators of domestic consumption. It has long been the everyday experience of many women to undertake both paid formal employment and unpaid work in the home. Moreover, local estate facilities helped to break down the threat of home-based isolation which, as we saw in Chapter 5, affected some women in Milton Keynes.[120] Together, this means that 'women tend to be more concerned than men with their local residential environment, and therefore more likely to be provoked to campaign in their communities for better and more equitably located services, for better home and estate maintenance, for housing construction and design that meets their needs'.[121]

There is a strong thread of continuity here with earlier postwar housing developments. For example, during the 1960s Max Lock, who was concerned with the relationship between planning and the planned, singled out the importance of what he termed 'classic citizen victories', confrontations which occurred when people felt aggrieved by decision-making which adversely affected them. He gave as his example 'the housewives of Stevenage New Town' who in 1952 campaigned hard to keep the main street of their shopping centre free from the proposed new volumes of traffic. That struggle anticipated traffic-free shopping centres, a point stressed in oral testimony from Stevenage.[122] The development corporation was forced to revise its plans and produce a pedestrian-only centre.[123] In Swindon, also during the 1950s, a number of women, this time with the support of the development corporation's neighbourhood workers, demonstrated outside the shop of a local trader 'who was exploiting his monopoly position by charging extortionate prices'.[124] A similar episode was provided by the writer Margaret Lassell in her jaded account of a 'typical' street in a working-class council estate on the edge of a large industrial town. One man who went to the shop for his wife was unable to get in because women were picketing the butcher's in protest at the prices: 'I nearly had my eyes torn out when I went to go in'.[125] Other examples, such as the formation of groups to challenge the negative labelling of estates by the local press, and in Kirkby's case by television, are the tip of an iceberg of local groups which form to agitate for a particular purpose, then disband, sometimes in defeat, sometimes in success.[126]

A second point of significance from the foregoing is the concerted, sustained and effective action of propinquitous people. To this extent, Webber's view that the 'local realm' would remain important may be empirically demonstrated. However, his stronger emphasis upon 'community without propinquity' and 'nonplace urban realms' were rhetorical phrases designed to highlight those very processes mentioned in this chapter, namely the widening of social networks and a growing diversity in bases for community. This is particularly evident in the sphere of leisure.

Leisure in Milton Keynes[127]

As a student of leisure in Milton Keynes argued during the 1980s, the planners of Milton Keynes envisaged social interaction less in terms of physical proximity and physical density, and more by common interests and voluntary association.[128] A belief in a growing level of 'free choice' in a situation of 'changing fashions in demand' underpinned MKDC's views that a 'high degree of flexibility should be built into the greater part of the provision' to meet both 'the majority of demand' and also the many requirements of specialised leisure groups.[129] MKDC also recognised that there were more profound trends in British society which were affecting the ways in which people used their leisure time. These were rising real wages, an expectation of more free time for most people, changes in working conditions and greater mobility. Public and private leisure providers had to respond to these changes.[130] MKDC was in agreement with the Central Council for Physical Recreation's (CCPR) recent report, which stated that 'increased affluence and car ownership have enabled more people to choose from a wider range of activities'.[131]

During the 1960s, local government was 'given progressively more direction in the use of the local rate to provide leisure activity' and the Sports Council was established in 1964 to promote leisure as part of a drive not simply to improve Britain's battered sporting reputation at that time, but also to improve the physical well-being of the British people.[132] As the CCPR argued, many British towns and cities had a 'strong demand' for more outdoor and indoor sports and recreational facilities. In a new city like Milton Keynes, starting from scratch in an under-provided region, the planned provision of leisure had to meet this demand. Earlier new towns had made some strides in this direction.[133] From the outset, MKDC's recreation strategy for the new city was twofold. One was institutional: to enhance existing facilities and provide new ones which would be available to all in local activity centres across the city. The second was more 'bottom upwards': the encouragement of more informal leisure. Both will now be discussed.

Leisure centres were planned and built for Bletchley and Wolverton, and the campus schools were given enhanced sporting and entertainments facilities. Golf courses, and small local pitches and playing fields on estates, were constructed. Together, these facilities accommodated the major participant sports: football, cricket, rugby, golf, swimming, outdoor bowls, hockey and lawn tennis. Outdoor water sports, especially fishing, were generously catered for, and other outdoor pursuits such as rambling, cycling, camping and caravanning made up 'miscellaneous provision'. The Sports Council was adamant that this provision should be completed, lest areas of sporting or recreational activity be discriminated against.[134]

Cultural provision, however, was less generous. The city centre, for example, retains a reputation both locally and nationally for limited leisure activities at night: cinema, clubs and bars only. No central theatre or arts complex had been built thirty years after the new city's designation. In 1980 MKDC admitted to 'the woeful lack of night life' in the centre.[135] This was worsened by the decision of the new owners of the shopping building, POSTEL, in 1990, to close off the shopping mall at night. That killed off the scope for developing its evening and night-time recreational potential. The privatisation of the city centre caused a great deal of disappointment and unsuccessful campaigning among many in the new city who wanted a more vibrant and varied night life.[136]

The prolonged failure to provide a varied menu of urban leisure facilities for a growing city undermined the goal of a dynamic city centre acting as an entertainments magnet within a fluid yet cohesive social system, a magnet which might have appealed to all classes and cultures. Until the opening of The Point multiplex cinema and leisure complex in 1985, there was little reason to go to the city centre once the shops had shut. It is within this context, then, that the contribution of those who made their own leisure deserves recognition. Self-help assisted social formation in Milton Keynes.

This indigenous contribution has been ignored by superficial accounts of life in the new city. Writers on town planning, such as David Lock and Colin Ward, who have been involved in the social development of Milton Keynes, were angered at knocking copy in *The Times* and *Guardian* during 1992 which stressed Milton Keynes's 'desolation and soulless atmosphere'.[137] Both Lock and Ward pointed to Ruth Finnegan's *The Hidden Musicians: Music Making in an English Town* (1989), which detailed the great diversity and enthusiasm of the musicians, making many different types of music, in Milton Keynes. Finnegan, a social anthropologist at the Open University, found that classical musicians, brass bands, folk music, country and western, church and religious music, and popular music, especially rock, were being practised, played, listened to and enjoyed in locations all over the city. Finnegan was particularly impressed by the number of rock bands, for example, who played in front rooms, garages, clubs and pubs to a teenage and twenty- or thirty-something audience. Milton Keynes's rock culture was sub-divided into punk, new wave, heavy metal, new romantics, funk, soul, reggae, futurist and sixties sounds 'to quote just a few'. The culture was mainly but by no means exclusively male.[138]

Music and those who made it represented a significant element in the social formation of a new city during its early decades. People formed groups and bands on the basis of friendship, and shared interests and tastes. They made their own entertainment by playing their own music or cover versions. This was done sometimes to make money, but always for enjoyment. This culture and its internal diversity lend support to Webber's predictions of voluntary and interest-based forms of association. Moreover, and equally significantly, this was a grassroots creativity in leisure, not really a 'top down' commercial provision. Hence Finnegan found that views about uniform leisure, pacified leisure and commercially provided 'youth cultural' forms of leisure were reductionist attempts to grasp the nature of recreation. There was little that was pacified or spoon-fed about such music-making.[139]

Music, moreover, dovetailed the private with the public sphere, for it was also listened to at home. By 1988 most Milton Keynes homes had record players and radios, and 20 per cent had a compact disc player. Moreover, almost 100 per cent of people watched television, which was slightly higher than the national average, a phenomenon in part explained by the cable facilities supplied to 55 per cent of Milton Keynes homes. Over 65 per cent of households possessed a video recorder and 35 per cent had a home computer. These statistics were above the national average, but similar to local South Eastern levels.[140] Other evidence, furthermore, illustrates the popularity of gardening in Milton Keynes and the considerable level of do-it-yourself activity at home,[141] both of which remain general enthusiasms in English recreational life.[142]

Beyond the home and garden, people's recreational choices reflected the love of the outdoor life, suburban-style. Parks with lakes and canals for walking, fishing and water sports were widely used. For example, as the *Walnut Tree* estate review of 1990 found, at the nearby Caldecotte Lake 'residents frequently meet informally to walk there'. Moreover, 'organised walks and nature days have been well attended with numbers frequently surpassing expectations'.[143] People enjoyed watching or participating in a wide variety of indoor and outdoor sports. The most commonly participated in were swimming, golf, roller skating, football, cricket, rugby in a variety of local teams, equestrianism, and other 'dry sports' played or practised in local leisure centres. The most common form of organised participation in leisure was within sports clubs, whose membership totalled 17 per cent of the population. Rosemary Deem's *All Work and No Play*, a mid-1980s study of women's leisure in Milton Keynes, found that female participation rates were lower than male rates, for both outdoor sports, dry sports and the use of leisure facilities in general. And when women were at leisure centres it was not always for their own entertainment, but because they were accompanying their children.[144] MKDC found a similar state of affairs in 1989: 'Males were more likely to use leisure centres for dry sports than females; generally twice as many males participate in dry sports than women. Females are slightly more likely to escort others to facilities, i.e., children.'[145]

Sociable indoor entertainments reflected national trends. For example, 15 per cent of people in Milton Keynes were members of social clubs. The Point cinema was visited at least once within a twelve-month period by 56 per cent of the local population. Drinking in public houses remained very popular, as did, especially for women, dancing.[146] Here too, levels of participation were broadly similar to sub-regional and South Eastern averages outside London.[147] They also bore similarities to the leisure practices of another third generation new town, Telford, whose 'rank order' of leisure activities in 1980 was dominated by watching television, listening to music, outdoor sports, local car trips and visits to friends, drinking, and a variety of other sociable and home-based pursuits.[148]

It is pertinent to note that people have not simply used their free time for leisure, but also for philanthropic voluntary activities, ranging from the informal unpaid helpers 'dropping in on a neighbour' to paid officials working for self-help and interest-based groups. This tradition has remained strong in twentieth-century Britain, as Suzanne Mackenzie and Frank Prochaska have shown.[149] Hence in Milton Keynes by 1990, 7 per cent of the population worked for voluntary groups; 5 per cent of all women actively belonged to mothers' or women's support groups; 5 per cent of elderly people participated in senior citizens' associations and clubs. 'Members' of places of worship numbered 13 per cent, and religion embraced pastoral as well as spiritual activity. Just 3 per cent of Milton Keynes residents were members of their estate's residents' association.[150] As noted above, however, a small number of pioneering spirits could effectively mobilise considerable levels of association and collective self-help. For example, the Borough Council reported in 1992 on 'community development' action in the year 1991–92. This included thirty-seven grants to neighbourhood and 'local self-help groups', and other practical and financial assistance had been provided for residents' associations. Grants were made to voluntary organisations including the Citizens' Advice Bureau, the Council for Voluntary Organisations, Age Concern, the Racial Equality Council, Relate, the Council of Disabled People, over-fifties groups, after school clubs, other self-help groups, playgroups, toy libraries, black and ethnic minority groups, community centre management committees, and groups run by and for people with physical disabilities.[151]

Milton Keynes shares in the growing national trend, since 1970, of participation in residents' and tenants' groups, and in the continued higher participation of women in voluntary philanthropic action.[152] There is little in Milton Keynes's short social evolution, therefore, to suggest a static social life, and certainly not a declining one. Hence, it is necessary to repudiate the view that Milton Keynes was a city of bleakness and anonymity 'rather than a living community'.[153] It would be more accurate to argue that the unique urban design of Milton Keynes has done nothing to diminish the continuities in suburban and new town social organisation that this book has traced back to the interwar years.

Conclusion: an associative culture

Social connections and social relations on the postwar new estates and neighbourhoods discussed here were not in decline. It is impossible, however, to boil them down to a simple base such as 'neighbourhood'. The pattern of social interaction as it evolved since 1945, and was already evolving anyway, modified the territorialism implied by the neighbourhood unit. Furthermore, it transcended the wistful anticipations of cross-class mixing and local community mobilisation beloved of wartime and early postwar planners, politicians and community workers.

There is no need to throw the baby out with the bath water, however. For the new estates and neighbourhoods did continue to act in certain circumstances as bases for local action. If needs dictated, people could come together across their ostensible class and tenure divisions to agitate for those needs to be met. People associated for a particular purpose. The idea of the fragmentation of urban social relations may be turned on its head. Instead, groups of people demonstrated an ability to merge and engage in meaningful action.

The postwar housing developments witnessed the flowering of an associative culture, and that metaphor further suggests roots and stems in history. Chapter 2 pointed to the associative nature of active social relations in Edwardian garden suburbs, for example.[154] More generally, as Joanna Bourke, Ross McKibbin and Mike Savage have argued, for the period from the mid-nineteenth century to the mid-twentieth, workers had long been drawn together around the basis of shared needs, interests or enthusiasms. The consequent association could be short-lived and informal, or longer-term and more structured. Moreover, the character of these levels of association was often specific and their membership often exclusionary.[155] It was noted above that some movements could embrace other social classes, but many did not, and that was just as pertinent for earlier periods: 'Associations, groups and classes', noted McKibbin, 'lived and let live'.[156]

Formality and informality overlapped. Within the new estate, and within the context of an association, be it for leisure, voluntary or agitational activity, people could make neighbours, pursue friendships, maintain a polite and cordial nexus, or keep themselves to themselves. In consequence, there has been no recent denouement in working-class social life, because there has been no fragmentation of social relations in conditions of urban change.

Finally, as Chapter 2 demonstrated, differentiation both between and within classes was endemic to town life in Victorian, Edwardian and interwar England. And Chapters 3, 4 and 5 pointed to divisions within working-class life, in slum and suburb, during the 'collectivist era' of the 1940s to the early 1970s. To emphasise these wider continuities demonstrates the relevance of social history in our own times.

Notes

1 J. Bourke, *Working-Class Cultures in Britain, 1890–1960: Gender, Class and Ethnicity* (London, 1994), p. 137.

2 P. Howlett, 'The "Golden Age", 1955–73', in P. Johnson (ed.), *Twentieth Century Britain: Economic, Social and Cultural Change* (London, 1994), p. 320.

3 A. H. Halsey, 'Social trends since world war two', in L. McDowell, P. Sarre and C. Hamnett (eds), *Divided Nation: Social and Cultural Change in Britain* (London, 1989), pp. 21–3.

4 T. Bendixson and J. Platt, *Milton Keynes: Image and Reality* (Cam-

bridge, 1992), pp. 167–80.

5 On Manchester, see A. J. P. Taylor, 'Manchester', in A. J. P. Taylor, *Essays in English History* (Harmondsworth, 1976), pp. 307–25. On Los Angeles, see E. W. Soja, 'Taking Los Angeles apart', in C. Jencks (ed.), *The Postmodern Reader* (London, 1992), pp. 277–98.

6 R. Clarke (ed.), *Enterprising Neighbours: The Development of the Community Associations Movement in Britain* (London, 1990), p. 36.

7 S. G. Jones, *Workers at Play: A Social and Economic History of Leisure, 1918–1939* (London, 1986), pp. 122–6; L. E. White, *Community or Chaos: Housing Estates and their Social Problems* (London, 1950), pp. 14–15.

8 White, *Community or Chaos*, pp. 14–15.

9 NCSS, *New Housing Estates and their Social Problems* (London, 1937), foreword by Professor Ernest Barker, p. 3.

10 Ibid., p. 7; see above, Chapter 5, pp. 131–2.

11 Clarke, *Enterprising Neighbours*, p. 40.

12 T. Young, *Becontree and Dagenham: A Report Made for the Pilgrim Trust* (London; 1934), pp. 88–90.

13 R. Durant, *Watling: A Survey of Social Life on a New Housing Estate* (London, 1939), pp. 22–45.

14 Political and Economic Planning (PEP), 'Watling revisited', *Planning*, 14:270 (1947), pp. 68–6.

15 Ibid., p. 68.

16 E. Barker, 'Community centres and the uses of leisure', *Adult Education*, 11:1 (1939), pp. 8–9.

17 Durant, *Watling*, p. ix; see also R. Durant, 'Community and community centres', *Adult Education*, 11:1 (1939), pp. 36–48.

18 R. Glass (ed.), *The Social Background of a Plan: A Study of Middlesbrough* (London, 1948), pp. 17–19.

19 NCSS, *The Size and Social Structure of a Town* (London, 1943), p. 5.

20 NCSS, *Community Centres and Associations Conference* (London, 1943), pp. 5–7.

21 Ibid., pp. 9–13.

22 NCSS, *Size and Social Structure*, pp. 8–9.

23 J. H. Forshaw and Sir L. P. Abercrombie, *County of London Plan* (London, 1943), pp. 28–30; Sir L. P. Abercrombie, *Greater London Plan, 1945* (London, 1945), pp. 113–14.

24 G. Herbert, 'The neighbourhood unit principle and organic theory', *Sociological Review* (New Series) 11:2 (1963), pp. 165–7.

25 See above, Chapter 2, p. 38.

26 M. Broady, *Tomorrow's Community: A Report of the Working Party set up by the National Federation of Community Associations* (London, 1979), p. 5.
27 Ibid., p. 3.
28 *Parliamentary Debates, House of Commons* (*Hansard*), Fifth Series, Vol. 422, 1945–46, cols 1089–90.
29 See, for example, Stevenage Development Corporation, *The New Town of Stevenage* (Stevenage, 1949), pp. 24–5.
30 Basildon Development Corporation, *Sixth Annual Report For the Period Ended March 31st, 1955* (*Parliamentary Papers*, 1955–56 (91) Vol. XXV, p. 41).
31 A. H. Halsey (ed.), *Trends in British Society Since 1900* (London, 1974), p. 551. Also, see below, pp. 170–1.
32 P. Willmott, 'Housing density and town design in a new town: a pilot study at Stevenage', *Town Planning Review*, 33:2 (1962), p. 125.
33 D. T. Herbert and H. B. Rodgers, 'Space relationships in neighbourhood planning', *Town and Country Planning*, 35:4 (1967), p. 198.
34 R. J. Hacon, 'Neighbourhoods and neighbourhood units', *Sociological Review* (New Series) 3:2 (1955), p. 238.
35 'Next door neighbours', *Mass Observation Bulletin* (New Series) 15, February 1948 (London, 1948).
36 Ibid.
37 Hacon, 'Neighbours and neighbourhood units', pp. 239, 245.
38 G. Gorer, *Exploring English Character* (London, 1955), p. 58.
39 Ibid., p. 58.
40 J. M. Mogey, F*amily and Neighbourhood: Two Studies of Oxford* (Oxford, 1956), p. 84.
41 Ibid., pp. 84–5.
42 See above, Chapter 4, pp. 112–13; Chapter 5, pp. 132–4.
43 E. Roberts, *Women and Families: An Oral History, 1940–1970* (Oxford, 1995), pp. 33, 210.
44 P. Willmott, *The Evolution of a Community* (London, 1960), p. 79.
45 J. Tucker, *Honourable Estates* (London, 1966), quote p. 27, and generally, pp. 23ff.
46 P. Collison, 'The Cutteslowe saga', *New Society*, 25 April 1963, pp. 18–20; see also P. Collison, *The Cutteslowe Walls* (London, 1963), passim.
47 P. Willmott and M. Young, *Family and Class in a London Suburb* (London, 1960), pp. 111–22.
48 NCSS, *Our Neighbourhood* (London, 1950), p. 15.

49 N. Dennis, F. Henriques and C. Slaughter, *Coal is Our Life* (London, 1956); N. Dennis, 'Changes in function and leadership renewal: a study of the Community Associations movement and problems of small voluntary groups in the urban locality', *Sociological Review* (New Series) 9:1 (1961), pp. 58–79.

50 G. D. Mitchell and T. Lupton, 'The Liverpool estate', in G. D. Mitchell, T. Lupton, M. W. Hodges and C. S. Smith, *Neighbourhood and Community: An Inquiry into Social Relationships on Housing Estates in Liverpool and Sheffield* (Liverpool, 1954), pp. 34–6

51 Dennis, 'Changes in function', pp. 71–4; Mitchell and Lupton, 'The Liverpool estate', pp. 25–33.

52 Dennis, 'Changes in function', p. 73.

53 Mogey, *Family and Neighbourhood*, pp. 113, 115.

54 See, for example, M. Jeffreys, 'Londoners in Hertfordshire: the South Oxhey estate', in R. Glass, E. Hobsbawm et al., *London: Aspects of Change* (London, 1964), p. 241; J. H. Nicholson, *New Communities in Britain: Achievements and Problems* (London, 1961), p. 140; N. H. Rankin, 'Social adjustment in a North-West newtown', *Sociological Review* (New Series) 11:3 (1963), p. 298.

55 E. M. B. Hamilton, 'On living in a new town', *Society of Housing Managers' Quarterly Review*, 4:4 (1956), p. 7.

56 Mogey, *Family and Neighbourhood*, p. 156 (emphasis added).

57 D. Donnison, 'Foreword' to Clarke, *Enterprising Neighbours*, p. ix; R. Frankenberg, *Communities in Britain: Social Life in Town and Country* (Harmondsworth, 1971), p. 233; Glass, *The Social Background of a Plan*, Chapter 4, n. 65 for example; J. H. Goldthorpe, D. Lockwood, F. Bechhofer and J. Platt, *The Affluent Worker: Political Attitudes and Behaviour* (Cambridge, 1968), p. 77; J. Klein, *Samples From English Cultures* (London, 1965), I, p. 231; Mitchell and Lupton, 'The Liverpool estate', pp. 76–7; Nicholson, *New Communities in Britain*, pp. 140–1; J. Platt, *Social Research in Bethnal Green* (London, 1971), p. 58; M. Stacey, E. Batstone, C. Bell and A. Murcott, *Power, Persistence and Change: A Second Study of Banbury* (London, 1975), pp. 50–69, 143–7; P. Willmott, *Community Initiatives: Patterns and Prospects* (London, 1989), p. 88.

58 J. H. Goldthorpe, D. Lockwood, F. Bechhofer and J. Platt, *The Affluent Worker in the Class Structure* (Cambridge, 1971), pp. 93–4. (The Luton team felt this was a low level of associational attachment.)

59 Goldthorpe, Lockwood, Bechhoffer and Platt, *The Affluent Worker: Political Attitudes and Behaviour*, p. 77; *The Affluent Worker in the Class*

Structure, p. 91.

60 Goldthorpe, Lockwood, Bechoffer and Platt, *The Affluent Worker in the Class Structure*, pp. 110–11, and Appendix B, p. 198.

61 Ibid., Appendix B, p. 198.

62 Ibid., pp. 110–11, and Appendix B, p. 198.

63 See, for example, Mitchell and Lupton, 'The Liverpool estate', pp. 20–43.

64 N. Dennis, 'The popularity of the neighbourhood community idea', in R. E. Pahl (ed.), *Readings in Urban Society* (Oxford, 1969), p. 84.

65 Ibid., pp. 91, 78; see also N. Dennis, 'Community and sociology', in P. Kuenstler (ed.), *Community Organisation in Great Britain* (London, 1961), pp. 130–1.

66 Cited in Dennis, 'Popularity of the neighbourhood community idea', p. 77.

67 P. H. Mann, 'The concept of neighbourliness', *American Journal of Sociology*, 60:2 (1954), p. 154.

68 M. Harloe, *Swindon: A Town in Transition. A Study in Urban Development and Overspill Policy* (London, 1975), p. 127.

69 Bracknell Development Corporation, *Fifth Annual Report for the Period Ended March 31, 1955* (*Parliamentary Papers* 1955–56 (91), Vol. XXV, p. 80).

70 See, for example, Harlow Development Corporation, *Ninth Annual Report for the Period Ended March 31, 1955* (*Parliamentary Papers* 1955–56 (91) Vol. XXV, p. 227); Crawley Development Corporation, *Eighth Annual Report For the Period Ended March 31, 1956* (*Parliamentary Papers* 1955–56 (91) Vol. XXV, p. 143).

71 S. Fielding, P. Thompson and N. Tiratsoo, *'England Arise': The Labour Party and Popular Politics in 1940s Britain* (Manchester, 1995), pp. 127–8.

72 M. Broady, 'Social change and town development', *Town Planning Review*, 36:4 (1966), pp. 270, 274–7.

73 Hemel Hempstead Development Corporation, *Eighth Annual Report for the Period Ended March 31, 1955* (*Parliamentary Papers* 1955–56 (91) Vol. XXV, p. 272).

74 Basildon Development Corporation, *Seventh Annual Report for the Period Ended March, 31, 1956* (*Parliamentary Papers* 1955–56 (365) Vol. XXV, p. 46).

75 P. Lucas, *Basildon: Behind the Headlines* (Basildon, 1985), pp. 57, 60.

76 Donnison 'Foreword', in Clarke, *Enterprising Neighbours*, p. ix.

77 This discussion is based upon the following articles by Melvin Webber:

'Planning in an environment of change, part 1: beyond the industrial age', *Town Planning Review*, 39 (1968–69), pp. 179–95; 'Planning in an environment of change, part 2: permissive planning', *Town Planning Review*, 39 (1968–69), pp. 277, 95; 'The urban place and the nonplace urban realm', in M. Webber et al. (eds), *Explorations into Urban Structure* (Philadelphia, 1971), pp. 79–153; 'Order in diversity: community without propinquity', in L. Wingo (ed.), *Cities and Space: The Future Use of Urban Land* (Baltimore, 1970), pp. 23–54.

78 See, for example, F. J. C. Amos, 'The planner's responsibility to the community', SSRC/CES Joint Weekend Conference, 5–7 July 1968 (Glasgow, unpublished papers, 1968), pp. 3–4.

79 Llewelyn-Davies, Weeks, Forestier-Walker and Bor (for MKDC), *The Plan for Milton Keynes* (Milton Keynes, 1970), II, pp. 122–35.

80 E. Hopkins, *The Rise and Decline of the English Working Classes, 1918–1990: A Social History* (London, 1991), p. 278.

81 P. Saunders, 'Beyond housing classes: the sociological significance of private property rights in means of consumption', in McDowell, Sarre and Hamnett, *Divided Nation*, pp. 205–6.

82 See the discussion by C. Hamnett, 'Consumption and class in contemporary Britain', in C. Hamnett, L. McDowell and P. Sarre (eds), *The Changing Social Structure* (London, 1993), pp 199–243.

83 J. Allen 'Fragmented firms, disorganised labour?', in J. Allen and D. Massey (eds), *The Economy in Question* (London, 1994), pp. 184–227.

84 MKDC, *The Plan for Milton Keynes*, II, p. 97; Milton Keynes and North Bucks TEC, *Economic Review 1993* (Milton Keynes, n.d.), p. 3.

85 A. G. Champion and A. E. Green, *In Search of Britain's Booming Towns: An Index of Local Economic Performance for Britain* (Newcastle, 1985), p. 33.

86 MKDC, *Seven Years On: Household Survey, 1976, Technical Report 3: Employment* (Milton Keynes, 1977), p. 42. M. S. Grieco, 'Corby: new town planning and imbalanced development', *Regional Studies*, 19:1 (1985), pp. 9–18.

87 G. Tweedale, 'Industry and de-industrialisation', in R. Coopey and N. Woodward (eds), *Britain in the 1970s: The Troubled Economy* (London, 1996), pp. 251–2.

88 MKDC, *Seven Years On: Household Survey, 1976, Technical Report 3: Employment*, p. 43.

89 MKDC, *Employer's Survey Report, 1987* (Milton Keynes, 1987), p. 19.

90 MKDC, *Employer's Survey Report, 1990* (Milton Keynes, 1990), p. 23.

91 MKDC, *Employer's Survey Report, 1987*, p. 9.

92 Ibid., p. 9.

93 S. Bowlby, 'From corner shop to hypermarket: women and food retailing', in J. Little, L. Peake and P. Richardson (eds), *Women in Cities: Gender and the Urban Environment* (London, 1988), p. 74.

94 MKDC, *Milton Keynes Household Survey, 1988, Employment Technical Report* (Milton Keynes, 1989), p. 1.

95 This is based on MKDC, *Labour Resources* (Milton Keynes, n.d. 1979?).

96 MKDC, *What's the Secret of Success in Milton Keynes?* (Milton Keynes, n.d. 1990?). This has no page numbers.

97 *Social Trends* 23 (London, 1993), pp. 158–9.

98 MKDC, *Milton Keynes Household Survey, 1988, Employment Technical Report*, pp. 20–1.

99 Ibid., p. 34.

100 D. C. Thorns, *Fragmenting Societies? A Comparative Analysis of Regional and Urban Development* (London, 1992), pp. 272–3.

101 *Milton Keynes Gazette*, 13 June 1980; 20 June 1980; 30 March 1984.

102 Milton Keynes Urban Studies Centre, *Notes on Milton Keynes* (Milton Keynes, 1981), p. 24.

103 Information on occupations comes from Milton Keynes Borough Council, *People and Work in Milton Keynes: A Profile of Settlements from the 1991 Census; 10% Sample, Part 2* (Milton Keynes, 1993), p. 15. Information on tenure is derived from Milton Keynes Borough Council, *People and Housing in Milton Keynes: A Profile of Settlements from the 1991 Census* (Milton Keynes, 1993), p. 27.

104 Also, see above, Chapter 4, p. 105.

105 N. Pevsner and E. Williamson, *The Buildings of England: Buckinghamshire* (Harmondsworth, 1993), p. 505.

106 *Milton Keynes Express*, 22 April 1977.

107 *Milton Keynes Express*, 22 October 1981.

108 See above, Chapter 3, pp. 68–9; Chapter 4, pp. 99–105.

109 *Milton Keynes Express*, 11 March 1982; *Milton Keynes Gazette*, 22 March 1985; 21 June 1985; *Milton Keynes Mirror*, 14 August 1986.

110 On local feeling against the cuts generally, see *Milton Keynes Citizen* and *Milton Keynes Gazette*, 7 and 14 January 1993.

111 *Milton Keynes Gazette*, 7 January 1993.

112 *Milton Keynes Gazette*, 13 November 1981.

113 Milton Keynes Borough Council, *People and Housing in Milton Keynes: A Profile of Settlements from the 1991 Census*, p. 99; Milton Keynes Borough Council, *People and Work in Milton Keynes: A Profile of Settlements from the 1991 Census; 10% Sample, Part 2*, p. 65.

114 Milton Keynes Borough Council, *People and Housing in Milton Keynes: A Profile of Settlements from the 1991 Census*, p. 163; Milton Keynes Borough Council, *People and Work in Milton Keynes: A Profile of Settlements from the 1991 Census; 10% Sample, Part 2*, p. 104.

115 *North Bucks Standard*, 18 April 1986.

116 *Milton Keynes Herald and Post*, 20 February 1987.

117 L. Bondi and L. Peake, 'Gender and the city: urban politics revisited', in Little, Peake and Richardson, *Women in Cities*, p. 35.

118 S. Mackenzie, 'Balancing our space and time: the impact of women's organisations on the British city, 1920–1980', in Little, Peake and Richardson, *Women in Cities*, p. 52.

119 Bondi and Peake, 'Gender and the city', p. 35.

120 Mackenzie, 'Balancing our space', pp. 51–2.

121 Quote from S. Mackenzie and D. Rose 'Industrial change, the domestic economy and home life' (1983) cited in Bondi and Peake, 'Gender and the city', p. 33.

122 H. and C. Rees, *The History Makers: The Story of the Early Days of Stevenage New Town* (Stevenage, 1991), pp. 85–9.

123 M. Lock, 'The planners and the planned', *Listener*, 18 March 1965, p. 398.

124 Harloe, *Swindon*, p. 120.

125 M. Lassell, *Wellington Road* (London, 1962), p. 28.

126 *Liverpool Daily Post*, 24 January 1962; 17 February 1962; J. B. Mays, 'New hope in newtown', *New Society*, 22 August 1963, p. 12; *Milton Keynes Citizen*, 13 January 1982.

127 The term 'leisure' often seems apparent at first, but when one considers the borderlines between work and non-work, the distinctions between the two are not so clear, and a great deal of sociological theory has been devoted to determining whether leisure time is really a time of 'leisure', or best seen as time when an amalgam of non-work activities, which are not all for fun, take place. Moreover, for the unemployed, non-work time in the sense of not going out to work is rarely 'leisure time' because of the search for work and the disappearance of the tangible distinction between work and leisure when people do not leave their home for their place of employment every day. In this section, leisure is taken to mean those activities which people choose to do, whether employed or unemployed, because they do not perceive those activities as 'work'. As John Wilson argues: 'we should not abandon the attempt to define leisure simply because exceptions to any definition we agree upon will always be

found. Leisure is essentially "autotelic" activity. In other words, it is chosen primarily for its own sake ... Leisure is to be distinguished from whatever has to be done, it is voluntary, and the motivation is intrinsic': J. Wilson, *Politics and Leisure* (London, 1988), p. 2.

128 S. Cox, 'Changing concepts and attitudes to the provision of leisure in a new town: Milton Keynes' (Ealing College of Higher Education, unpublished BA (Hons) Humanities project, n.d.), p. 79.

129 Llewelyn-Davies, Weeks, Forestier-Walker and Bor, *Milton Keynes Plan: Interim Report to the Milton Keynes Development Corporation* (London, 1968), p. 9.

130 Ibid., p. 83.

131 In MKDC et al., *Recreation: Recreation Plan for Milton Keynes* (Milton Keynes, 1970), p. 1.

132 J. Clarke and C. Critcher, *The Devil Makes Work: Leisure in Capitalist Britain* (London, 1985), p. 87; on the Sports Council, see T. Mason, *Sport in Britain* (London, 1988), pp. 81–3.

133 Bracknell and Harlow, for example, were among the first towns in Britain to be provided with comprehensive sports centres: MKDC et al., *Recreation Plan for Milton Keynes*, pp. 2–3.

134 Ibid., pp. 11–21.

135 D. White, 'What's so bad about Milton Keynes?', *New Society*, 17 April 1988, p. 97.

136 C. Ward, *New Town, Home Town* (London, 1993), pp. 99–102.

137 D. Lock, 'MK, new towns, and the British spirit', *Town and Country Planning* (April 1992), p. 108; Ward, *New Town*, pp. 61–2.

138 R. Finnegan, *The Hidden Musicians: Music Making in an English Town* (Cambridge, 1989), pp. 104–6.

139 Ibid., p. 123.

140 MKDC, *Milton Keynes Insight, 1988* (Milton Keynes, 1989), p. 4.

141 As at September 1996, Milton Keynes New City contained seven DIY superstores, plus a host of hardware merchants, ironmongers, home inprovement centres and tool merchants. The new city and the borough of Milton Keynes, which includes the nearby rural district, contained seven sizeable garden centres with nurseries, and a host of other smaller outlets. See the *Thomson Local: Milton Keynes, Towcester and Buckingham Area, 1996–97* (Farnborough, 1996), pp. 59, 95. See also above, Chapter 4, pp. 103–4.

142 E. Jacobs and R. Worcester, *We British: Britain Under the Moriscope* (London, 1990), p. 126.

143 MKDC, *Walnut Tree Neighbourhood Review* (Milton Keynes, 1990),

p. 4.

144 R. Deem, *All Work and No Play: The Sociology of Women and Leisure* (Milton Keynes, 1986), pp. 1–7.

145 MKDC, *Milton Keynes Household Survey, 1988: Leisure and Recreation, Technical Report*, p. 15.

146 This discussion is based on MKDC, *Milton Keynes Household Survey, 1988: Leisure and Recreation, Technical Report*, pp. 1–19; Milton Keynes Borough Council, *Household Survey, 1990* (Milton Keynes, 1990), pp. 43–46; J. Bishop, *Milton Keynes: The Best of Both Worlds: Public and Professional Views of the New City* (Bristol, 1986), pp. 92–3, and the writer's participant observation of the new city's pubs since 1986.

147 *Social Trends* 21 (London, 1991), pp. 178–9.

148 J. R. Kelly, *Leisure Identities and Interactions* (London, 1983), pp. 16–17.

149 Mackenzie, 'Balancing our space', pp. 41–60; F. Prochaska, *The Voluntary Impulse* (London, 1988), pp. 2–7.

150 Milton Keynes Borough Council, *Household Survey, 1990*, p. 46.

151 Milton Keynes Borough Council, *Community Development Strategy: Summary* (Milton Keynes, 1992), p. 3.

152 L. Cairncross, D. Clapham and R. Goodlad, 'The origins and activities of tenants' associations in Britain', *Urban Studies*, 29:5 (1992), p. 710, *Social Trends* 23 (London, 1993), pp. 154–5

153 J. Stevenson, 'The Jerusalem that failed? The rebuilding of post-war Britain', in T. Gourvish and A. O'Day (eds), *Britain Since 1945* (London, 1991), p. 102.

154 See above, Chapter 2, pp. 31–2.

155 Bourke, *Working-Class Cultures*, p. 169; R. McKibbin, 'Work and hobbies in Britain, 1880–1950', in R. McKibbin (ed.), *The Ideologies of Class: Social Relations in Britain, 1880–1950* (Oxford, 1991), pp. 165–6; M. Savage and A. Miles, *The Remaking of the British Working Class, 1840–1940* (London, 1994), pp. 65–8.

156 McKibbin, 'Work and hobbies', p. 166.

7

Invincible suburbs? Brave new towns? Some conclusions and connections

Synopsis

The former Secretary of State for the Environment, John Selwyn Gummer, argued that historians should be among many different professional groups included in the current debates about urban growth and town design.[1] Alongside historians of planning and architecture, social historians have much to offer to these debates. For there are practical lessons to be learned by policy-makers from past experiences in urban migration. Social change is inextricably linked with town development. There is much evidence to show that for many people, the well-planned and provisioned suburban and new town context is much sought after and perceived as a good place in which to live. Hence, discussions on town design which take knee-jerk reactions against suburbanism and dispersal, and which ignore these general findings, may result in unpopular new housing developments. It is a shame that Gummer himself set his face against 'the suburbs'. His rationale, manifesting no originality at all, was that they are 'soulless' and that many suburban estates are not integrated within their wider 'communities'. Gummer also articulated some disquiet about dispersal in general, and new towns are in themselves impossible without dispersal.[2]

The findings of this book contradict such gloomy perspectives. Chapter 2 demonstrated that postwar urban dispersal was the continuation both of a popular trend to suburban living and of official housing policies. Chapter 3 argued that working-class households moved out for a number of reasons, foremost of which was the desire for improved housing. As Chapter 4 showed, the new house and the improved residential environment made an important contribution to the ease with which the majority of people settled down. When housing failed to meet expectations, however, discontent could and did ensue, as Chapter 5 demonstrated. Yet the house, despite its undoubted importance, did not foster an overly home-centred and desiccated privatism among the postwar working classes. Chapter 6 emphasised the lively and diverse social life on the postwar new estates, and pointed to the flowering of an associative culture. Privatism and participation in a wide range of social activities were not, then, mutually exclusive. This important understanding explains why the grim diagnoses of suburban neurosis and new town blues, discussed in Chapter 4, were misleading. The undoubted problems of moving on and settling in were, for the majority, overcome as newcomers sought to make a fresh life for themselves. They attempted to achieve a meaningful balance between home, wider family and the social and material opportunities offered by the suburban and new town context.

Balance

Suburban and new town migration may be regarded, indeed 'must be regarded as being composed of working-class people in search of a new equilibrium'.[3] That important observation, first made for Liverpudlians displaced by war work and relocated Sheffield slum dwellers, is strongly relevant to the wider changes and continuities discussed here. Moreover, the pursuit of a new social equilibrium has been empirically identified in other countries. Hence the English experience has been part of a wider trend. For example, during the 1960s, the American sociologist Herbert J. Gans stressed the importance of the quest for balance, and the stable conditions which that term implied, in his study of 'a much maligned part of America, suburbia'.[4] This quest was actively pursued by people with 'the most urgent space needs, large families and blue-collar workers'. Gans did not wax hyperbolic about the intrinsic suburban appeal of his case study town – Levittown, in New York state – but his findings indicated the synthesis of motives behind the aspiration to live there. The majority of Levittowners, he wrote, 'did not regret leaving the city':

> nor did they flee from it. [They] were not looking for roots or a rural idyll, not for a social ethic or a consumption-centred life, not for civic participation or for sense of community. They wanted the good or comfortable life for themselves and their families.[5]

The pursuit of material domestic improvement was also evident in a later 1950s study of auto-workers in a Californian suburban town. It was clear that the quest for a better home life was evident before the workers and their families moved away, and they were prepared to move as a group of workers in order to enjoy a new life. There is a certain similarity here, therefore, with the aspirations and experiences of groups of workers prepared to move with the Industrial Selection Scheme and the Direct Nominations Scheme in England. As with car workers in Luton, England, moreover, there was no *embourgeoisement* of American blue-collar suburbanites.[6] (There is scope for further comparative historical study in both respects.) In both countries, there was a continuity of working-class norms and preferences, not a radical alteration of them, within improved material and residential conditions.

These findings were relevant to English working-class migrants during the later 1950s and 1960s. Yet Gans and others who were sympathetic to working-class suburbs were marginalised within the popular sociological debates in England during the 1960s. The continuing textual hegemony of Michael Young and Peter Willmott was in no small part responsible for that. Gans's analysis, however, has since evoked greater enthusiasm. Writing about Milton Keynes in the mid-1980s, Jeff Bishop, of Bristol University's School for Advanced Urban Studies, noted that Gans's findings were very applicable to that suburban new city and its 'balances between public and private, local and area-wide activity'.[7] That is, people wanted convenient access to local facilities, but they also wanted to enjoy leisure opportunities elsewhere, and to participate in kinship and friendship networks which were wider than the local context. This notion also involved a further dovetailing between the enjoyment of urban amenities and convenient access to the countryside. Balance is, furthermore, a useful term to describe the negotiation between private and associational life on the postwar new estates, because it has important implications for a wider understanding of contemporary social relations in a changing society. For if the balance is upset, it may trigger an associative response which seeks to restore equilibrium to the estate.

Challenges to the social equilibrium came in the form of riots in suburban council estates during the 1980s and early 1990s. The writer Beatrix Campbell, observing 'Britain's dangerous places', has shown how a small number of activists – usually committed female residents – were able to mobilise enough people to take action to address the crisis of morale and to improve the inadequate or burnt-out facilities of the estates. This was often in the face of confused or prating politicians. Residents' associations also had to negotiate the uncoordinated apparatus of both statutory and voluntary agencies.[8] Recent studies of unpopular and declining council estates made for the Joseph Rowntree Foundation demonstrate similar efforts of a small number of committed residents, again usually women, addressing the social and resource problems of their estates.[9] Without the centrality of residents' associations, initiatives adopted to solve an estate's problems have foundered. Moreover, although the act of organisation on estates was left to a few, Ann Holmes's study of peripheral estates showed that 87 per cent of her sample knew that residents' groups were more likely to take effective action than individuals. Furthermore, over three-quarters of residents liked their estates: they wanted to see them regenerated.[10]

These are important continuities in social action on new estates. But they exist in conditions of structural change. Since 1979, with the decline in the provision and consumption of council housing, there has been an increasing emphasis upon networks and partnerships, involving local government, central government, private companies, voluntary agencies and, at the hub of this, the residents themselves. Many estates have seen housing managers appointed within a growing emphasis upon 'estate management', and the more residents are involved in the management process, the more successful estate management is.[11] Furthermore, since 1981 increasing numbers of council estates throughout England have been 'privatised', sold off to housing associations in order to off-load the economic costs from the state. Housing associations are responsible for growing numbers of new starts in house building, whereas councils are, for the time being at least, unable to commit to mass house building.[12]

On a different level, the economic determinants affecting many estates have undergone considerable alteration and decline since 1970. Many of the poorer council estates are prevalent in the suburban rings around the old heartlands of the industrial revolution, but they are also to be found in most towns where economic insecurity has taken root. Hence the poor inner cities and the poor outer suburbs share a common danger. Once smart new suburban estates have been transformed as unemployment has, literally, struck home.[13]

There is a further continuity between inner urban areas and the outer estates from the 1920s to the present: gender has been important in the organisation of residents from below. Support networks of women have grown and adapted as the capacity for mutual self-help to protect the needs of women and their families has continued to evolve. This last point must also be considered in relation to the growth of the welfare state and its agencies. These have increasingly taken over key primary caring and health-related roles once largely the domain of women in poor areas. As Chapter 6 showed, greater dependency on these services has led to a more associative localism in their defence, rather than the close reliance upon those women who performed such vital roles in pre welfare state slums.[14] As these communities dispersed, the roles of women underwent subtle changes in common with the wider context of working-class life. Yet the basic position of women as the health-keepers and home-keepers of their families remains evident in the working-class estates of suburbs and new towns, as was evident in Chapter 6.[15]

Throughout the twentieth century, the types of local action described in this book have sometimes been successful, sometimes partly successful, and occasionally unsuccessful, as work by the Lancaster Regionalism Group has demonstrated.[16] However, success, or the lack of it, in local action is historically less significant than the act of organisation itself. For when the balancing of space and time required for the reproduction of the family or the household is taken into account, and when the problems facing poorer women in terms of travel mobility are considered, the extra efforts required for informal political action are, to say the least, impressive.[17]

This general point was ignored by Bob Mullan in his 1970s study of local political action in Stevenage. He examined a number of associations, mostly but not solely middle-class in membership, who challenged the expansion of the new town. Mullan argued that 'social base' had failed to become a 'social force' due to leadership difficulties, and to the problems of liaison both within groups and between those groups and the local authority. His pessimistic conclusion and prediction was that society would become 'increasingly focused on urban issues' and that, if the Stevenage example was anything to go by, there was little hope for a 'united front of protest (of middle-class conservationists, "ecologists", and the working class), or indeed a working-class response ...'.[18] Such reductionism failed to recognise the historical significance of association in the first place. And historical and sociological evidence from elsewhere, both at the time Mullan was writing and before it, proved that united fronts could sometimes be formed, and were successful. The rather grim view of economic and political structures – in Mullan's term 'Stevenage Limited' – endlessly defeating the weak forces of fractured social relations among apathetic town dwellers gains little support in this book, a point emphasised in Chapter 6.

This generally more optimistic viewpoint has wider relevance for social change in relation to housing. It is also relevant to politics, both locally and nationally. For example, a recent textbook on British society in the twentieth century has argued that during the postwar years the working classes have been indifferent to protest groups, popular campaigning and radical politics in general. Comparing middle-class activism on 'post-materialist' issues such as the environment and nuclear disarmament with the working-class contribution, one historian has argued that the working classes 'could better be described as "apathetic" rather than "alternative"'.[19] This is a depressing and inaccurate characterisation, which appropriates radicalism and action for a middle-class agenda. Moreover, it implies that the experience of working-class people on new estates is not very important, and that is a puzzling position for a social historian to take. It ignores the very real material issues and problems faced by many working-class households on declining postwar new estates, and fails to recognise the political strategies adopted to address them.

Moreover, other political positions adopt equally misleading and simplistic perspectives upon the suburbs and, by implication, the new and expanded towns: 'Fifty years from now, Britain will still be the country of long shadows on county grounds, warm beer, invincible green suburbs, dog lovers, and – as George Orwell once said – old maids bicycling to holy communion through the morning mist'.[20] This was John Major's conservative and mystical vision of England. The reference to our 'invincible suburbs' may be taken to mean either the Conservative Party's invincible constituencies or the country's invincible suburban backbone. On both levels, political and social, he was wrong, and he was not alone in his errors.

The political evolution of the new estates of postwar England was repeatedly subject to considerable contemporary misunderstanding since the 1950s. Political scientists, concerned to assess the impact of postwar socio-economic changes on voting behaviour, have emphasised rising levels of affluence, the break-up of traditional urban-industrial communities because of dispersal, and the 'new breed' of affluent, skilled manual workers who have become especially concentrated in the South East as a consequence of the drift from the declining industrial areas.[21] Moreover, the growth of home ownership has been held responsible for new divisions of self-interest within the working classes. The collectivist 'neighbourhood effect' of council estate tenants, and its effect on voting behaviour, is compared with the self-interest of home buyers who have, allegedly, become more 'middle-class' on private estates.[22] Hence, the 1951, 1955, 1959, and more recently the 1979, 1983, 1987 and 1992 general election victories of the Conservatives have been seen as strong evidence of these growing trends.

Therefore, as Steven Fielding has shown, Labour's inability during the 1950s to win many new town constituencies, despite the largely working-class composition of the new towns, appeared to confirm to psephologists and political commentators Labour's failure to appeal to the 'new' working class.[23] Stuart Laing has made a similar point for the suburban new estates in affluent towns and cities during the 1950s. The Conservative Party appeared to have developed a more successful language and imagery of affluence which caught the imagination of the newly comfortable working classes.[24] During the Macmillan years, Stevenage, comprised largely of Londoners who had moved to the Hertfordshire new town, symbolised to many on the Left a political incorporation into conservatism of the better-off sections among the working classes.[25] In the 1987 and 1992 elections, the symbol of affluent working-class conservatism was another new town, Basildon.[26]

The history of working-class evolution presented in this book, however, presents complications for such interpretations. First, it is romantic and misleading to accept that a once greater solidarism and homogeneity was broken by urban dispersal and settlement on the new estates. The slums were no more nor less friendly than the new estates, and the propensity for association and mutuality has persisted, but in combination with the growth of wider social relationships and the much-welcomed higher levels of privacy which new housing offered when compared to many poorer housing areas.[27] Moreover, during the decades of 'collectivist consumption', divisions and tensions on council estates were strongly in evidence, as Chapter 5 made clear. Hence, the 'neighbourhood effect' within working-class areas, pre or post dispersal, may be inferred to have had no real effect on voting behaviour.

A second reason for repudiating any notion of the quintessential conservatism of new estates and new towns is their anti-conservative majority. Few postwar working-class suburban or new town constituencies have returned Conservative candidates at 50 per cent of the vote or above.[28] Third, there have been many straws in the wind to indicate a gathering yet unpredictable complexity in the political composition of postwar working-class peripheral housing developments, and in the new and expanded towns. Stevenage, for example, shared in the general swing to Labour in Southern Hertfordshire in the 1964 general election.[29] Moreover, a study of Basingstoke, an expanded town in a largely rural area, found that the constituency, which had returned a Conservative MP since 1885, had swung towards Labour during the 1964 general election because of the incoming numbers of dispersed Londoners. In common with Stevenage, a majority of the local electorate voted against the Conservatives. And that was in spite of a better organised and longer-established Conservative election machine.[30]

More recent political behaviour has produced some profound results. Following the local elections of 1994, 1995 and 1996, huge swathes of both middle- and working-class suburbia, and new and expanded town constituencies, were controlled by the Labour or Liberal Democrat parties, either in majorities or in alliance with each other. And Basildon, symbol of the Thatcherite victories of the 1987 and 1992 general elections, had removed all Conservative local councillors in May 1996.[31] To take another new town example, in the new town (as opposed to rural borough) wards of Milton Keynes, no Conservative councillors remained after the local elections of May 1996. As the local newspaper reported, during the count 'the faces of the Conservative candidates darkened', especially when they heard that Labour had won the three seats of the Loughton Park ward.[32] In Loughton Park, over 70 per cent of economically active householders worked in the service sector, and its housing tenure was over 75 per cent owner-occupied.[33] Writing in the *New Statesman*, Paul Barker of the ICS has stressed the 'untraditional' political eclecticism of Milton Keynes.[34] It returned a female Labour Euro MP to the European Union Parliaments in 1994, in place of the well-known Tory candidate, Edwina Currie. And in the general election on 1 May 1997 Labour won both Milton Keynes's parliamentary seats from the Conservatives. This was merely one example of a massive national swing which devastated the Tory vote in the new towns and in many suburban areas. Post-election analyses in newspapers (for example the *Guardian* and the *Independent* on 3 and 4 May) highlighted the electoral demise of 'Basildon Man', that is, the demise of the affluent working-class Tory voter. On 8 June 1997 the *Sunday Telegraph*, a Conservative newspaper, went so far as to argue that the 'very rootlessness' of 1970s estates and new towns explained their switch to Labour. There was no attempt to justify this statement.

John Major was mistaken, therefore, if he implied that the suburbs were invincibly Conservative. He was equally mistaken if he was implying that the English suburbs – and by implication the new towns – were somehow socially and economically forever comfortable and well-off. Housing conditions remain vastly unequal. Moreover, working-class council estates have experienced flash points of disorder brought about by economic demise and social deprivation. For these reasons at least, this is not a Whig history of postwar working-class urban dispersal: there is no reason to assume that the undoubted gains made in the housing of the English working classes since 1945 will continue unabated. In this connection, it is important to emphasise the role of associative action. It articulates aspirations and complaints from below, and provides the means to correct poor provision and indifference from above.

Connections: the recent past, the present and the future

The findings of this book are strongly relevant to the present and the future, for urban dispersal is a continuing phenomenon. It is generated by the factors described in Chapters 2 and 3, but also by more recent social changes. The increasing divorce rate and the growing number of people who prefer to stay single are social changes which are engendering greater urbanisation in England. Hence, for example, over twenty-four new towns are now mooted to provide many of the four million new and smaller households which government has predicted for the early decades of the next century.[35] Structurally, furthermore, urban dispersal has been coterminous with key changes, notably the decentralisation of production and employment to outer labour markets and to the new and expanded towns.[36] Since the 1970s a proliferation of small-batch hi-tech companies, distribution centres and other workplaces on the peripheries of towns has occurred, where the land is cheaper to purchase or rent. And these economic developments followed the peak of the postwar economy's industrial prowess during the 1950s. Since then, England underwent a faster decline and a more radical de-industrialisation process than other advanced industrial nations.[37] The experiences in Milton Keynes provide some important indicators of social formation within a transitional economic context.

The final two decades of this century have witnessed a further pressure for dispersal. Out-of-town shopping in hypermarkets and shopping villages, and the infrastructure required for it, have extended development on the urban edges.[38] This has meant extensions to already extensive suburban areas. Urban sociologists have, in consequence, recently introduced the notions of 'edge cities' or 'outer cities', which are now buzz-phrases in urban theory, planning theory and urban history.[39] Where are edge cities? Who lives in them? Simply, they are taken to mean those living in suburbs and in new settlements of new estates which no longer depend upon the central zones for employment, shopping, leisure and essential services. Thanks to out-of-town shopping malls and supermarkets, and as a result of heightened rapidity in electronic communications and accelerated mobility via faster motor cars, new settlements have come into existence which may be sustained without reference to the older town centres: people can live and work within a realm which is independent of those centres.

The South East of England has seen the most rapid expansion of outer developments. They have grown most extensively in those areas of the South East whose local economies are increasingly comprised of service sector employment and the more mobile industries, especially those of computing and electronic communications. In the so-called M4 corridor, for example, thousands of acres of fields and woodlands nestling around the River Loddon disappeared during the 1970s and 1980s as once distinctive outer suburbs of Reading and Wokingham all but merged near the Winnersh Triangle business park. There, out-of-town shopping centres, leisure facilities and easy access to the national road network means, in theory at least, that no one needs to visit the town centres of Reading or Wokingham.[40]

In edge cities, too, it may be inferred that associations of residents will be central to the articulation of their needs within a socio-economic system which increasingly involves new systems of negotiation and resource management, to wit, 'network' and 'partnership' agreements between a range of official and private agencies. Tenants' associations and voluntary associations will remain important in articulating needs from below. The example of Milton Keynes demonstrates that they have usually continued to be formed when required. The growth of Milton Keynes since 1970 manifests a number of edge city characteristics outlined above.[41]

There is a danger, however, in viewing such urban developments as a wholly recent and distinctly postwar phenomenon with dangerous and unforetold implications for future urban and social change. As one urban historian has recently argued, for example, the garden city principle itself contained characteristics of the edge city, with its emphasis upon sub-rural and sub-urban settlement, and upon self-sufficiency. These developments were intended to exist beyond the old urban centres.[42] Hence, the postwar new towns, planned and built within the garden city lineage, were to a considerable extent new urban developments whose social and economic life occurred away from existing towns and cities. Moreover, there was a strong requirement for social and family facilities to exist in the new towns and expanded towns and peripheral projects. To this extent, new towns have manifested edge city characteristics. Yet wider kinship and social networks were accepted by new town residents, and have been maintained. There was, then, no purely 'edge' existence, a point also germane to peripheral projects since Watling.

Further suburban housing developments, and the likelihood of further new towns, are proof of a continuing momentum for urban dispersal, and of a popular desire for suburban or quasi-suburban living. Statistics in *Social Trends* confirm the continuing decline of the metropolitan cores as a consequence of growing internal migration.[43] Moreover, in both the developed and the developing world, dispersal migration is a common demographic feature, and a growing one.[44] The findings of this book, for the postwar period of accelerated and expanded urban dispersal in England, may have a wider relevance to the continuing phenomenon in two important ways. First, if housing conditions are perceived to be good, and if the authorities are responsive to needs articulated from below, then urban dispersal fosters positive social and material results.

Second, the English working classes have, once more, been placed at the forefront of a considerable historical transition. Oral historians of the experience of moving to suburbs and new towns often refer to their subjects as 'pioneers' or 'history makers'.[45] And many people who have moved into new housing estates have described themselves as pioneers.[46] There should be little doubt of the historical significance of these well-chosen terms. For two centuries ago, England was a pioneer nation. It witnessed the formation of the first urban-industrial working classes, and their paradigmatic urban-industrial communities have been the subject of a great many historical studies. These studies stressed their significance as expressions of a mature proletarian culture which had adapted to the rapidly growing urban and economic conditions of Victorian England.[47] Since the interwar years, those communities were evacuated by working-class migrants seeking a better life for themselves. In both experiencing and negotiating this profound social transition, with all its advantages and also disadvantages, the English working classes have moved on. They have driven ahead of the romantic misunderstanding and elitist contempt of cultural critics who failed to understand the substantive changes taking place in the suburban new estates, and in the new and expanded towns, of *fin de siècle* England.

Notes

1 R. Fyson, 'Campaigning for the inexclusive in urban design', *Planning Week*, 4:41 (1996), p. 7.

2 J. Meikle, 'Gummer attacks executive homes', *Guardian*, 1 October 1996; M. Wainwright, 'Community life in a cul-de-sac', *Guardian*, 1 October 1996; *Today*, BBC Radio 4, 25 and 26 November 1996.

3 E. I. Black and T. S. Simey, 'Introduction', in G. D. Mitchell, T. Lupton, M. W. Hodges and C. S. Smith, *Neighbourhood and Community: An Inquiry into Social Relationships on Housing Estates in Liverpool and Sheffield* (Liverpool, 1954), p. 9.

4 H. J. Gans, *The Levittowners: Ways of Life and Politics in a Suburban Community* (London, 1967), p. 37.

5 Ibid., p. 37.

6 See B. M. Berger, 'Suburbia and the American dream', in I. L. Allen (ed.), *New Towns and the Suburban Dream:, Ideology and Utopia in Plan-*

ning and Development (New York, 1977), pp. 229–40; see also B. M. Berger, *Working-Class Suburb* (Los Angeles, 1960), passim.

7 J. Bishop, *Milton Keynes: The Best of Both Worlds? Public and Professional Views of the New City* (Bristol, 1986), pp. 78, 99.

8 B. Campbell, *Goliath: Britain's Dangerous Places* (London, 1995), pp. 226–53.

9 A. Power and R. Tunstall, *Swimming Against the Tide: Polarisation or Progress on 20 Unpopular Council Estates, 1980–1995* (York, 1995), passim; M. Taylor, *Unleashing the Potential: Bringing Residents to the Centre of Regeneration* (York, 1995), passim.

10 A. Holmes, *Limbering Up: Community Empowerment on Peripheral Estates* (1992), cited in Taylor, *Unleashing the Potential*, pp. 10, 16.

11 Power and Tunstall, *Swimming Against the Tide*, pp. 36–56; see also J. Charlesworth and A. Cochrane, 'Tales of the suburbs: the local politics of growth in the South East of England, *Urban Studies*, 31:10 (1994), pp. 1723–31.

12 P. Balchin, *Housing Policy: An Introduction* (London, 1995), pp. 143–52.

13 See Power and Tunstall, *Swimming Against the Tide*, passim; Taylor, *Unleashing the Potential*, passim.

14 C. Chinn, *They Worked All Their Lives: Women of the Urban Poor, 1880–1939* (Manchester, 1988), passim; E. Roberts, *A Woman's Place: An Oral History of Working-Class Women, 1890–1940* (Oxford, 1984), passim.

15 See above, Chapter 6, pp. 179–80. See also H. Graham, 'Women, poverty and caring', in C. Glendinning and J. Millar (eds), *Women and Poverty in Britain* (Brighton, 1987), pp. 221–40.

16 J. Mark-Lawson, M. Savage and A. Warde, 'Gender and local politics: struggles over welfare policies, 1918–1939', in L. Murgatroyd, M. Savage, D. Shapiro, J. Urry, S. Walby, A. Warde and J. Mark-Lawson, *Localities, Class and Gender* (London, 1985), pp. 195–215.

17 L. Pickup, 'Hard to get around: a study of women's travel mobility', in J. Little, L. Peake and P. Richardson (eds), *Women in Cities: Gender and the Urban Environment* (London, 1988), pp. 98–108.

18 B. Mullan, *Stevenage Limited: Aspects of the Planning and Politics of Stevenage, 1945–78* (London, 1980), p. 287.

19 P. Byrne, 'Pressure groups and popular campaigns', in P. Johnson (ed.), *Twentieth Century Britain: Economic, Social and Cultural Change* (London, 1994), p. 458.

20 *Daily Telegraph*, 23 April 1993.

21 A. Heath, R. Jowell and J. Curtice, *How Britain Votes* (Oxford, 1985), p. 8.

22 Ibid., pp. 46, 78.

23 S. Fielding, '"White heat and white collars": the evolution of "Wilsonism"', in R. Coopey, S. Fielding and N. Tiratsoo (eds), *The Wilson Governments, 1964–1970* (London, 1993), p. 31.

24 S. Laing, *Representations of Working-Class Life, 1957–64* (London, 1986), p. 13.

25 See, for example, R. Samuel, 'The deference voter', *New Left Review*, 1 (January–February 1960), pp. 9–13.

26 *The Times*, 3 May 1996; 4 May 1996.

27 See above, pp. 103, 133.

28 This point is evident from the post-election surveys of *General Election Statistics*, or simply from *The Times*'s breakdowns of election results.

29 D. E. Butler and A. King, *The British General Election of 1964* (London, 1965), p. 314.

30 Ibid., pp. 254–5.

31 *The Times*, 3 May 1996.

32 *Milton Keynes Herald*, 9 May 1996.

33 Milton Keynes Borough Council, *People and Housing in Milton Keynes: A Profile of Settlements From the 1991 Census* (Milton Keynes, 1993), pp. 142–3; Milton Keynes Borough Council, *People and Work in Milton Keynes: A Profile of Settlements From the 1991 Census* (Milton Keynes, 1993), pp. 92–3.

34 P. Barker, 'Though unEnglish and much sneered at, Milton Keynes is a success ...', *New Statesman*, 4 October 1996, p. 54.

35 R. Fyson, 'Deadline set for homes document', *Planning Week*, 4:43 (1996), p. 1; C. Pepinster, 'Divorce and single life bring back the new town', *Independent on Sunday*, 4 February 1996.

36 M. Savage, 'Spatial differences in modern Britain', in C. Hamnett, L. McDowell and P. Sarre (eds), *The Changing Social Structure* (London, 1993), pp. 255–8.

37 G. Tweedale, 'Industry and de-industrialisation in the 1970s', in R. Coopey and N. Woodward (eds), *Britain in the 1970s: The Troubled Economy* (London, 1996), pp. 251–5.

38 A. Minton, 'Shopping around', *Planning Week*, 2:10 (1994), p. 10; Savage, 'Spatial differences', pp. 255–8.

39 See Joel Garreau, *Edge City: Life on the New Frontier* (New York, 1991); John Herington, *The Outer City* (London, 1984).

40 This description is based partly upon Herington, *Outer City*, pp. 1–4, 6–9, and the writer's knowledge of Reading.
41 Charlesworth and Cochrane, 'Tales', pp. 1723, 1734.
42 G. Hise, 'The airplane and the garden city: regional transformations during World War 2', in D. Albrecht (ed.), *World War Two and the American Dream: How Wartime Building Changed a Nation* (Cambridge, Mass., 1995), p. 174.
43 *Social Trends* 23 (London, 1993) pp. 16–18; *Social Trends* 25 (London, 1995), p. 18.
44 Point made by John de Monchaux in M. Clapson, M. Dobbin and P. Waterman (eds) *The Best Laid Plans ... Milton Keynes Since 1967* (Luton, 1997).
45 See, for example, J. Turner and B. Jardine, *Pioneer Tales: A New Life in Milton Keynes* (Milton Keynes, 1985); H. and C. Rees, *The History Makers: The Early Days of Stevenage New Town* (Stevenage, 1991).
46 E. Harvey, 'The post-war pioneers', *Town and Country Planning*, 41:9 (1973); A. Hughes and K. Hunt, 'A culture transformed? Women's lives in Wythenshawe in the 1930s', in A. Davies and S. Fielding (eds), *Workers' Worlds: Cultures and Communities in Manchester and Salford, 1880–1939* (Manchester, 1992), p. 85.
47 See Chapter 3, notes 2–4.

Bibliography

Abercrombie, Sir L. P., *Greater London Plan, 1945* (London, 1945).

Abrams, M., 'The home centred society', *Listener*, 26 November 1959.

Age Exchange, *Just Like the Country: Memories of London Families Who Settled the New Cottage Estates, 1919–1939* (London, 1991).

Alcan Industries Limited with Cullen, G., *A Town Called Alcan* (London, 1964).

Allen J., 'Fragmented firms, disorganised labour?', in J. Allen and D. Massey (eds), *The Economy in Question* (London, 1994).

Amos, F. J. C., 'The planner's responsibility to the community', SSRC/CES Joint Weekend Conference, 5–7 July 1968 (Glasgow, unpublished papers, 1968).

Anderson, C., 'London government in transition: LCC to GLC, 1962–1967' (University of Luton, unpublished Ph.D. thesis, 1996).

Anstis, G., *Redditch: Success in the Heart of England. The History of Redditch New Town* (Stevenage, 1985).

Ashton, P. J., 'The political economy of suburban development', in W. K. Tabb and L. Sawers (eds), *Marxism and the Metropolis: New Perspectives in Urban Political Economy* (New York, 1978).

Astley, J., *Pleasant Vices* (London, 1995).

Balchin, P., *Housing Policy: An Introduction* (London, 1995).

Ballard, R., 'The Pakistanis: stability and introspection', in C. Peach (ed.), *Ethnicity in the 1991 Census. Vol. II: The Ethnic Minority Populations of Great Britain* (London, 1996).

Barker, E., 'Community centres and the uses of leisure', *Adult Education*, 11:1 (1939).

Barker, P., 'Though unEnglish and much sneered at, Milton Keynes is a success...' *New Statesman*, 4 October 1996.

Barnes, J., 'Books and journals', in A. Seldon (ed.), *Contemporary History: Practice and Method* (Oxford, 1988).

Barnes, J., *Metroland* (London, 1990).

Barwick, S., 'In the circles of Pooter's inferno', *Independent*, 28 March 1992.

Basildon Development Corporation, *Seventh Annual Report for the Period Ended March 1956* (*Parliamentary Papers* 1955–56 (91) Vol. XXV).

Basildon Development Corporation, *Sixth Annual Report For the Period Ended March 31st, 1955* (*Parliamentary Papers* 1955–56 (91) Vol. XXV, p. 41).

Bayley, S., 'The Garden City', unit 23, Open University third level course *A305: History of Architecture and Design, 1890–1939* (Milton Keynes, 1975).

Beatson-Hird, J. F., 'Case history of "newstate"', *Town and Country Planning*, 25:8 (1967).

Bédarida, F., *A Social History of England, 1951–1990* (London, 1991).

Bendixson, T. and Platt, J., *Milton Keynes: Image and Reality* (Cambridge, 1992).

Bentley, I., 'The owner makes his mark', in P. Oliver, I. Davis and I. Bentley (eds), *Dunroamin: The Suburban Semi and its Enemies* (London, 1994).

Berger, B. M., 'Suburbia and the American dream', in I. L. Allen (ed.), *New Towns and the Suburban Dream: Ideology and Utopia in Planning and Development* (New York, 1977).

Berger, B. M., *Working-Class Suburb* (Los Angeles, 1960).

Bergonzi, B., *The Situation of the Novel* (Harmondsworth, 1972).

Berthoud, R. and Jowell, R., *Creating a Community: A Study of Runcorn New Town* (London, 1973).

Betjeman, J., 'City and Suburban' columns, *Spectator*, 15 February 1957; 22 February 1957; 1 March 1957.

Betjeman, J., 'Slough', in R. Skelton (ed.), *Poetry of the Thirties* (Harmondsworth, 1985).

Bishop, J., *Milton Keynes: The Best of Both Worlds? Public and Professional Views of a New City* (Bristol, 1986).

Blackwell, T. and Seabrook, J., *A World Still to Win: The Reconstruction of the Postwar Working Class* (London, 1985).

Blowers, A., 'London's out-county estates: a reappraisal', *Town and Country Planning*, 41:9 (1973).

Blur, 'Stereotypes' and 'Ernold Same', on Blur, *The Great Escape* CD (Parlophone, 1995, 7243 8 35235 28).

Bondi, L. and Peake, L., 'Gender and the city: urban politics revisited', in J. Little, L. Peake and P. Richardson (eds), *Women in Cities: Gender and the Urban Environment* (London, 1988).

Bonzo Dog Band, The, 'My pink half of the drainpipe', on *Cornology: Vol. 1: The Intro* CD (EMI, 1992, 0777 7 99596 2 4).

Booker, C., *The Neophiliacs: A Study of the Revolution in English Life in the Fifties and Sixties* (London, 1970).

Bott, E., *Family and Social Network: Roles, Norms and External Relationships in Ordinary Urban Families* (London, 1968).

Bourke, J., *Working-Class Cultures in Britain, 1890–1960: Gender, Class and Ethnicity* (London, 1994).

Bowlby, S., 'From corner shop to hypermarket: women and food retailing', in J. Little, L. Peake and P. Richardson (eds), *Women in Cities: Gender and the Urban Environment* (London, 1988).

Bracey, H. E., *Neighbours on New Estates and Subdivisions in England and the USA* (London, 1964).

Bracknell Development Corporation, *Fifth Annual Report for the Period Ended March 31, 1955* (*Parliamentary Papers* 1955–56 (91), Vol. XXV).

Brannigan, J., 'Literature's poor relation: history and identity in the writing and criticism of 1950s literature' (University of Luton, unpublished Ph.D. thesis, 1996).

Briggs, A., *Victorian Cities* (Harmondsworth, 1990).

Brinig, D., 'What it's really like to live in Milton Keynes', *Over 21*, July 1978.

Britain 1970: An Official Handbook (London, 1970).

British Medical Journal, 'Demolition melancholia', 15 July 1939.

Broady, M., 'Social change and town development', *Town Planning Review*, 36:4 (1966).

Broady, M., 'The organisation of Coronation street parties', *Sociological Review* (New Series) 4:2 (1956).

Broady, M., *Tomorrow's Community: A Report of the Working Party set up by the National Federation of Community Associations* (London, 1979).

Brooke-Taylor, G., 'Social problems of new towns', in P. Kuenstler (ed.), *Community Organisation in Great Britain* (London, 1961).

Brooke-Taylor, G., 'The social effect of dispersal', *Town and Country Planning*, 2:1 (1961).

Brookes, B. and Lewis, J., 'A reassessment of the work of the Peckham Health Centre, 1926–1951', *Milbank Memorial Fund Quarterly, Health and Society*, 61:2 (1983).

Brooks, C., 'The Lakes Estate, Bletchley: a case study of a GLC overspill development designed on Radburn principles' (Oxford Polytechnic, unpublished Diploma in Urban Planning dissertation, 1990).

Brown, A., 'Dead bored and other common problems', *Independent*, 8 August 1992.

Burke, T., *Son of London* (London, n.d. 1947?).

Burnett, J., *A Social History of Housing 1815–1985* (London, 1991).

Butler, D. E. and King A., *The British General Election of 1964* (London, 1965).

Buttimer, A., 'Sociology and planning', *Town Planning Review*, 42:2 (1971).

Byrne, P., 'Pressure groups and popular campaigns', in P. Johnson (ed.), *Twentieth Century Britain: Economic, Social and Cultural Change* (London, 1994).

Cairncross, L., Clapham, D. and Goodlad, R., 'The origins and activities of tenants' associations in Britain', *Urban Studies*, 29:5 (1992).

Calder, A., 'Introduction' to Charles Dickens, *Great Expectations* (Harmondsworth, 1984).

Campbell, B., *Goliath: Britain's Dangerous Places* (London, 1995).

Campbell, B., *Wigan Pier Revisited: Poverty and Politics in the 80s* (London, 1984).

Carey, J., *The Intellectuals and the Masses: Pride and Prejudice among the Literary Intelligentsia, 1880–1939* (London, 1992).

Carey, L. and Mapes, R., *The Sociology of Planning: A Study of Social Activity on New Housing Estates* (London, 1972).

Caunce, S., *Oral History and the Local Historian* (London, 1994).

Central Housing Advisory Committee, *Moving From the Slums: Seventh Report of the Housing Sub-Committee of the Central Housing Advisory Committee* (London, 1956).

Champion, A. G. and Green, A. E., *In Search of Britain's Booming Towns: An Index of Local Economic Performance for Britain* (Newcastle, 1985).

Champion, T. and Dorling, D., *Population Change for Britain's Functional Regions, 1951–1991* (London, 1994).

Chance, J., 'The Irish: invisible settlers', in C. Peach (ed.), *Ethnicity in the 1991 Census. Vol. II: The Ethnic Minority Populations of Great Britain* (London, 1996).

Chapman, D., *The Home and Social Status* (London, 1955).

Charlesworth, J. and Cochrane, A., 'Tales of the suburbs: the local politics of growth in the South East of England, *Urban Studies*, 31:10 (1994).

Chave, S. P. W., 'Mental health in Harlow new town', *Journal of Psychomatic Research*, 10:1 (1966).

Cherry, G., *Cities and Plans: The Shaping of Urban Britain in the Nineteenth and Twentieth Centuries* (London, 1993).

Cherry, G., 'Homes for heroes: semis for bypasses', *New Society*, 1 February 1979.

Cherry, G., 'Influences on the development of town planning in Britain', *Journal of Contemporary History*, 4:3 (1969).

Cherry, G., 'New towns and inner city blight', *New Society*, 8 February 1979.

Childs, D., *Britain Since 1945: A Political History* (London, 1992).

Chinn, C., *Better Betting With a Decent Feller: Bookmaking, Betting and the British Working Class, 1750–1990* (Hemel Hempstead, 1991).

Chinn, C., *Homes for People: 100 Years of Council Housing in Birmingham* (Birmingham, 1991).

Chinn, C., *They Worked All Their Lives: Women of the Urban Poor, 1880–1939* (Manchester, 1988).

Chinn, C., 'Women in their own words', *Social History Society Bulletin*, 20:20 (1995).

Christie, C., 'Welfare work in housing management', in R. J. Rowles (ed.), *Housing Management* (London, 1959).

City of Sheffield Housing Management Committee, *City of Sheffield Municipal Tenant's Handbook* (Gloucester, 1964) .

Clapson, M., *A Bit of a Flutter: Popular Gambling and English Society, 1823–1961* (Manchester, 1992).

Clapson, M., Dobbin, M. and Waterman, P. (eds), *The Best Laid Plans ... Milton Keynes Since 1967* (Luton, 1997).

Clapson, M. and Emsley, E., 'Street, beat and respectability', *Criminal Justice History: An International Annual*, forthcoming.

Clark, H., 'Problems of the housing manager today', *Society of Housing Managers' Quarterly Bulletin*, 4:7 (1957).

Clarke, J. and Critcher, C., *The Devil Makes Work: Leisure in Capitalist Britain* (London, 1985).

Clarke, R. (ed.), *Enterprising Neighbours: The Development of the Community Associations Movement in Britain* (London, 1990).

Coates, K. and Silburn, R., *Poverty: The Forgotten Englishmen* (Harmondsworth, 1973).

Coleman, D. A., 'Population', in A. H. Halsey (ed.), *British Social Trends Since 1900: A Guide to the Changing Social Structure of Britain* (London, 1988).

Collison, P., 'The Cutteslowe saga', *New Society*, 25 April 1963.

Collison, P., *The Cutteslowe Walls* (London, 1963).

Constantine, S., 'Amateur gardening and popular recreation in the nineteenth and twentieth centuries', *Journal of Social History*, 14:3 (1981).

Constantine, S., *Unemployment in Britain Between the Wars* (London, 1980).

Coopey, R., Fielding, S. and Tiratsoo, N. (eds), *The Wilson Governments, 1964–1970* (London, 1993).

Cox, S., 'Changing concepts and attitudes to the provision of leisure in a new town: Milton Keynes' (Ealing College of Higher Education, unpublished BA (Hons) Humanities project, n.d.).

Craft, M. (ed.), *Family, Class and Education: A Reader* (London, 1970).

Crawley Development Corporation, *Ninth Annual Report For the Period Ended March 31, 1956* (*Parliamentary Papers* 1955–56 (91) Vol. XXV).

Cresswell, P., *The New Town Goal of Self Containment* (Milton Keynes, 1974).

Cruickshank, R. J., *The Moods of London* (London, 1951).

Cullingworth, J. B., *Housing Needs and Planning Policy: A Reassessment of the Problems of Housing Need and 'Overspill' in England and Wales* (London, 1960) .

Cullingworth, J. B., 'Social implications of overspill: the Worsley social survey', *Sociological Review* (New Series) 8:1 (1960).

Cullingworth, J. B., 'The Swindon social survey: a second report on the social implications of overspill', *Sociological Review* (New Series) 9:2 (1961).

Cullingworth, J. B., *Town and Country Planning in Britain* (London, 1974).

Danaher, D. and Williamson, J. D., '"New town blues": planning versus mutual', *International Journal of Social Psychiatry*, 29:2 (1983).

Darley, G., *Villages of Vision* (London, 1975).

Davies, A., 'Leisure in the classic slum', in A. Davies and S. Fielding (eds), *Workers' Worlds: Cultures and Communities in Manchester and Salford, 1880–1939* (Manchester, 1992).

Davies, D., *Kink: An Autobiography* (London, 1996).

Davis, I., 'A celebration of ambiguity: the synthesis of contrasting values held by builders and house purchasers', in P. Oliver, I. Davis and I. Bentley (eds), *Dunroamin: The Suburban Semi and its Enemies* (London, 1994).

Davis, I., '"One of the greatest evils..." Dunroamin and the modern movement', in P. Oliver, I. Davis and I. Bentley (eds), *Dunroamin: The Suburban Semi and its Enemies* (London, 1994).

De Wofle, I. with Nairn, I., *Civilia: The End of Suburban Man* (London, 1971).

Deakin, N. and Ungerson, C., *Leaving London: Planned Mobility and the Inner City* (London, 1977).

Deem, R., *All Work and No Play: The Sociology of Women and Leisure* (Milton Keynes, 1986).

Delafons, J., 'Brentham estate: a new community, 1901', *Town and Country Planning*, 61:11/12 (1992).

Delderfield, R. F., *The Avenue Story* (London, 1964).

Denham, C., 'Urban Britain', *Population Trends*, 36 (1984).

Dennis, N., 'Changes in function and leadership renewal: a study of the Community Associations movement and problems of small voluntary groups in the urban locality', *Sociological Review* (New Series) 9:1 (1961).

Dennis, N., 'Community and sociology', in P. Kuenstler (ed.), *Community Organisation in Great Britain* (London, 1961).

Dennis, N., *People and Planning: The Sociology of Housing in Sunderland* (London, 1970).

Dennis, N., 'The popularity of the neighbourhood community idea', in R. E. Pahl (ed.), *Readings in Urban Society* (Oxford, 1969).

Dennis, N., 'Who needs neighbours?', *New Society*, 25 July 1963.

Dennis, N., Henriques, F. and Slaughter, C., *Coal is Our Life* (London, 1956).

Department of the Environment, *English House Condition Survey, 1991* (London, 1993).

Department of the Environment, *Housing in England, 1994–95* (London, 1996).

Devine, F., *Affluent Workers Revisited: Privatism and the Working Class* (Edinburgh, 1992).

Donnison, D. with Soto, P., *The Good City: A Study of Urban Development and Policy in Britain* (London, 1980).

Douglas, J. W. B., *The Home and the School: A Study of Ability and Attainment in the Primary School* (London, 1976).

Duff, A. C., *Britain's New Towns: An Experiment in Living* (London, 1961).

Durant, R., 'Community and community centres', *Adult Education*, 11:1 (1939).

Durant, R., *Watling: A Survey of Social Life on a New Housing Estate* (London, 1939).

Dyos, H. J., 'The slums of Victorian London', *Victorian Studies*, 11:1 (1967).

Dyos, H. J., *Urbanity and Suburbanity* (Leicester, 1979).

Eade, J., Vamplew, T. and Peach, C., 'The Bangladeshis: the encapsulated community', in C. Peach (ed.), *Ethnicity in the 1991 Census. Vol. II: The Ethnic Minority Populations of Great Britain* (London, 1996).

Empson, M., 'The housing manager's contribution to estate planning', in R. J. Rowles (ed.), *Housing Management* (London, 1959).

English J., Madigan R. and Norman P., *Slum Clearance: The Social and Administrative Context in England and Wales* (London, 1976).

Evans, H. and Self, P. (eds), *New Towns Come of Age* (London, 1968).

Fava, S. F., 'The pop sociology of suburbs and new towns', in I. L. Allen (ed.), *New Towns and the Suburban Dream: Ideology and Utopia in Planning and Development* (New York, 1977).

Fielding, S., '"White heat and white collars": the evolution of "Wilsonism"', in R. Coopey, S. Fielding and N. Tiratsoo (eds), *The Wilson Governments, 1964–1970* (London, 1993).

Fielding, S., Thompson, P. and Tiratsoo, N., *'England Arise': The Labour Party and Popular Politics in 1940s Britain* (Manchester, 1995).

Finnegan, R., *The Hidden Musicians: Music Making in an English Town* (Cambridge, 1989).

Fletcher, R., *The Family and Marriage in Modern Britain* (Harmondsworth, 1974).

Flint, K., 'Fictional suburbia', *Literature and History*, 8:2 (1982).

Forman, C., *Industrial Town: Self Portraits of St. Helens in the 1920s* (London, 1979).

Forshaw, J. H. and Abercrombie, Sir L. P., *County of London Plan* (London, 1943).

Frankenberg, R., *Communities in Britain: Social Life in Town and Country* (Harmondsworth, 1971).

Fyson, R., 'Campaigning for the inexclusive in urban design', *Planning Week*, 4:41 (1996).

Fyson, R., 'Deadline set for homes document', *Planning Week*, 4:43 (1996).

Fyvel, T., 'The stones of Harlow', *Encounter*, 33 (1956).

Fyvel, T., 'Thoughts about suburbia', *Socialist Commentary*, January 1961.

Galbraith, J. K., *The Affluent Society* (Harmondsworth, 1958).

Gans, H. J., *The Levittowners: Ways of Life and Politics in a Suburban Community* (London, 1967).

Garreau, J., *Edge City: Life on the New Frontier* (New York, 1991).

Gaskell, S. M., 'Housing and the lower middle class, 1870–1914', in G. Crossick (ed.), *The Lower Middle Class in Britain, 1870–1914* (London, 1977).

Gaskell, S. M., '"The suburb salubrious": town planning in practice', in A. Sutcliffe (ed.), *British Town Planning: The Formative Years* (Leicester, 1981).

Gavron, H., *The Captive Wife: Conflicts of Housebound Mothers* (London, 1983).

Geddes, P., 'City survey for town planning purposes, of municipalities and government', in R. T. Legates and F. Stout (eds), *The City Reader* (London, 1996).

Gibson, G., 'New town ghettoes', *Socialist Commentary*, April 1959.

Giles, J. and Middleton, T., *Writing Englishness, 1900–1950: An Introductory Sourcebook on National Identity* (London, 1995).

Glass, R., *Newcomers: The West Indians in London* (London, 1960).

Glass, R. (ed.), *The Social Background of a Plan: A Study of Middlesbrough* (London, 1948).

Glendinning, C. and Millar, J. (eds), *Women and Poverty in Britain* (Brighton, 1987).

Goldthorpe, J. H., Lockwood, D., Bechhofer, F. and Platt, J., *The Affluent Worker: Political Attitudes and Behaviour* (Cambridge, 1968).

Goldthorpe, J. H., Lockwood, D., Bechhofer, F. and Platt, J., *The Affluent Worker in the Class Structure* (Cambridge, 1971).

Goodey, B., 'Social research in the new communities', *Built Environment*, 2:4 (1973).

Gorer, G., *Exploring English Character* (London, 1955).

Gosling, R., *Personal Copy* (London, 1980).

Graham, H., 'Women, poverty and caring', in C. Glendinning and J. Millar (eds), *Women and Poverty in Britain* (Brighton, 1987).

Graham, S. and Marvin, S., *Telecommunications and the City: Electronic Spaces, Urban Places* (London, 1996).

Graves, R. and Hodge, A., *The Long Weekend: A Social History of Great Britain, 1918–1939* (London, 1985).

Greed, C., *Women and Planning: Creating Gendered Realities* (London, 1994).

Grieco, M. S., 'Corby: new town planning and imbalanced development', *Regional Studies*, 19:1 (1985).

Hacon, R. J., 'Neighbourhoods or neighbourhood units?', *Sociological Review* (New Series) 3:2 (1955).

Hall, C., 'Married women at home in Birmingham in the 1920s and 1930s', *Oral History*, 5:2 (1977).

Hall, P., 'Moving on', *New Society*, 24 November 1977.

Hall, P., 'Some clinical aspects of moving house as an apparent precipitant', *Journal of Psychomatic Research*, 10:1 (1966).

Hall, P., 'The people: where will they go?', *Planner*, 71:4 (1985).

Hall, P., *Urban and Regional Planning* (London, 1992).

Hall, S., 'Lodging house zone', *Listener*, 23 February 1967.

Hall, S., 'The supply of demand', in E. P. Thompson (ed.), *Out of Apathy* (London, 1960) .

Halliwell, L., *Halliwell's Film Guide* (London, 1986).

Halsey, A. H., 'Leisure', in A. H. Halsey (ed.), *Trends in British Society Since 1900* (London, 1974).

Halsey, A. H., 'Social trends since world war two', in L. McDowell, P. Sarre and C. Hamnett (eds), *Divided Nation: Social and Cultural Change in Britain* (London, 1989).

Halsey, A. H., 'Statistics and social trends in Britain', in A. H. Halsey (ed.), *British Social Trends Since 1900: A Guide to the Changing Social Structure of Britain* (London, 1988).

Hamilton, E. M. B., 'On living in a new town', *Society of Housing Managers' Quarterly Bulletin*, 4:4 (1956).

Hamnett, C., 'Consumption and class in contemporary Britain', in C. Hamnett, L. McDowell and P. Sarre (eds), *The Changing Social Structure* (London, 1993).

Hamnett, C., 'Social change – London', *Urban Studies*, 13 (1976).

Hare, E. H., 'Mental health in new towns: what next?', *Journal of Psychosomatic Research*, 10:1 (1966).

Hare, E. H. and Shaw, G. K., *Mental Health on a New Housing Estate: A Comparative Study of Health in Two Districts of Croydon* (London, 1965).

Harloe, M., *Swindon: A Town in Transition. A Study in Urban Development and Overspill Policy* (London, 1975).

Harlow Development Corporation, *Ninth Annual Report for the Period Ended March 31, 1955* (*Parliamentary Papers* 1955–56 (91) Vol. XXV).

Harlow, J., 'One new town', *Universities and Left Review*, 5 (1958).

Harris, J., 'Between civic virtue and Social Darwinism: the concept of the residuum', in D. Englander and R. O'Day (eds), *Retrieved Riches: Social Investigation in Britain, 1840–1914* (Aldershot, 1995).

Harrison, M., 'Housing and town planning in Manchester before 1914', in A. Sutcliffe (ed.), *British Town Planning: The Formative Years* (Leicester, 1981).

Harvey, E., 'The post-war pioneers', *Town and Country Planning*, 41:9 (1973).

Hasegawa, J., *Replanning the Blitzed City Centre* (Buckingham, 1992).

Heath, A., Jowell, R. and Curtice, J., *How Britain Votes* (Oxford, 1985).

Hemel Hempstead Development Corporation, *Eighth Annual Report for the Period Ended March 31, 1955* (*Parliamentary Papers* 1955–56 (91) Vol. XXV).

Heraud, B. J., 'Social class and the new towns', *Urban Studies*, 5:1 (1968).

Heraud, B. J., 'The end of a planner's dream', *New Society*, 11 July 1968.

Herbert, D. T. and Rodgers, H. B., 'Space relationships in neighbourhood planning', *Town and Country Planning*, 35:4 (1967).

Herbert, G., 'The neighbourhood unit principle and organic theory', *Sociological Review* (New Series) 11:2 (1963).

Herington, J., *The Outer City* (London, 1984).

Hill, M., *Bigger, Brighter, Better: The Story of Bletchley 1946–1966 Told by its Residents* (Milton Keynes, 1996).

Hise, G., 'The airplane and the garden city: regional transformations during world war two', in D. Albrecht (ed.), *World War Two and the American Dream: How Wartime Building Changed a Nation* (Cambridge, Mass., 1995).

Holmes, A., 'Better than no place', *New Society*, 15 April 1971.

Hopkins, E., *The Rise and Decline of the English Working Classes, 1918–1990: A Social History* (London, 1991).

Howlett, P., 'The "Golden Age", 1955–1973', in P. Johnson (ed.), *Twentieth Century Britain: Economic, Social and Cultural Change* (London, 1994).

Hughes, A. and Hunt, K., 'A culture transformed? Women's lives in Wythenshawe in the 1930s', in A. Davies and S. Fielding (eds), *Workers'*

Worlds: Cultures and Communities in Manchester and Salford, 1880–1939 (Manchester, 1992).

Humphries, S. and Taylor, J., *The Making of Modern London, 1945–1985* (London, 1986).

Husain, J., 'Londoners who left', *New Society*, 7 July 1977.

Hutton, W., 'Angst in Acacia Avenue', *Guardian*, 2 August 1994.

Ineichen, B., 'Home ownership and manual workers' lifestyles', *Sociological Review* (New Series) 20:3 (1972).

Ineichen, B., 'Neurotic wives in a modern residential suburb', *Social Science and Medicine*, 9 (1975).

Ineichen, B. and Hooper, D., 'Wives' mental health and children's behaviour problems in contrasting residential estates', *Social Science and Medicine*, 8 (1974).

Jackson, A. A., *Semi Detached London: Suburban Development, Life and Transport, 1900–1939* (London, 1991).

Jackson, A. A., *The Middle Classes, 1900–1950* (Nairn, 1991).

Jackson, B., *Working-Class Community* (Harmondsworth, 1972).

Jackson, B. and Marsden, D., *Education and the Working Class* (Harmondsworth, 1976).

Jacobs, E. and Worcester, R., *We British: Britain Under the Moriscope* (London, 1990).

Jahn, M., 'Suburban development in outer west London', in F. M. L. Thompson (ed.), *The Rise of Suburbia* (Leicester, 1982).

Jeffrey, T., 'The suburban nation: politics and class in Lewisham', in D. Feldman and G. S. Jones (eds), *Metropolis. London: Histories and Representations Since 1800* (London, 1989).

Jeffreys, M., 'Londoners in Hertfordshire: the South Oxhey estate', in R. Glass, E. Hobsbawm et al. (eds), *London: Aspects of Change* (London, 1964).

Jennings, H., *Societies in the Making: A Study of Development and Redevelopment Within a County Borough* (London, 1962).

Johnson P., 'Introduction', in P. Johnson (ed.), *Twentieth Century Britain: Economic, Social and Cultural Change* (London, 1994).

Johnston, R. J., *Urban Residential Patterns: An Introductory Review* (London, 1971).

Jones, G. S., *Outcast London: A Study in the Relationship between Classes in Victorian Society* (Harmondsworth, 1983).

Jones, S. G., *Workers at Play: A Social and Economic History of Leisure, 1918–1939* (London, 1986).

Karn, V. A., *Aycliffe Housing Survey: A Study of Housing in a New Town* (Birmingham, 1970).

Karn, V. A., *Stevenage Housing Survey: A Study of Housing Development in a New Town* (Birmingham, 1970).

Kelly J. R., *Leisure Identities and Interactions* (London, 1983).

Kent, R. A., *A History of British Empirical Sociology* (Aldershot, 1983).

Kirp, D. L., Dwyer, J. P. and Rosenthal, L. A., *Our Town: Race, Housing and the Soul of Suburbia* (New Jersey, 1995).

Kitchen, R., 'Doing a moonlight' (Milton Keynes, unpublished manuscript, 1975, held at the Living Archive Project).

Kitchen, R., 'Moving to Milton Keynes', *New Society*, 22 August 1974.

Klein, J., *Samples From English Cultures* (London, 1965), I.

Kosmin, B. A. and de Lange, D. J., 'Conflicting urban ideologies: London's new towns and the metropolitan preference of London's Jews', *London Journal*, 6:2 (1980).

Kuper, L., 'Blueprint for living together', in L. Kuper (ed.), *Living in Towns* (London, 1953).

Kureishi, H., *The Buddha of Suburbia* (London, 1989).

Laing, S., *Representations of Working-Class Life, 1957–64* (London, 1986).

Lancet, 'Psychiatric illness in a new town practice', 31 March 1967.

Lancet, 'Suburban neurosis up to date', I, 18 January 1958.

Lassell, M., *Wellington Road* (London, 1962).

Lawless, P., *Britain's Inner Cities: Problems and Policies* (London, 1981).

Legatte, J., 'Out of the closet and into the commuter belt', *Guardian*, 12 April 1993.

Lewis, J., 'Social facts, social theory and social change: the ideas of Booth in relation to those of Beatrice Webb, Octavia Hill and Helen Bosanquet', in D. Englander and R. O'Day (eds), *Retrieved Riches: Social Investigation in Britain, 1840–1914* (Aldershot, 1995).

Lewis, J., *Women in Britain: Women, Family, Work and the State in the Postwar Years* (Oxford, 1993).

Lewis, J., *Women in England: 1870–1950* (Hemel Hempstead, 1984).

Lewis, J. and Brookes, B., 'A reassessment of the work of the Peckham Health Centre, 1926–1951', *Milbank Memorial Quarterly; Health and Society*, 61:2 (1983).

Lewis, R. and Maude, A., *The English Middle Classes* (Harmondsworth, 1953).

Liddiard, P., *Milton Keynes Felt Needs Project: A Preliminary Study of the Felt Health Needs of People Living in Relative Poverty on a Milton Keynes Housing Estate* (Milton Keynes, 1988).

Liepmann, K. K., *The Journey to Work: Its Significance for Industrial and Community Life* (London, 1944).

Ling, A., 'The newest towns', *New Society*, 9 July 1964.

Living Archive Project, Milton Keynes: selected taped interviews.

Llewelyn-Davies, R., 'Town design', *Town Planning Review*, 37:3 (1966).

Llewelyn-Davies, Weeks, Forestier-Walker and Bor, *Milton Keynes Plan: Interim Report to the Milton Keynes Development Corporation* (London, 1968).

Llewelyn-Davies, Weeks, Forestier-Walker and Bor, *The Plan for Milton Keynes* (Milton Keynes, 1970), II.

Lock, D., 'MK, new towns, and the British spirit', *Town and Country Planning*, April 1992.

Lock, M., 'The planners and the planned', *Listener*, 18 March 1965.

Lockwood, D., 'Sources of variation in working-class images of society', *Sociological Review* (New Series) 14:3 (1966).

Lockwood, D., 'The new working class', *European Journal of Sociology*, 1:2 (1960).

Lucas, P., *Basildon: Behind the Headlines* (Basildon, 1985).

MacDonald, I., *Revolution in the Head* (London, 1995).

Mackenzie, S., 'Balancing our space and time: the impact of women's organisations on the British city, 1920–1980', in J. Little, L. Peake and P. Richardson (eds), *Women in Cities: Gender and the Urban Environment* (London, 1988).

MacTaggart, R., 'Newcomers to Milton Keynes: getting their housing priorities right', *Architectural Design*, 45 (1975).

Manfred Mann, 'Semi-detached suburban Mr James', *Ages of Mann* CD (Polygram, 1993, 514 326–2).

Mann, P., 'The concept of neighbourliness', *American Journal of Sociology*, 60:2 (1954).

Mark-Lawson, J., Savage, M. and Warde, A., 'Gender and local politics: struggles over welfare policies, 1918–1939', in L. Murgatroyd, M. Savage, D. Shapiro, J. Urry, S. Walby, A. Warde and J. Mark-Lawson, *Localities, Class and Gender* (London, 1985).

Mars, T., 'Little Los Angeles in North Bucks', *Architect's Journal*, 15 April 1992.

Martin, B., *A Sociology of Contemporary Cultural Change* (Oxford, 1985).

Martin, F. M., 'An inquiry into parent's preferences in secondary education', in D. V. Glass (ed.), *Social Mobility in Britain* (London, 1954).

Marwick, A., *British Society Since 1945* (Harmondsworth, 1987).

Mason, T., *Sport in Britain* (London, 1988).

Mass Observation, 'Marriage and divorce in post-war Britain', in *The Changing Nation: A Contact Book* (London, 1947).

Mass Observation Bulletin (New Series) 15, 'Next door neighbours, February 1948' (London, 1948).

Maule, H. G. and Martin, F. M., 'Social and psychological aspects of rehousing', *Advancement of Science*, 12:48 (1956).

Mays, J. B., 'New hope in newtown', *New Society*, 22 August 1963.

Mays, J. B., *The Introspective Society* (London, 1968).

McGovern, P., 'Social facilities in new and expanded towns', *Town and Country Planning*, 35:8 (1967).

McKenna, M., 'The suburbanisation of the working-class population of Liverpool between the wars', *Social History*, 16:2 (1991).

McKibbin, R. (ed.), *The Ideologies of Class: Social Relations in Britain, 1880–1950* (Oxford, 1991).

Meikle, J., 'Gummer attacks executive homes', *Guardian*, 1 October 1996.

Members, The, 'The sound of the suburbs' single (Virgin Music, 1979, VS242).

Men Only, 57:1 (1992).

Merret, S. with Gray, F., *Owner-Occupation in Britain* (London, 1979).

Milton Keynes and North Bucks TEC, *Economic Review 1993* (Milton Keynes, n.d.).

Milton Keynes Borough Council, *Community Development Strategy: Summary* (Milton Keynes, 1992).

Milton Keynes Borough Council, *Household Survey, 1990* (Milton Keynes, 1990).

Milton Keynes Borough Council, *People and Housing in Milton Keynes: A Profile of Settlements from the 1991 Census* (Milton Keynes, 1993).

Milton Keynes Borough Council, *People and Work in Milton Keynes: A Profile of Settlements From the 1991 Census* (Milton Keynes, 1993).

Milton Keynes Development Corporation, *Employer's Survey Report, 1987* (Milton Keynes, 1987).

Milton Keynes Development Corporation, *Employer's Survey Report, 1990* (Milton Keynes, 1990).

Milton Keynes Development Corporation, *Four Years On: The Milton Keynes Household Survey, 1973* (Milton Keynes, 1974).

Milton Keynes Development Corporation, *Labour Resources* (Milton Keynes, n.d. 1979?).

Milton Keynes Development Corporation, *Milton Keynes* (Milton Keynes, 1988).

Milton Keynes Development Corporation, *Milton Keynes Household Survey, 1976, Technical Supplement no. 2* (Milton Keynes, 1977).

Milton Keynes Development Corporation, *Milton Keynes Household Survey, 1983, Demographic Report* (Milton Keynes, 1985).

Milton Keynes Development Corporation, *Milton Keynes Household Survey,*

1988, Demography Technical Report (Milton Keynes, 1989).

Milton Keynes Development Corporation, *Milton Keynes Household Survey, 1988, Employment Technical Report* (Milton Keynes, 1989).

Milton Keynes Development Corporation, *Milton Keynes Household Survey, 1988, Leisure and Recreation Technical Report* (Milton Keynes, 1989).

Milton Keynes Development Corporation, *Milton Keynes Insight* (Milton Keynes, 1989).

Milton Keynes Development Corporation, *Milton Keynes Population Bulletin* (Milton Keynes, 1990).

Milton Keynes Development Corporation, *New City, Milton Keynes* (Milton Keynes, 1974).

Milton Keynes Development Corporation, *New City, Milton Keynes,* (Milton Keynes, 1975).

Milton Keynes Development Corporation, *Recreation: Recreation Plan for Milton Keynes* (Milton Keynes, 1970).

Milton Keynes Development Corporation, *Residential Design Feedback: Report of Studies* (Milton Keynes, 1975).

Milton Keynes Development Corporation, *Seven Years On: The Summary Report of the 1976 Household and Employers Surveys* (Milton Keynes, 1977).

Milton Keynes Development Corporation, *Seven Years On: Household Survey, 1976, Technical Report 2: The Move to Milton Keynes* (Milton Keynes, 1977).

Milton Keynes Development Corporation, *Seven Years On: Household Survey, 1976, Technical Report 3: Employment* (Milton Keynes, 1977).

Milton Keynes Development Corporation, *The Plan for Milton Keynes* (Milton Keynes, 1970), II.

Milton Keynes Development Corporation, *Walnut Tree Neighbourhood Review* (Milton Keynes, 1990).

Milton Keynes Development Corporation, *Walnut Tree Neighbourhood Review, July Through December 1990: A Report on the Community Development Programme Undertaken by Milton Keynes Development Corporation Between 1987 and 1990* (Milton Keynes, 1991).

Milton Keynes Development Corporation, *What's the Secret of Success in Milton Keynes?* (Milton Keynes, n.d. 1990?).

Milton Keynes Urban Studies Centre, *Notes on Milton Keynes* (Milton Keynes, 1981).

Ministry of Housing and Local Government, *The First Hundred Families* (London, 1965).

Ministry of Housing and Local Government, *The Needs of New Communities: A Report on Social Provision in New and Expanding Communities* (London, 1967).

Ministry of Housing and Local Government, *The South East Study, 1961–1981* (London, 1964).

Ministry of Town and Country Planning, *Final Report of the New Towns Committee* (London, 1946, Cmd 6876).

Ministry of Town and Country Planning, *Report of the Committee on the Qualification of Planners* (London, 1950, Cmd 8059).

Minton, A., 'Shopping around', *Planning Week*, 2:10 (1994).

Mitchell, G. D., Lupton, T., Hodges, M. W. and Smith, C. S., *Neighbourhood and Community: An Inquiry into Social Relationships on Housing Estates in Liverpool and Sheffield* (Liverpool 1954).

Mogey, J. M., 'Changes in family life experienced by English workers moving from slums to housing estates', *Marriage and Family Living*, 17:2 (1955).

Mogey, J. M., *Family and Neighbourhood: Two Studies of Oxford* (Oxford, 1956).

Mogey, J. M., 'The climate of opinion on housing estates', *Sociological Review* (New Series) 4:1 (1956).

Moravia, A., *The Woman of Rome* (Harmondsworth, 1958).

Morris, R. J. and Rodger, R. (eds), *The Victorian City: A Reader in British Urban History, 1820–1914* (London, 1993).

Morrison, Lord, *Herbert Morrison: An Autobiography* (London, 1960).

Mowat, C. L., *Britain Between the Wars* (London, 1976).

Muggeridge, M., 'England, whose England?', *Encounter*, 118 (1963).

Mullan, B., *Stevenage Limited: Aspects of the Planning and Politics of Stevenage, 1945–78* (London, 1980).

Mumford, L., *The City in History* (Harmondsworth, 1979).

Nairn, I., *Outrage* (London, 1955).

National Council of Social Service, *Community Centres and Associations Conference* (London, 1943).

National Council of Social Service, *Dispersal: An Enquiry into the Advantages of the Permanent Settlement Out of London and Other Great Cities of Offices, Clerical and Administrative Staffs* (London, 1944).

National Council of Social Service, *New Housing Estates and Their Social Problems* (London, 1937).

National Council of Social Service, *Our Neighbourhood* (London, 1950).

National Council of Social Service, *The Size and Social Structure of a Town* (London, 1943).

Nicholson, J. H., *New Communities in Britain: Achievements and Problems* (London, 1961).

Norris, J., *Human Aspects of Redevelopment* (Birmingham, 1962).

Office of Population Censuses and Surveys, *Demographic Review: A Report of Population in Great Britain* (London, 1987).

Orlans, H. J., *Stevenage: A Sociological Study of a New Town* (London, 1952).

Orwell, G., *Homage to Catalonia* (London, 1971).

Owens, R., 'The Great Experiment', *Architect's Journal*, 15 April 1993.

Parker, B. J., 'Some sociological implications of slum clearance programmes', in D. Donnison and D. Eversley (eds), *London: Urban Patterns and Problems* (London, 1973).

Parker, J. and Mirrlees, C., 'Housing', in A. H. Halsey (ed.), *British Social Trends Since 1900: A Guide to the Changing Social Structure* (London, 1988).

Parliamentary Debates, House of Commons (*Hansard*); Fifth Series, Vol. 422, 1945–46, cols 1089–90.

Peach, C., 'Black Caribbeans: class, gender and geography', in C. Peach (ed.), *Ethnicity in the 1991 Census. Vol. II: The Ethnic Minority Populations of Great Britain* (London, 1996).

Penney, M. C., 'Tenant's views on house design', *Society of Housing Managers' Quarterly Bulletin*, 3:17 (1955).

Pepinster, C., 'Divorce and single life bring back the new town', *Independent on Sunday*, 4 February 1996.

People's Press, *This Place Has Its Ups and Downs, Or Kids Could Have Done It Better* (Milton Keynes, 1977).

Pet Shop Boys, 'Suburbia', on The Pet Shop Boys, *Discography* (Parlophone, 1991, TCPMTV 3).

Pevsner, N. and Williamson, E., *The Buildings of England: Buckinghamshire* (Harmondsworth, 1993).

Philipson, G., *Aycliffe and Peterlee New Towns, 1948–1988: Swords into Ploughshares and Farewell Squalor* (Cambridge, 1988).

Pickup, L., 'Hard to get around: a study of women's travel mobility', in J. Little, L. Peake and P. Richardson (eds), *Women in Cities: Gender and the Urban Environment* (London, 1988).

Platt, J., *Social Research in Bethnal Green* (London, 1971).

Platt, S., 'Goodbye council housing', *New Society*, 26 February 1988.

Pocock, D. C. D., 'Some features of the population of Corby new town', *Sociological Review* (New Series) 8:2 (1960).

Police, The, 'Synchronicity 2', on *The Police: Greatest Hits* CD (A & M Records, 1992, 540 030-2).

Political and Economic Planning, 'Watling revisited', *Planning*, 14:270 (1947).

Power, A. and Tunstall, R., *Swimming Against the Tide: Polarisation or Progress on 20 Unpopular Council Estates, 1980–1995* (York, 1995).

Priestley, J. B., *English Journey* (London, 1937).

Prochaska, F., *The Voluntary Impulse* (London, 1988).

Pym, B., *Crampton Hodnet* (London, 1986).

Rankin, N. H., 'Social adjustment in a North-West newtown', *Sociological Review* (New Series) 11:3 (1963).

Rapoport, A., *The Meaning of the Built Environment: A Non-Verbal Communication Approach* (Beverley Hills, 1982).

Ravetz, A., *The Government of Space: Town Planning in Modern Society* (London, 1986).

Rawcliffe, J. M., 'Bromley: Kentish market town to London suburb, 1841–81', in F. M. L. Thompson (ed.), *The Rise of Suburbia*, (Leicester, 1982).

Read, D., *The Age of Urban Democracy, 1868–1914* (London, 1994).

Reade, E., *British Town and Country Planning* (Milton Keynes, 1987).

Ree, D., Lazell, B. and Osborne, R., *The Complete NME Singles Charts* (London, 1995).

Reeder, D., 'Representations of metropolis: descriptions of the social environment in *Life and Labour*', in D. Englander and R. O'Day (eds), *Retrieved Riches: Social Investigation in Britain, 1840–1914* (Aldershot, 1995).

Reeder, D., *Suburbanity and the Victorian City* (Leicester, 1980).

Rees, H. and C., *The History Makers: The Story of the Early Days of Stevenage New Town* (Stevenage, 1991).

Reisman, D., *The Lonely Crowd* (Yale, 1970).

Reisman, D., 'The suburban sadness', in W. M. Dobriner (ed.), *The Suburban Community* (New York, 1958).

Rex, J. and Moore, R., *Race, Community and Conflict: A Study of Sparkbrook* (Oxford, 1979).

Rhodes, G., 'Research in London, 1952–1977', *London Journal*, 5:1 (1979).

Roberts, E., *A Woman's Place: An Oral History of Working-Class Women, 1890–1940* (Oxford, 1984).

Roberts, E., 'Neighbours: North West England 1940–70', *Oral History*, 21:2 (1993).

Roberts, E., *Women and Families: An Oral History, 1940–1970* (Oxford, 1995).

Roberts, R., *The Classic Slum: Salford Life in the First Quarter of the Twentieth Century* (Harmondsworth, 1983).

Robinson, V., 'The Indians: onward and upward', in C. Peach (ed.), *Ethnicity in the 1991 Census. Vol. II: The Ethnic Minority Populations of Great Britain* (London, 1996).

Rodwin, L., *The British New Towns Policy: Problems and Implications* (Harvard, 1956).

Rose, G., *The Working Class* (London, 1968).

Rose, M. E., *The Relief of Poverty, 1834–1914* (London, 1977).

Rowe, D. J., 'The North East', in F. M. L. Thompson (ed.), *The Cambridge Social History of Britain, 1750–1950. Vol. I: Regions and Communities*

(Cambridge, 1993).

Rowntree, B. S. and Lavers, G. R., *English Life and Leisure: A Social Study* (London, 1951).

Royal Commission on the Distribution of the Industrial Population: Report (London, 1940, Cmd 6153).

Royle, E., *Modern Britain: A Social History, 1750–1985* (London, 1991).

Sainsbury, P. and Collins, J., 'Some factors relating to mental illness in a new town', *Journal of Psychomatic Research*, 10:1 (1966).

Saint, A., '"Spread the people": the LCC's dispersal policy, 1889–1965', in A. Saint (ed.), *Politics and the People of London: The London County Council, 1889–1965* (London, 1989).

Salt, J. and Flowerdew, R., 'Labour migration from London', *London Journal*, 6:1 (1980).

Samuel, R., 'The deference voter', *New Left Review*, 1 (January–February 1960).

Sarkissian, W., 'The idea of social mix in town planning: an historical view', *Urban Studies*, 13 (1976).

Saunders, P., 'Beyond housing classes: the sociological significance of private property rights in means of consumption', in L. McDowell, P. Sarre and C. Hamnett (eds), *Divided Nation: Social and Cultural Change in Britain* (London, 1989).

Savage, J., *England's Dreaming: The Sex Pistols and Punk Rock* (London, 1992).

Savage, M., 'Spatial differences in modern Britain', in C. Hamnett, L. McDowell and P. Sarre (eds), *The Changing Social Structure* (London, 1993).

Savage, M., 'The missing link? The relationship between spatial mobility and social mobility', *British Journal of Sociology*, 39:4 (1988).

Savage, M. and Miles, A., *The Remaking of the British Working Class, 1840–1940* (London, 1994).

Sayer, K., 'Feminism and History', *Modern History Review* (November 1994).

Schaffer, F., *The New Town Story* (London, 1972).

Schnore, L. F., 'Satellites and suburbs', in W. M. Dobriner (ed.), *The Suburban Community* (New York, 1958).

Seabrook, J., 'Milton Keynes: a mirror of England', *Observer Magazine*, 5 October 1978.

Self, P., *Cities in Flood: The Problems of Urban Growth* (London, 1957).

Seymour Smith, M., review of J. Burke, *The Suburbs of Pleasure*, in the *Spectator*, 3 March 1967.

Siouxsie and the Banshees, 'Suburban relapse', on *The Scream* CD (Polydor, 1989, 839 008-2).

Smailes, A., 'Balanced towns: their bases and occurence in England and

Wales', *Journal of the Town Planning Institute*, 32 (1945).

Smith, S., 'A London suburb', in S. Smith, *Me Again: The Uncollected Writings of Stevie Smith* (London, 1988).

Society of Housing Managers, *Report of Conference, 'Housing in Towns', 28/29 January, 1965* (London, 1965).

Society of Housing Managers, *Report of Conference, 'Housing Management', 10/11, January 1957* (London, 1957) .

Society of Housing Managers, *Report of Conference 'Management Problems Arising Out of the Housing Repairs and Rents Act, 1954, 28/29 January 1955* (London, 1955).

Society of Housing Managers, *Report of Conference 'Tomorrows Homes', 25/26 January, 1962* (London, 1962).

Soja, E. W., 'Taking Los Angeles apart', in C. Jencks (ed.), *The Postmodern Reader* (London, 1992).

Solomon, M. C., 'Public and private housing authorities', in R. J. Rowles (ed.), *Housing Management* (London, 1959).

Stacey, M., *Tradition and Change: A Study of Banbury* (Oxford, 1960).

Stacey, M., Batstone, E., Bell, C. and Murcott, A., *Power, Persistence and Change: A Second Study of Banbury* (London, 1975).

Stern, J. and M., *Sixties People* (London, 1990).

Stern, R. M., with Massengale, J. M., *The Anglo-American Suburb* (London, 1981).

Stevenage Development Corporation, *The New Town of Stevenage* (Stevenage, 1949).

Stevenson, J., *British Social History, 1914–45* (Harmondsworth, 1990).

Stevenson, J., 'The Jerusalem that failed? The rebuilding of post-war Britain', in T. Gourvish and A. O'Day (eds), *Britain Since 1945* (London, 1991).

Stevenson, J. and Cook, C., *The Slump: Society and Politics during the Depression* (London, 1979).

Style Council, The, 'Come to Milton Keynes', on *Our Favourite Shop* CD (Polydor, 1985, 825 700-2).

Suede, 'The power', on *Dog Man Star* CD (Nude, 1995, 3CD).

Swenarton, M. and Taylor, S., 'The scale and nature of the growth of owner-occupation in Britain between the wars', *Economic History Review*, 37:3 (1983).

Taylor, A. J. P., 'Manchester', in A. J. P. Taylor, *Essays in English History* (Harmondsworth, 1976).

Taylor, Lord and Chave, S., *Mental Health and Environment* (London, 1964).

Taylor, M., *Unleashing the Potential: Bringing Residents to the Centre of Regen-*

eration (York, 1995).

Taylor, P., 'British local government and housebuilding during the second world war', *Planning History*, 17:2 (1995).

Tebbutt, M., 'Gossip and "women's words" in working-class communities, 1880–1939', in A. Davies and S. Fielding (eds), *Workers' Worlds: Cultures and Communities in Manchester and Salford, 1880–1939* (Manchester, 1992).

Tebbutt, M., *Making Ends Meet: Pawnbroking and Working Class Credit* (London, 1984).

Thomas, R., *London's New Towns: A Study of Self-Contained and Balanced Communities* (London, 1969).

Thompson, F. M. L., 'Introduction: The rise of suburbia', in F. M. L. Thompson (ed.), *The Rise of Suburbia* (Leicester, 1982).

Thompson, F. M. L. (ed.), *The Cambridge Social History of Britain, 1750–1950. Vol. I: Regions and Communities* (Cambridge, 1993).

Thorns, D. C., *Fragmenting Societies? A Comparative Analysis of Regional and Urban Development* (London, 1992).

Thorns, D. C., *Suburbia* (London, 1972).

Tiratsoo, N., *Reconstruction, Affluence and Labour Politics: Coventry, 1945–60* (London, 1990).

Titmuss Collection at the British Library of Political and Economic Science.

Todd, N., 'The uses of contemporary suburban history, 1918–1950', *Local Historian*, 11:5 (1975).

Tsubaki, T., 'Postwar reconstruction and the questions of popular housing provision, 1939–51' (University of Warwick, unpublished Ph.D. thesis, 1993), I.

Tucker, J., *Honourable Estates* (London, 1966).

Turner, J. and Jardine, B., *Pioneer Tales: A New Life in Milton Keynes* (Milton Keynes, 1985).

Tweedale, G., 'Industry and de-industrialisation', in R. Coopey and N. Woodward (eds), *Britain in the 1970s: The Troubled Economy* (London, 1996).

Vahimagi, T. for the British Film Institute, *British Television: An Illustrated Guide* (Oxford, 1994).

Vaughan, P., 'Linoleum, cigarette card pictures, and the glorious whiff of suburbia', *Daily Mail*, 19 February 1994.

Vincent, D., *Poor Citizens: The State and the Poor in the Twentieth Century* (London, 1991).

Wainwright, M., 'Community life in a cul-de-sac', *Guardian*, 1 October 1996.

Walker, D., *The Architecture and Planning of Milton Keynes* (London, 1981).

Walton, J. K., *Lancashire: A Social History, 1558–1939* (Manchester, 1987).

Walvin, J., *Leisure and Society, 1830–1950* (London, 1978).

Ward, C., *New Town, Home Town* (London, 1993).

Ward, C., *Welcome Thinner City: Urban Survival in the 1990s* (London, 1989).

Waterhouse, K., *Billy Liar* (Harmondsworth, 1985).

Waterhouse, K., *Streets Ahead: Life After City Lights* (London, 1995).

Waterhouse, K., T*he Billy Liar Novels* (Harmondsworth, 1993).

Webber, M., 'Order in diversity: community without propinquity', in L. Wingo (ed.), *Cities and Space: The Future Use of Urban Land* (Baltimore, 1970).

Webber, M., 'Planning in an environment of change, part 1: beyond the industrial age', *Town Planning Review*, 39 (1968–69).

Webber, M., 'Planning in an environment of change, part 2: permissive planning', *Town Planning Review*, 39 (1968–69).

Webber, M., 'The urban place and the nonplace urban realm', in M. Webber et al. (eds), *Explorations into Urban Structure* (Philadelphia, 1971).

Weinreb, B. and Hibbert, C. (eds), *The London Encyclopaedia* (London, 1987).

Weldon, F., 'Letter one: the city of invention', in *Letters to Alice on First Reading Jane Austin* (London, 1993).

Weldon, F., *Life Force* (London, 1992).

White, D., 'Metroland', *New Society*, 1 July 1971.

White, D., 'What's so bad about Milton Keynes?', *New Society*, 17 April 1980.

White, J., *The Worst Street in North London: Campbell Bunk, Islington, Between the Wars* (London, 1986).

White, L. E., *Community or Chaos: Housing Estates and Their Social Problems* (London, 1950).

White, L. E., 'Good kitchens and bad towns', *Town and Country Planning*, 19:89 (1951).

Whyte, W. H., *The Organisation Man* (Harmondsworth, 1965).

Wicks, B., *No Time to Wave Goodbye: True Stories of Britain's 3,500,000 Evacuees* (London, 1988).

Wilkinson, R. K. and Sigsworth, E. M., 'Attitudes to the housing environment: an analysis of private and local authority households in Batley, Leeds and York', *Urban Studies*, 9 (1972).

Wilkinson, R. K. and Sigsworth, E. M., 'Slum dwellers of Leeds', *New Society*, 4 April 1963.

Williams, N., *East of Wimbledon* (London, 1993).

Williams, N., *The Wimbledon Poisoner* (1990).

Williams, N., *They Came From SW19* (London, 1992).

Williams, R., *Culture and Society, 1780–1950* (Harmondsworth, 1984).

Williams-Ellis, C., *Around the World in Ninety Years* (Portmeirion, 1996).

Williams-Ellis, C., 'To hell with subtopia', *New Statesman and Nation*, 23 March 1957.

Willmott, P., *Community Initiatives: Patterns and Prospects* (London, 1989).

Willmott, P., 'Housing density and town design in a new town: a pilot study at Stevenage', *Town Planning Review*, 33:2 (1962).

Willmott, P., 'Social research in the new communities', *Journal of the American Institute of Planners*, 33:6 (1967).

Willmott, P., *The Evolution of a Community* (London, 1960).

Willmott, P. and Young, M., *Family and Class in a London Suburb* (London, 1960).

Wilson, A., *Late Call* (Harmondsworth, 1992).

Wilson, J., *Politics and Leisure* (London, 1988).

Wilson, R., 'Difficult housing estates', *Human Relations*, 16:1 (1963).

Wood, B., 'Urbanisation and local government', in A. H. Halsey (ed.), *British Social Trends Since 1900* (London, 1988).

Young, M., 'Must we abandon our cities?', *Socialist Commentary*, September 1954.

Young, M. and Willmott, P., *Family and Kinship in East London* (Harmondsworth, 1979).

Young M. and Willmott, P., 'The old East End', *New Society*, 18 April 1986.

Young, M. and Willmott, P., *The Symmetrical Family: A Study of Work and Leisure in the London Region* (London, 1973).

Young, T., *Becontree and Dagenham: A Report Made for the Pilgrim Trust* (London, 1934).

Zweig, F., *The Worker in an Affluent Society* (London, 1961).

Index

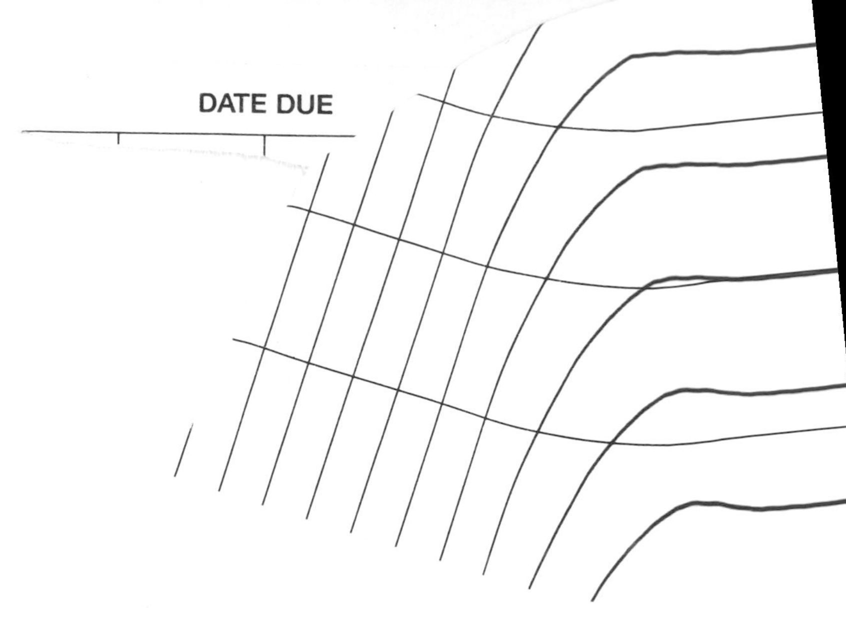
DATE DUE